DAILY LIFE IN
Chaucer's England

**Recent Titles in
The Greenwood Press "Daily Life Through History" Series**

Daily Life in Elizabethan England
Jeffrey L. Singman

DAILY LIFE IN

Chaucer's England

JEFFREY L. SINGMAN
AND WILL McLEAN

The Greenwood Press "Daily Life Through History" Series

GREENWOOD PRESS
Westport, Connecticut • London

Library of Congress Cataloging-in-Publication Data

Singman, Jeffrey L.
  Daily life in Chaucer's England / Jeffrey L. Singman and Will
McLean.
    p.   cm.—(The Greenwood Press "Daily life through history"
series, ISSN 1080–4749)
  Includes bibliographical references and index.
  ISBN 0–313–29375–9 (alk. paper)
  1. England—Social life and customs—1066–1485.   2. Chaucer,
Geoffrey, d. 1400—Contemporary England.   I. McLean, Will.
II. Title.   III. Series.
DA185.S48   1995
942.03'7—dc20   95–7568

British Library Cataloguing in Publication Data is available.

Library of Congress Catalog Card Number: 95–7568
ISBN: 0–313–29375–9
ISSN: 1080–4749

First published in 1995

Greenwood Press, 88 Post Road West, Westport, CT 06881
An imprint of Greenwood Publishing Group, Inc.

Printed in the United States of America

Contents

Acknowledgments   vii

Introduction   ix

1. Historical Background to Chaucer's England   1

2. Chaucer's World   9

3. The Course of Life   39

4. Cycles of Time   61

5. The Living Environment   79

6. Clothing and Accessories   93

7. Arms and Armor   137

8. Food and Drink   159

9. Entertainments   179

Glossary   215

Appendix A: The Medieval Event   221

Appendix B: Contacts   226

Appendix C: Suppliers   228

Notes   231

Bibliography   241

Index   247

Acknowledgments

The authors wish to thank the following: Robert Charrette for his purse design; Robert MacPherson for his breech design; Daniel Jennings for his shirt design; Karen Walter for her design for a veil and wimple and for her instructions on gussets; David Meddows-Taylor and John Vernier for their work on earlier drafts of the section on Shoes and Pattens; David Kuijt for the original draft of the section on Cards and for the rules for Karnoeffel and Glic; David Tallan for the original draft of the chapter on Food and Drink and of the recipes for Salad and Mustard; Kitten Reames for the original draft of the section on Spoons; Maren Drees for her work on the recipes; Trish Postle for her research into songs; and Karen Weatherbee for the original draft of the text and illustrations on handwriting.

Illustrations by Poul Norlund of the Herjolfsnes garments appear by permission of *Meddelelser om Groenland*.

Special credit is due to Kitten Reames for her illustrations of spoons, and to John Vernier for his illustrations of shoes and pattens and of arms and armor.

Special credit is also due to Trish Postle for her settings of "Kyrie Eleyson" and "The False Fox."

The authors also wish to thank the following individuals who assisted in this book in its various incarnations: Elizabeth Bennett, Robert Charrette, David Carroll-Clark, Susan Carroll-Clark, Gerry Embleton, Jeremy Graham, Victoria Hadfield, Marianne Hansen, Tara Jenkins, Daniel Jennings, Wendy McLean, Aryeh Nusbacher, and Karen Walter.

Daily Life in Chaucer's England is a revised and expanded version of *The Chaucerian Handbook,* itself a revision and expansion of *The Tabard Inn,* a manual for Chaucerian living history published by the University Medieval and Renaissance Society of Toronto in February 1991 for its "Tabard Inn" living history event.

Introduction

The life of medieval people has exercised a fascination for English speakers for two hundred years, since the romantics and antiquarians of the late eighteenth century began to rediscover the medieval past. There is indeed good reason why we should be so interested in the Middle Ages. Childhood plays an enormous role in shaping adult life, and in many respects the Middle Ages were the infancy of the society we know today. Between us and the classical world there lies a real historical break, for the fall of the Roman Empire broke off the development of Greco-Roman culture. Since the Middle Ages, however, there has been more of a historical continuum. The institutions that shape our world evolved during the medieval period: cities, universities, nation-states, and the common law are all inherited from the medieval world. Today, even people from lands unknown to medieval Europe are profoundly influenced by the medieval heritage. The language of the Beatles and of Martin Luther King is the language they inherited from Chaucer—the medieval world shapes our own in ways that are more far-reaching than we can ever fully perceive.

This book focuses on the daily life of people during a particularly fascinating period of the English Middle Ages. By custom, the Middle Ages in England are reckoned to have lasted from the fall of Rome (roughly the fifth century A.D., depending on what historical event one chooses as the moment of Rome's fall), until the end of the Wars of the Roses, with the accession of Henry VII in 1485. Sometimes the term is used in a more limited sense to indicate the period after the Norman Conquest in 1066. In either case, the Middle Ages spanned a number of centuries. In order to focus this book sufficiently to make meaningful statements about people's lives, it concentrates on the period of a single man's lifetime, from 1342 to 1400.

This man is Geoffrey Chaucer, generally considered the first great poet in English since the time of the Conquest and unsurpassed until the time of Shakespeare. This book is about ordinary people rather than about Chaucer, but he is a particularly apt choice as a figure around which to center the text. His *Canterbury Tales* are in many ways about ordinary people, whom he portrayed with a vividness that brings them alive even today; and the tales are themselves a rich source of information on people's daily lives.

The latter part of the fourteenth century is also a very effective vantage point from which to observe medieval life. Many major events of the English Middle Ages happened during Chaucer's lifetime. The English archers of the Hundred Years' War won their great victories at Crécy and Poitiers, the Black Plague swept across Europe, the peasantry of England rose in revolt against their feudal overlords, the Papacy was split in two, and Henry Bolingbroke unseated Richard II as king, an act that to lead to the Wars of the Roses in the fifteenth century. In social and cultural terms, the fourteenth century offers an opportunity to see the medieval world at its fullest. On the one hand, the traditional feudal structures were still at work, the Catholic Church held sway over the religious life of the nation, the French language enjoyed the prestige it had acquired since French-speaking Normans conquered the Anglo-Saxons in 1066, and Latin was the international language of learning. At the same time, new, market-oriented arrangements were reshaping the old feudal system, London and its merchant class were becoming a significant political force, John Wycliffe and his Lollards were challenging the teachings of the Catholic Church, and English was reasserting itself as a language of law, culture, and education.

In fact, quite a number of books have already been written about daily life in Chaucer's England. However, this book differs from any that has gone before, for it is the first such book to be written from the perspective of "living history." Living history encompasses a broad range of activities. In its most general sense, it can include any attempt to recreate materially some aspect of the past. In this sense, playing medieval music or practicing medieval calligraphy are both living history activities. In its most comprehensive form, living history tries to recreate an entire historical milieu.

Living history of this last sort is relatively rare for the medieval period, partly because the lack of information makes it rather difficult. This book began as a brief manual written by members of the University Medieval and Renaissance Association of Toronto (now called the Tabard Inn Society) for a Chaucerian-period event held at the University of

Toronto in 1991. It included information on clothing, games, songs, dances, and historical background, so that the participants could recreate the atmosphere of an evening at a London inn in 1391.

That original manual has undergone many substantial revisions since 1991, and very little of this book comes from that document, but the connection with living history remains. It has shaped this book in two important ways. First, living history encourages a hands-on approach to the past. Whereas other books on medieval daily life will tell you what kinds of clothes people wore, what kinds of games they played, or what kinds of songs they sang, this book includes actual patterns for medieval clothes, rules for medieval games, and music for medieval songs. History need not only live on the pages of books: there is both fun and learning to be had from trying it out first-hand.

Second, living history is a great means of focusing one's attention on the essential facts of daily life. Engaging in living history doesn't itself teach us how people lived their lives, but it does help us decide what sorts of questions we might want to ask about the past. When you spend a day trying to live as a medieval person would, you soon discover what sorts of information are really important. For this reason, you will find that this book is much more focused on crucial aspects of daily life than is generally the case, and that it offers information on significant subjects that have tended to be overlooked in the past.

One final important feature of this book is the quality of scholarship. While we have tried to make the text accessible and enjoyable for a wide audience, we have also tried to ensure that it is written to a high standard of fidelity to the sources. Of course, we can never fully recover the past: even if all the necessary information were available, it would be impossible for anyone to master all of it, and in the case of the Middle Ages our information is often fragmentary or inaccessible. However, we can ensure that we remain as faithful as we can to our available primary sources (i.e., original documents or artifacts from the period), so the margin of error is kept to a minimum.

This is precisely what we have striven to do in this book. Moreover, we have included a few of the sources (such as original medieval food recipes and patterns of surviving clothes) to allow the reader even closer contact with the original material. In some of the hands-on sections, we have had to use other sorts of sources (some of the rules for games, for example, are based on later texts), but in each case we felt that the degree of conjecture was justifiable and we have been careful to make it clear where the information is coming from if not from contemporary sources. For those who want to pursue a particular topic more deeply, we have added footnotes and a bibliography to help point you in the right direction.

This book has been a labor of love in which quite a number of hands have had a part over the years. We hope it will give you as much enjoyment in reading and using it as it has given us in creating it, and that for you, as for us, it will help make history come alive.

Geoffrey Chaucer, after a fifteenth-century manuscript illustration [Furnivall (1885)].

DAILY LIFE IN
Chaucer's England

1

Historical Background to Chaucer's England

The Middle Ages in England, in their broadest sense, are generally taken to begin in the fifth century A.D. at the time of the Roman withdrawal from Britain and the invasion of the country by Angles, Saxons, and Jutes from what is now Denmark and northern Germany. Over the following centuries, the invaders expanded their area of control at the expense of the native Celtic Britons and eventually consolidated into a single Anglo-Saxon kingdom of England. By the last years of this kingdom in the first half of the eleventh century the Anglo-Saxons had established control over all of present-day England, including western Cornwall, which still spoke Cornish, a descendant of the language of the Britons. They also had considerable authority over Wales, whose inhabitants spoke Welsh, another descendant of the British language. To the north, Scotland was an independent kingdom albeit with close ties to England.

In 1066, King Edward the Confessor died, and there was a dispute over the English crown between an English lord, Harold Godwinson, and William, Duke of Normandy. William invaded England, and Harold was defeated and killed at the Battle of Hastings. William became king, and the native English aristocracy was largely supplanted by French-speaking Normans.

Under the Norman kings, England began to expand its authority. In 1166 Norman lords under Henry II invaded and conquered Ireland, although over the centuries many of the invaders assimilated to the native Irish culture and effective English control came to be limited to parts of the eastern coast. Henry also succeeded in acquiring most of northern and western France, establishing an Anglo-French empire that was to remain a recurring dream of English monarchs for the rest of the Middle Ages.

Henry II's empire disintegrated after his death, and in 1204 his youngest son, King John, lost the Duchy of Normandy, leaving only a distant holding in southwestern France under English control. However, this loss actually opened the way for a new flourishing of English national identity. No longer did the English aristocracy have close connections and lands in France, and over the following century they became increasingly likely to speak English as their native tongue.

English imperial ambitions were revived during the reign of John's grandson, Edward I, in the late thirteenth century. Edward at last succeeded in subjecting Wales in 1284, and in 1301 the title of the Prince of Wales was given to his son, the future Edward II; the eldest son of the English monarch has held this title ever since. In 1296 Edward managed to subject the King of Scotland to the English crown, but this English overlordship was lost in 1314 by Edward II at the battle of Bannockburn.

The young Edward III came to the throne in 1327 in a coup d'état against his father, Edward II, who had become quite unpopular with the English aristocracy. The coup was led by Edward II's wife, Isabella, the daughter of King Philip IV (Philip the Fair) of France, and by Roger Mortimer, the Earl of March, who was Isabella's lover. Edward was forced to abdicate, then imprisoned, and secretly murdered. Mortimer and Isabella became the effective rulers of England but soon managed to antagonize the nobles themselves. In 1330 Edward assumed the royal authority in person: Mortimer was executed, and Isabella was confined for the remainder of her life.

As Isabella's son, Edward had French royal blood as well as English. In 1328, when the French king Philip IV's sons had all died without male issue, the French crown passed to Philip VI, the son of Philip IV's younger brother, Charles of Valois. In 1337 Philip declared Edward's French holdings confiscated over a legal squabble, and later that year Edward took the offensive by claiming the French throne for himself. He invaded France from the Low Countries in 1339, starting the Hundred Years' War.

The early years of the war went well for England. In 1340 Edward won a major naval victory at Sluys (in the Low Countries), securing control over the English Channel. At Crécy in 1346 his archers and dismounted knights soundly defeated a much larger force of French knights and noblemen, whose losses were catastrophic. Edward's eldest son, Edward of Woodstock, the Prince of Wales, distinguished himself in the battle, marking the beginning of a lasting military reputation; he came to be known in later centuries as the Black Prince. In the aftermath of the battle Edward captured Calais. At Poitiers in 1356, English archers once again defeated a larger French force, and King John of France, the son and heir of Philip VI, was among those captured. By the terms of the Treaty of

Bretigny signed in 1360, Edward renounced his claim to the French throne but was to hold Calais and his lands in southwestern France independently of the King of France.

Simultaneous with the war with France was the ongoing conflict with Scotland, which was increasingly allying itself with France against England. Edward III had more success against the Scots than had his father. His victory at Halidon Hill in 1333 re-established English overlordship over the King of Scotland, and at the battle of Neville's Cross in 1346 the Scots king, David II, was captured.

In 1347, in the middle of these wars, Europe was hit by the Black Plague, which reached England in 1348. This disease had come from the east and decimated Europe, killing as many as a third to a half of the population. The sudden collapse in the population sent prices skyrocketing; it greatly increased the value of labor, while it decreased the value of land—much land went uncultivated for lack of people to till it. In response, the government instituted a series of measures to keep wages at their pre-plague levels. Such legislation proved impossible to enforce in the face of market pressures, and its primary effect may have been to inflame anti-government sentiment among wage-earning commoners.

Nonetheless, Edward III enjoyed considerable popularity among his subjects largely as a result of his military successes, and this popularity was shared by the Prince of Wales. However, public euphoria waned in the later years of Edward's reign. In 1367 the Prince of Wales led an expedition to Spain in aid of Pedro the Cruel, King of Castile, whose throne had been seized by his brother Henry, with French support. The campaign was successful, but the Prince financed it by imposing heavy taxes in Gascony. The Gascon lords refused to pay and appealed to King Charles V of France, son of King John. Charles gave judgment in favor of the Gascons. The move was a direct infringement of Edward III's sovereignty in his French holdings. Edward resumed his claim to the French throne, and the war began again in 1369.

This time, things did not go nearly so well. The French had learned the lessons of Crécy and Poitiers: they avoided large pitched battles, relying instead on smaller raids to eat away at Edward's control. In 1371 the Prince of Wales, debilitated with disease, returned to England. The aging Edward III was losing effective control over his government, which came to be dominated by factions led by his mistress Alice Perrers, and his youngest son, John of Gaunt. The Prince of Wales died in 1376, and Edward III a year later. By this time, all that remained of their French conquests were Calais and a thin strip of the Gascon coast.

Edward was succeeded by Richard II, son of the late Prince of Wales. Richard was still underage, and the early years of his reign continued to be dominated by factions. The reign was also dogged by chronic revenue shortages. To redress this problem the government instituted the Poll Tax in 1377; the tax was tripled in 1380. This annual tax on every head fell especially hard on the poorest people, and helped spark the Peasants' Revolt in 1381. The rebels were concentrated in the east and southeast. A force of peasant rebels from Kent actually managed to capture London and force the King to promise the abolition of villeinage and reduction of rents. However, their leader, Wat Tyler, was killed in parlay with the King, and the rebellion collapsed. The King abandoned his promises, and harsh reprisals followed.

Richard had shown some personal courage at a very young age during the Peasants' Revolt, but the remainder of his reign proved rather unsuccessful. He allowed himself to be dominated by factions and favorites, which alienated many of his subjects, and he failed to revive the military successes of his father's reign. In 1385 he and John of Gaunt conducted an expensive and unsuccessful invasion of Scotland, and in 1388 an English army was severely defeated by the Scots at the Battle of Otterburn. Anglo-French relations were largely peaceful. Indeed, in 1396 Richard married a French princess, temporarily sealing a peace between England and France.

The last decade of Richard's reign was dogged by problems in Ireland, where English control was progressively weakening. In 1394 Richard led an expedition that succeeded in subduing the Irish lords for a time. In 1399 another rebellion erupted, and he set out to suppress it. During his absence Henry of Bolingbroke, the eldest son of John of Gaunt, returned from exile to claim estates belonging to his father that had been unjustly seized by Richard at John's death that year. The invasion quickly became a rebellion. Richard returned to England but was captured and forced to abdicate. With the approval of Parliament, Henry assumed the crown as Henry IV, first of the Lancastrian kings of England, and Richard died in prison the following year.

Richard II's reign had lacked political success, but it was a high point in the history of English culture. Richard was a generous patron of the arts, and it was during his reign that Geoffrey Chaucer produced most of his work. Chaucer was probably born in 1342, the son of a London wine merchant. His life demonstrated to the full the possibilities that were opening up for the middle classes in late medieval England. He received an excellent education at the school of St. Paul's Cathedral in London, followed by a few years in royal service and some study of law at the Inns of Court. During his long career of service to the crown he traveled in France and Italy. He married a woman from Hainault (in modern-day Belgium), whose sister eventually became the wife of John of Gaunt. However, his chief claim to fame is his extensive and diverse body of writings, ranging from devotional poems to a technical treatise on the use of the astrolabe, in addition to his renowned *Canterbury Tales*. Chaucer died in 1400.

By the time of Chaucer's death, England had a new king and a new dynasty on the throne. The dubiousness of Henry IV's claim to the crown helped provoke the Wars of the Roses in the fifteenth century, which pitted Henry's Lancastrian heirs against the Yorkist descendants of Lionel Duke of Clarence, the second son of Edward III. These civil wars finally ended with the accession of Henry Tudor in 1485. Henry was a descendant of John of Gaunt by his second wife; his accession is customarily taken to mark the end of the Middle Ages in England.

A CHRONOLOGY OF CHAUCERIAN ENGLAND

1327	Edward III is brought to power in a coup d'état against his father, Edward II.
1330	Edward III assumes royal authority.
1339	Edward III invades France, beginning the Hundred Years' War.
1340	English naval victory at Sluys.
1342	?Birth of Chaucer.
1346	Battle of Crécy, France. English archers soundly defeat French knights. Battle of Neville's Cross, England. English troops defeat Scottish invasion force.
1347	Truce between England and France. Plague arrives in Italy.
1348	Plague reaches England.
1351	Parliament passes the Statute of Laborers to keep down wages.
1353	Boccaccio's *Decameron*.
1356	Battle of Poitiers, France.
1360	Treaty of Bretigny ends the first phase of the Hundred Years' War.
1361	Outbreak of plague.
1362	First version of *Piers Plowman*, the first major literary work to be written in English since the Norman Conquest.
1367	Edward Prince of Wales leads an expedition to Spain in aid of Pedro the Cruel, the deposed King of Castile.
1369	Outbreak of plague. Hostilities resume in the Hundred Years' War.
1375	Outbreak of plague.

1376	Death of the Prince of Wales. Parliament impeaches royal servants belonging to the faction of John of Gaunt, the king's fourth son.
1377	Death of Edward III, accession of his grandson Richard II, still only 11 years of age. Poll Tax levied. The papacy returns to Rome from Avignon, where it had resided since 1309.
1378	Pope Gregory XI dies. The French-dominated College of Cardinals is intimidated by the Roman mob into electing an Italian as Pope, Urban VI. Urban antagonizes the cardinals, who declare him deposed, and elect a Frenchman, Clement VII. Clement moves to Avignon, but Urban remains as Pope in Rome. England, as well as the countries of Scandinavia, Germany, and northern Italy, support the Roman Pope; France, Scotland, Naples, Sicily, and the kingdoms of Spain follow the Pope of Avignon. This schism is not healed until the fifteenth century.
1380	John Wycliffe, an advocate of religious reform, is forced to stop teaching at Oxford.
1381	Peasants' Revolt.
1382	Richard II marries Anne of Bohemia. John Wycliffe and his Lollard followers complete the first full English translation of the Bible.
1384	Death of Wycliffe.
1385	Richard II and his uncle, John of Gaunt, undertake a fruitless military campaign in Scotland.
1386	John of Gaunt leads an expensive and unsuccessful expedition to Spain in an effort to win the crown of Castile, which he claims by right of his second wife. Chaucer produces the first sections of the *Canterbury Tales*.
1388	Scottish victory at Otterburn. Parliament impeaches several of the king's favorites.
1389	Richard II reaches the age of majority and assumes the functions of government in person. Boniface IX becomes Pope at Rome.
1390	Outbreak of plague.
1394	Richard II campaigns in Ireland. Death of Queen Anne.
1396	Richard II marries Isabella of France.

1399   Death of John of Gaunt.
            Richard II is deposed by Henry of Bolingbroke (John of
            Gaunt's son), who becomes King Henry IV.
1400   Death of Richard II.
            Death of Chaucer.
            Outbreak of plague.

2

Chaucer's World

SOCIETY

At the time of Chaucer's birth in about 1342, the population of England was around 3.75 million, although the ravages of the plague reduced it to about 2.25 million by the latter part of the century. This population represented a wide range of conditions, from the king to the destitute pauper.

Medieval political theory divided society by function into three "estates." The first estate was the clergy, who were responsible for people's spiritual well-being. The second estate was the aristocracy, who were supposed to defend the nation through their military might. The third estate was the commons, whose role was to labor and produce the country's wealth.

In theory, every English man and woman had a well-defined position in the social hierarchy, reflected in forms of address, in clothing, and in precedence in public places. People's positions in the hierarchy were considered to be of great importance, but sometimes the precise gradations weren't entirely clear. A wealthy commoner might live more richly than a poor aristocrat. It was generally clear who held an actual title—bishops, knights, and other titled persons received their titles through a clearly formalized system. However, it might be hard to tell whether the local miller was a more important man than the local smith. Disputes about who had the right to go into church first on Sunday could sometimes come to blows.

Social confusion was aggravated by social mobility. It was possible, although hardly easy, to rise in social rank. Sir John Hawkwood, the greatest English mercenary captain of the age, was a tanner's son who eventually married the daughter the Duke of Milan. On the other hand, people could lose social status if they failed to maintain a mode of living appropriate to their rank.

An aristocratic household at table. The lord and lady of the house sit in the center, with their sons and daughter-in-law on the right, two Dominican friars on the left, and two servants waiting table. English, before 1340 (LP, f. 208) [McLean].

The Clergy The theory of the three estates was essentially a clerical invention, so it is no wonder that the clergy constituted the first estate. Their major part in this theory also reflected the importance of religion in medieval society. The idea of a separation between church and state was unthinkable, and the Church was firmly embedded in the structures of society and government.

There were two sorts of clergy in the fourteenth century. The "secular" clergy, such as the parish priest, lived *in seculo*, "in the world." Their primary responsibility was to attend to the spiritual needs of the laity, the nonclerical people of the other two estates. The "regular" clergy consisted of monks and friars, who were regulated by rules that dictated lives of asceticism and discipline. In all, the clergy may have accounted for some 1.5% of the population of England. The clergy were instantly recognizable by their "tonsure," or clerical haircut. Their heads were shaven on top, with the rest of the hair worn short, and their facial hair was shaven too. In addition, members of the regular clergy wore "habits," or special clothing indicating the order to which they belonged. These clergy were all male and sworn to a life of celibacy.

Unlike the other two estates, nobody was born into the clergy. Every clergyman had been raised either as an aristocrat or as a commoner, and this distinction often played a role in their clerical life. Aristocratic clergymen tended to gravitate towards the upper levels of the clergy and to the more coveted positions. At the top of the secular clergy in England were the "prelates," two archbishops and about two dozen bishops under them. On a par with the prelates were the abbots of great monastic houses. Such clerics had incomes and status comparable to that of a duke or earl, and indeed they sat in Parliament in the House of Lords.

Below them were the lesser officers of the complicated church hierarchy, such as the dean who supervised a bishop's or archbishop's cathedral, or the archdeacon who helped administer the bishopric. Likewise, an abbot would have a prior and several other important officers to help administer the monastery. Such officers might have incomes and lifestyles that ranged from gentle to lordly. Clerics in such privileged positions often had more in common with the aristocracy than with the lesser clergy. Such was the priest William of North Berwick, who, according to the chronicler Jean Froissart, distinguished himself fighting beside the Earl of Douglas at the battle of Otterburn in 1388, and "thereby the same year he was made archdeacon of Aberdeen."

Commoners tended to have a harder time rising in the clerical establishment. Simple parish priests of rural parishes were often from peasant families and lived a life not much different from their peasant neighbors. Still, a clerical career was the best chance many commoners had for social advancement.

Towards the bottom end of the church hierarchy was the parish priest. There were some 8500 parishes in **The Parish Priest** England in Chaucer's day. The parish was the smallest unit of church organization, typically corresponding to a village in the countryside or to a neighborhood in the towns; it had its own church and, theoretically, its own priest. Some parishes produced revenues of hundreds of pounds, but most were worth less than £10 a year. Often much of the revenue was siphoned off to an absentee "rector." The rector might be a clergyman working at the royal court, a worthy clerk pursuing higher learning, or even a monastery or cathedral which used the funds to support its expenses. The actual care of the souls in the parish would then be in the hands of a "vicar," whose income might be as little as £4 a year. The poorest must have been particularly dependent on the harvest from the parson's share of the village fields (called a "glebe"). Many had to work those fields themselves, and some kept beasts or threshed corn in the churchyard or stored malt in the church.

On such low wages it was hard to attract good help. One chronicler complained that many of the men who became priests after the plague "knew nothing except how to read to some extent." Medieval clerics were expected not simply to be able to read and write but to be able to do so in Latin—a fourteenth-century clerical "illiterate" might not have been so by twentieth-century standards. Still, the poorer parishes can hardly have attracted well-educated parsons.

It is difficult to judge the moral quality of the fourteenth-century priesthood at a distance of six centuries. Certainly contemporaries thought there was a problem. In 1373 ten priests were accused of unchastity in Norwich alone, one of them with two women. In some ways the character of priestly offenses is more informative than their number: charges included haunting taverns, dicing, theft, assault, and poaching. Yet there must also have been many priests like the early fourteenth-century vicar of Staverton in Devon, who, according to his parishioners, "behaves himself well and honestly, and informs them excellently in spiritual matters, nor, as they say, is he at fault in that. They know nothing of any hidden mortal sin."

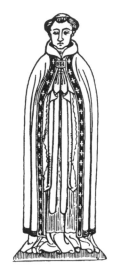

A priest in ordinary priestly garments. [Clinch]

Minor Orders At the very base of the secular clergy were the clerics in minor orders. They were ordained but not sworn to celibacy, so they could marry. They bore only a small tonsure at the crown of their head instead of the full tonsure of the priest. Many were acolytes and readers, assisting in church services; physicians, university students, and ordinary clerks were likely to be in minor orders as well.

Monks and Friars The oldest form of the regular clergy were the monks, who had been present since the early Middle Ages. The original intent of monasticism had been to foster spirituality by placing the monks in a monastery, secluded from the world outside, where they would lead austere lives devoted to prayer and holy contemplation. Every monastery and every monk belonged to a particular order, which had its own administration and its own rules governing the monks' way of life. The oldest order was the Benedictines; more recent orders included the Carthusians and Cistercians. The principal responsibility of monks was originally a daily cycle of prayers called the canonical hours, but over the centuries they had assumed important roles as scribes, teachers, and healers, and it was by no means unusual for them to be seen outside their monasteries.

The thirteenth century had witnessed the emergence of a new kind of regular clergy, known as the mendicant orders or friars. Friars, like monks, lived under the authority of the rule of their order; in particular, they were not allowed to own private property—all their possessions belonged to their order. However, rather than retiring from the world, their mission was to minister to the spiritual needs of the public, particularly through preaching, teaching, and hearing confession. There were two principal mendicant orders: the Dominicans, also known as the black friars or friars-preachers, and the Franciscans, also called gray friars or friars-minor. In all, there may have been some 12,000 monks and friars in England towards the end of the Middle Ages.

The ideals of the regular clergy were difficult to sustain, especially when pious bequests made it easy to enjoy a comfortable life in the cloister. Few abbeys were as lax as Flaxley in 1397, where nine monks were unchaste and where the abbot was found to have slept with three different women. Gross immorality was a less common problem than creeping worldliness, a falling away from the austere ideals that had defined the monks and friars in the first place. On the whole, monks and friars were probably no more worldly than other men—most were probably less so—but their failings were considered much more grievous because of their religious profession. However, the worldliness of the regular clergy had its benefits too, since friars and monks contributed significantly to society as teachers, physicians, and administrators.

A nun and monk in the stocks [Wright].

In addition to the male clergy there were nuns, whose place in the social structure was less obvious. In effect they belonged to **Nuns** the first estate, but they did not enjoy the same privileges as the male clergy. They could not become priests, their abbesses did not have a place in the House of Lords, and in general they were attached to the clerical hierarchy rather than integrated into it. Nonetheless, some nunneries were quite wealthy; the abbess of such an establishment could be an important woman in her own right, enjoying a degree of authority rare for a medieval woman. The activities of a nun's life were in many ways similar to those of monks, and, like monks, they were not always confined to their nunneries. Nuns also belonged to orders and wore special habits, and their hair was cropped close under their veils.

The Feudal System

The second and third estates, the aristocracy and commons, were defined by the institution of feudalism, perhaps the most distinctive social phenomenon of the Middle Ages. The feudal system was in its prime in England from the eleventh to the thirteenth century. Already in Chaucer's England the classical feudal system was past its heyday, yet it remained an important force in shaping society.

At its heart feudalism was simply a series of contracts, of payment for services and payment for the use of land. Feudalism had arisen out of the social arrangements of the early Middle Ages (roughly the second half of the first millennium A.D.) and took its peculiar character from the social and economic conditions of that time. First, warfare in the early Middle Ages was frequent and widespread, and central authorities were weak or nonexistent. At every level of society the constant and immediate threat of attack generated a pressing need for military power. Second, early medieval society was almost entirely agrarian. People made their livings either by controlling the use of agricultural land or by working on land controlled by others. Third, coinage was scarce, so it was impractical to make payments in cash. Lastly, literacy was so rare that written contracts were impractical.

The feudal system created a hierarchy in which the right to use land was exchanged for labor and military service in accordance with established customs. At the top of the feudal hierarchy was the king, who was the theoretical owner of all the land in the country. The king granted "holdings" of land to aristocratic "tenants" in exchange for military support. The aristocracy had evolved from the warrior class of barbarian Europe. An aristocrat "paid" for his landholding by promising the king military service in time of war, bringing a stipulated number of armed followers to fight under the king's command for a specified number of days. The aristocrat would in turn grant landholdings to lesser aristocrats under similar terms. Such aristocratic landholdings were often termed "manors."

At the bottom of the feudal chain, aristocratic landholders granted landholdings to commoners, people outside the warrior class, in exchange for specified labor services that enabled the lord to maintain and cultivate his estate. Such tenants were required to work for the lord a certain number of days each week and might have to perform special labor during the course of the year, such as harvesting or repairing roads or bridges. The distinction between landholding by military service and landholding by labor service defined the line between the aristocrat and the commoner, although custom also allowed commoners to be pressed into service as footsoldiers in a feudal levy when the lord needed to assemble a military force.

Instead of written contracts, the terms of a landholding were made binding by public oath and by custom. The commoner's main assurance that his landlord would not extort extra labor services was not a written contract but the fact that since time out of mind the holding had entailed certain services and no more. A lord's main security that his knight would not default on his service was not a document but the knight's public promise to serve, sworn in front of people whose respect he valued. Custom was a powerful force in a society in which other mechanisms to preserve stability were weak.

Partly because contracts were based on custom, land was "held" rather than owned. Landholders were not free to buy or sell their landholdings at will: the laws and customs governing transference of landholdings were extremely restrictive. A landholder inherited the right to a landholding much as he might inherit owned property; if he fulfilled the customary services required by his holding, he kept that right for life and passed it on to his heir on the same terms. A lord was not free to grant landholdings at will under terms of his own choosing. Indeed, the holding was not necessarily a right but a responsibility, since villeins, or unfree tenants, could not give up their holding without their lord's permission. Even a great lord might be unable to transfer his holding to someone else if the condition of the holding required that it remain in the family.

Feudalism had never been a convenient or flexible system; it had simply evolved in a conservative society in response to prevailing social and economic conditions. By Chaucer's day, various pressures were undermining its viability. Subsistence agriculture was no longer the rule. Even ordinary peasants were producing goods for sale rather than sustenance, and agrarian crop-raising was beginning to wane slightly in favor of the lucrative pursuit of sheep-farming for the wool trade. Coin was more plentiful, and commerce and even rudimentary industry were becoming significant elements in the economy. Increased literacy and a more developed legal system made it more practical to use and enforce written contracts. At the same time warfare was becoming increasingly professionalized, so that the fixed, part-time service of the feudal host had been almost entirely replaced by long-term service for cash wages, often by full-time professional soldiers.

In an increasingly market-oriented economy, the rigid arrangements of feudalism were unsatisfactory for everyone. Both landlords and tenants found it increasingly convenient to change service-rents to more flexible cash payments. The arrival of the Black Plague in 1349 hastened the decline of feudalism. With the sudden drop in population, there was intense competition for labor and tenants. This made it all but impossible to continue exacting unpopular service-rents, and prompted landowners to convert arable land into pasture, exchanging labor-intensive agriculture for labor-minimal pastoralism. Yet although service-rents were disappearing, the traditional feudal link between the individual and the land persisted. Service-rents may have been commuted to money rents, but tenancy remained a legal right and responsibility, and the relationship between people and the land they held was still relatively restrictive.

Meanwhile, feudal military service was being replaced by a system of written contracts, typically called "indentures." When the king needed an army, he would draw up contracts with his commanders, experienced captains or great lords to whom he promised a specified payment for a specific number of men. In this way the king was assured willing soldiers who would serve as long as required. The commanders would provide part of the force from their own personal followings and would subcontract the rest.

The usual arrangement under such subcontracts was that the lord or captain would retain men to serve under him, paying them a fixed annual fee to hold themselves ready to serve when required, plus set wages for each actual day served. The arrangement was much like the retainer paid to a modern lawyer. The advantage of the system was that the men were not expensive full-time employees, but were paid wages only when they were actually needed. The larger subcontractors might in turn subcontract a portion of their own obligation.

A knight in full armor.
German, 1369 [Hewitt].

No prudent man trusts his life to total strangers if he can avoid it, and such retainers, or retinues, were recruited from a man's relatives, tenants, and neighbors whenever possible. They were given badges or distinctive clothing, called livery, to indicate their allegiance. The retainers became a sort of extension of a great man's household: not precisely part of it, but connected to it. The lord would typically give his patronage as well, supporting his followers in legal or political matters, and they would return the favor where they could.

Modern historians call this practice "bastard feudalism," since subordinates were paid in money rather than landholdings and were bound by written contracts rather than oaths of fealty. Contemporaries called it "livery" or "maintenance." Like the new relationship between the lord and his peasant tenants, bastard feudalism was a distinctly market-oriented arrangement, since it was not bound by the traditions of inheritance or the physical tenancy of land which were a part of true feudalism.

Bastard feudalism allowed the king to put a large force into the field quickly without incurring the expense of a standing army, and the links of kinship and service that knit it together avoided the worst vices of a purely mercenary force. Yet the system also had weaknesses. The maintenance of retinues encouraged the corruption of legal and political institutions, as powerful lords would bend the rules in favor of their followers. Armies raised by indenture tended to find unpleasant alternate employment when they were put out of work, turning to brigandage and pillage to support themselves. Above all, bastard feudalism made it all too easy for turbulent subjects to raise troops on their own account. This aggravated the factional strife of Richard II's reign and helped tear the country apart when the houses of York and Lancaster struggled for supremacy in the Wars of the Roses during the following century.

In all, the aristocracy probably accounted for about 1% of the total population, spanning a vast economic **The Aristocracy** range, from incomes of about £20 to incomes of £3,000 or even £12,000. The aristocracy included both the titled nobility and those who were simply "of gentle birth," meaning that their forebears had belonged to the warrior class. According to the doctrine of the three estates, the purpose of the aristocracy was to fight on behalf of the kingdom: war was its profession and justification. In practice, the aristocracy was beginning to lose its pre-eminence on the battlefield. Yet if the aristocratic man-at-arms was no longer the only kind of soldier that mattered, he was still a force to be reckoned with; and in the cultural sphere the aristocrat enjoyed a kind of prestige that even the richest commoner lacked. Although diverse in power and wealth, the aristocracy were unified by a set of shared ideals. These included the martial virtues of prowess and courage, but also the outward signs that a person came of a certain station in life and could comfortably maintain it: social graces and a certain generosity of spirit. Not all aristocrats lived up to these ideals, but they remained a unifying principle nonetheless.

The monarch was lord of all England, hedged about with the glory of kingship, yet his power was far from absolute. The **The King** great lords of England were not afraid to rebel against a truly unpopular king. Edward III had come to the throne in one such rebellion, and his successor, Richard II, lost the throne in another. The king also needed to worry about his relations with the petty aristocracy and the more powerful commoners. His normal revenue, derived principally from crown lands and various tolls and customs, was greater than any subject's;

but it was not enough to run a country, especially in time of war. He had to rely on the consent of Parliament to levy taxes to make up the difference, and the lower house of Parliament consisted of the lowest echelons of the aristocracy and the upper ranks of the commons. Even with tax revenues, medieval monarchs were chronically short of money.

The Nobility Below the king were the titled nobility, beginning with a handful of dukes who were only slightly less wealthy and powerful than the king himself. They could be numbered on the fingers of one hand, had incomes of thousands of pounds, and were almost always close relatives of the king. The dozen or so earls were only slightly less splendid. These were the equivalent of the continental count, and their wives were called countesses. A few dozen barons, with incomes of several hundred pounds a year, rounded out the lay peerage—that is, the major feudal lords who received summons to Parliament. The entire lay peerage amounted to only some fifty lords at this time.

Knights Below the nobility were the aristocracy without hereditary titles. Knights ranked highest in this group. A knight received his title during his lifetime and did not pass it on to his heirs. In earlier centuries, the knights of England had been more or less all those men whose lands yielded enough income that they could afford a horse and armor. By the fourteenth century this was no longer the case. Any man who had lands worth £40 a year could become a knight. In fact, the king would fine him if he didn't. Yet many who could be knighted declined the honor. The rank was both prestigious and burdensome. The ceremony was expensive; knighthood entailed a number of local administrative and legal duties, mostly unpaid; and land held by knight-tenure exposed the owner to various feudal expenses that the ordinary landholder could avoid.

There were something less than 1,000 knights in Chaucer's England. The most important, able to afford to raise substantial retinues to fight under their banner, were called "knights banneret," the remainder "knights bachelor." The distinguishing symbol of knighthood was a pair of golden spurs, buckled on as part of the knighting ceremony. Also during the ceremony the new knight would be "belted" with a sword belt, often white in token of purity. The spurs were sometimes worn afterwards on ceremonial occasions, although this does not appear to have been the case with the belt.

Squires As the chivalry decreased in numbers, squires rose in status to fill the gap they had left. Originally, a squire had been a gentle-born assistant to a knight—the word meant "shield-carrier." The term was still used in this way, but it was also applied generally to men of gentle birth who were not knights. Many were wealthy enough to become knights. The great majority of fully armored horsemen, or men-at-arms, were squires. In most fourteenth-century armies they outnumbered the knights by three to one or more. Along with the knights they formed the backbone of the English and French armies, took part in tournaments, and shared a chivalric set of values. While some squires eventually became knights, most did not.

Most squires were drawn from the ranks of the moderate landowners. Some had incomes of £40 a year or more from land, enough to become knights if they wished. In 1436, fully 1,200 reported landed incomes of £15 or more. But many were younger sons, or had not yet inherited, or had lands that would not support them as they wished to live. These took service with richer men. They might serve as men-at-arms or superior domestic servants. They might also be bureaucrats or diplomats or independent military commanders, or they might be several of these in turn.

The theory of the three estates was weakest in accounting for the people who were neither clergy nor **The Commons** aristocrats, who were lumped together as "the commons." In fact, the commons constituted over 97% of the population, and in Chaucer's day they were becoming an increasingly diverse group; indeed, some were beginning to acquire real power in their own right. The commons were subdivided into two distinct social structures, that of the town and that of the country.

Over 95% of England's population lived in the countryside. The peasantry constituted the lowest level **Rural Commons** of the feudal hierarchy, itself subdivided by wealth and legal status. The terms of rental for any peasant's landholding varied enormously in accordance with the specific customs associated with it. In principle, there was a fundamental distinction between a "free" holding and an "unfree" or "servile" one. A free holding involved only limited services to the lord, entitled the holder to recourse to the king's courts, and might require only nominal rents. A servile holding involved more services and certain special taxes (for example, upon inheritance of the holding or marriage of the holder's daughter). The holder was entirely under the civil jurisdiction of the lord's manorial court and needed his lord's permission to move, to marry outside the lord's manorial landholding, or to enter the priesthood—although this permission could usually be secured for a fee. The tenant of a free holding was called a freeman; the tenant of a servile holding was called a villein or bondman. The villein was the closest English equivalent of the Continental serf. The situation was sometimes complex, as it was not unknown for a single individual to hold both free and unfree land. Since free or unfree status was a condition that attached to particular holdings, such a man would owe bond service only for his bond lands.

Villeinage was felt to be burdensome, and when the English peasantry revolted in 1381, one of their main demands was the abolition of villeinage. But a peasant's free or unfree status was ultimately less significant than the size of his holding. Although it was easier and more pleasant to be a freeholder with thirty acres than a bondsman with the same lands, the villein with thirty acres was better off than a free man with ten and probably carried more weight in local affairs. It was by no means unusual for a villein to be a man of considerable wealth and standing in the community.

A villein's labor services were always roughly proportional to the size of the holding. The services were essentially a rent surcharge paid in labor rather than money, although some or all of the services could be changed to a money payment by mutual consent. The services were rigidly fixed by custom, and villeinage was very poorly suited to the needs of a changing economy. Although half the peasantry may have been bondsmen during the early fourteenth century, this figure declined rapidly by the end of the century. With the drop in population after the Black Plague, landlords found themselves competing for tenants and it became even harder to continue exacting the services associated with villeinage. In another two centuries villeinage would disappear entirely. It was a slow process, and not obvious at the time. The peasants who risked their lives in a vain attempt to abolish villeinage in the revolt of 1381 probably did not realize that the institution was already dying a natural death.

A husbandman reaping grain. Italian, c. 1400 (TS Casanatense, f. lxxvi) [McLean].

At the top of the peasant hierarchy were the franklins or yeomen, freemen with holdings of 50 acres or more, enough **Franklins or Yeomen** to offer the prospect of economic advancement. Such men lived comfortably by the standards of the age, and many were wealthier than some squires. "Yeoman" was traditionally the term for the servant that ranked below a squire, and in this period the word was coming to be applied to the class of people from which such servants were drawn. This class also provided the deadly archers who distinguished themselves in the wars against France. Perhaps a fifth of the peasantry were yeomen in the early fourteenth century, and the number appears to have grown during the century.

Below the franklins were the husbandmen, who were freemen or villeins with holdings typically ranging from 10 **Husbandmen and Cottars** to 40 acres, a size sufficient to maintain a peasant family. Such men may have constituted a third of the peasant population in the early fourteenth century. The smallest landholders were commonly known as cottars. They held little more than their cottages— generally 5 acres or less, which was too little to live on—so they needed to supplement their land-based income by selling their labor. Probably about half the peasantry were cottars in the early fourteenth century, many of them villeins, although the lot of such people likely improved in the latter half of the century. At the bottom of rural society were those who held no land at all and were entirely dependent on their earnings as laborers: carters, plowmen, herdsmen, threshers, and other hired hands.

An olive oil vendor. Italian, c. 1390 (TS Paris, f. 15) [McLean].

Townsmen
Less numerous but increasingly important were the inhabitants of the towns. In all, less than 5% of the population lived in towns; a total of 1.5% resided in London, and another 1% in Bristol, York, and Norwich combined. Yet as centers of trade and commerce, towns exercised an influence beyond their actual populations. They were also a magnet for people. In fact, the urban population was in constant flux. Health conditions were especially poor, and towns would continually have declined in population were it not for an ongoing process of immigration from the countryside to the town, as people came in search of work or social advancement.

The medieval town was different from the country not only in its density of population but in its social structure as well. The town was by definition independent of the feudal structure, owing minimal feudal responsibilities to its overlord, usually the king himself. Therefore towns enjoyed considerable privileges of self-government, and town-dwellers were not confined within the feudal hierarchy. However, towns had a hierarchy of their own. Only a portion of the population of a town were "citizens" or "burgesses" with full rights and a say in the town's governance. In London less than half were citizens. The rest were apprentices, laborers, servants, and "aliens" from outside the town.

A riot in town [Ashdown].

Citizenship could be purchased, or it could be acquired by rising through the hierarchy of a trade. Each trade in a city had its own "mistery," or guild, which regulated the practice of the trade within that city. People entered the trade as apprentices and, if they were fortunate, might rise to the position of master.

Servants
An important social class in fourteenth-century England that has largely disappeared today was the servants. Servants were a common feature of medieval society, and there was nothing demeaning about domestic service. Indeed, service to a prestigious employer, especially the king, could raise one's status. Even a young aristocrat might spend time in service in some noble household, a boy as a page and later as a squire, a girl as a lady-in-waiting, acquiring social polish and learning the skills appropriate to their class. For commoners,

Table 2.1: The Social Hierarchy

FIRST ESTATE	SECOND ESTATE	THIRD ESTATE		
Clergy	Aristocracy	Rural Commons	Urban Commons	Landless Commons
	King, Queen			
Archbishop	Duke, Duchess			
Bishop	Earl, Countess			
Major Abbot	Baron, Lady		Mayor of London	
Abbot, Prior	Knight Banneret, Lady		Alderman of London, Mayor of great town, major legal officer	
Archdeacon, Dean	Knight Bachelor		Other mayor or civic or legal officer, great merchant	
Priest, Master of Arts	Squire		Lesser merchant	
Monk, Friar		Franklin, Yeoman	Craftsman	Yeoman (servant)
		Husbandman	Journeyman	Groom (servant)
		Cottar	Apprentice	Page, Laborer
				Vagrant

A schematized table of the social hierarchy. Ranks at the same horizontal level were considered to be roughly equivalent to each other.

service could be a means of saving up money and making useful contacts in aristocratic society. Thus, servants were not necessarily permanently in that social class; they might be young people with prospects of social and economic advancement.

In addition to those who had a place, however precarious, in the social structure, there were the genuinely destitute who **The Poor** had no reliable livelihood, whose survival depended on the charity of others. Many were physically unable to labor. The injured, infirm, and elderly were all vulnerable to poverty if they had no independent source of income. Prisoners relied entirely on charity, as they had to pay for their own provisions. Widows and orphans were also vulnerable to poverty if the man of the family died without leaving them a secure income. In addition, the laboring poor in both town and country invariably went through periods of unemployment. Living at the margin of subsistence, they were always at risk of slipping into destitution; however, this risk was considerably lower in the latter half of the century, once the plague had reduced the supply of labor far below the level of demand.

Women
In addition to the division of society by function and status, there was a fundamental division by gender. Medieval England was a very male-dominated society, at least at the level of official structures. In principle, every woman was supposed to be under the authority of a man. A girl was subject to her father until she married, at which time she would become subject to her husband. She did not normally inherit land unless her father died without leaving any sons. Women did not officially participate in governmental activities, were almost never allowed to become citizens of a town, and had only limited independent standing under the law.

However, the official structure was not the entire story. Chaucer's England was not like the United States of a generation or so ago, when men typically did most of their work outside the household and were paid money wages, and women typically did most of their work inside the household and were not. As in much of the world before the Industrial Revolution, the bulk of production in the Middle Ages occurred within the household. Food, fuel for heat and cooking, water, clothing, and shelter were in great part produced and processed within the family. The same was true of education, child care, and medical care. Work done inside the household was not a special case but the norm

A peasant woman feeding chickens. English, before 1340 (LP, f. 166v) [Bateson].

for both sexes. Further, money was as likely to come into the home from a wife's spinning or weaving as from the sale of surplus food. All this gave a woman influence in practice that she was not supposed to have in theory.

Some women sought opportunity by moving to a town, where the social structures were somewhat less rigid. Here a woman of some means might be able to engage in trade, property speculation, retailing, or brewing, and a poorer woman might find work as a spinster, vendor, or servant. Other women achieved independence in widowhood, a state that was all too common in this age of high mortality. A widow was guaranteed a share of her husband's property for support during her lifetime; if her husband had practiced a craft or trade, she might take over the business after his death and might even be admitted into the guild.

The fundamental building block of society was the family. The medieval family was not necessarily a nuclear family but a household. At the upper end of the **The Household** social spectrum it might include relatives beyond the immediate nuclear family, although this was not so common among ordinary people, and it was generally rare for two married couples to live in the same house. However, it was common for servants or apprentices to live with the family. Even a family of modest means might have a servant. A lesser gentleman might have 7 or 8 people in his household, a wealthy knight 12-30, a baron 20 or more, a major aristocrat 40 to 150, and the king around 400. Among commoners, the family was the typical unit of economic production: the family business was the rule rather than the exception.

An evening at home. Italian, c. 1395 (TS Vienna, f. 100v) [McLean].

A well-run aristocratic household was also a unit of production. One contemporary, Christine de Pisan, described how a lady living on a manor should not only carefully oversee the agricultural production, but in winter "she will reflect that labor is cheap" and put her men to work cutting firewood and making vine props for later sale, or threshing in the barn if the weather is bad. She will put her women to work in the herb garden, and work with them spinning and weaving, and making clothing for the household, "or to sell if she needs to do so." De Pisan noted with approval the Countess of Eu, who ran her household so well that she received more income from it than from her lands.

Different social classes tended to marry at different ages, and family sizes varied accordingly. An aristocratic woman, married in her teens, might have a fairly large family, but a commoner would not usually have the means to marry until she was in her twenties. With the high rate of child mortality, it was typical for such a woman to have no more than two children in her family.[1]

RELIGION AND COSMOLOGY

Probably one of the deepest differences between Chaucer's world and ours was the degree to which religion permeated society. Being a part of society in medieval England was in fact the same as being part of the church. All Christians in Western Europe were subject to the spiritual authority of the Pope (the Catholic Church was the only officially accepted church in Western Europe, although there were other churches in Eastern Europe and elsewhere). In spite of the disgraceful state of papal politics in the fourteenth century (which resulted in a prolonged period during which there were two popes, one in Rome, another in Avignon), the ideal of religious unity remained very important to medieval thought. Only the Pope could maintain unity in the Church; and in a world that made very little distinction between church and state, religious disunity was considered equivalent to social anarchy.

Every child was supposed to have a basic religious education. This included learning the proper means of crossing oneself and learning how to recite (in Latin) the Pater Noster, the Ave Maria, and the Credo (all of which are reproduced here in Latin and in Middle English).[2] It was also considered important to know the meaning of the Latin, especially in the case of the Credo, which formed the definitive statement of Christian belief.

Children's religious education also included the basic elements of Christian belief. These had been identified by the Lambeth Council in 1281 as

> —the Fourteen Articles of the Faith (which are the statements in the Apostles' Creed)
> —the Ten Commandments
> —the Two Laws of the Gospel ("Love God" and "Love Thy Neighbor")

The Lord's Prayer (Pater Noster)

Pater noster qui es in coelis	Fader oure that art in heven,
Sanctificetur nomen tuum	halwed be thi name;
Adveniat regnum tuum	come thi kyngdom,
Fiat voluntas tua	fulfild by thi wil
et in terra sicut in coelo	in hevene as in erthe;
Panem nostrum quotidianum	oure ech-day bred
da nobis hodie	yef us to day,
Et dimitte nobis debita nostra	and foryeve us oure dettes
sicut et dimittemus debitoribus nostris	as we foryeveth to oure detoures;
Et ne nos inducas in tentationem,	and ne led us nought in temptacion,
sed libera nos a malo. Amen.	bote delivere us of evel. So be it.

Hail Mary (Ave Maria)

Ave Maria, gratia plena	Heil Marye, ful of grace
Dominus tecum	God is with the [thee]
Benedicta tu in mulieribus	of alle wymmen thou art most blessid
Et benedictus fructus ventris tui.	and blessid be the fruyt of thi wombe, Ihesus.
Amen.	So mote it be.

—the Seven Virtues (Faith, Hope, Charity, Justice, Temperance, Prudence, Fortitude)

—the Seven Deadly Sins (Pride, Sloth, Envy, Avarice, Lust, Wrath, and Covetousness)

—the Seven Sacraments (Baptism, Confirmation, Confession, Communion, Ordination, Matrimony, and Extreme Unction)

—the Seven Works of Bodily Mercy (feeding the hungry, giving drink to the thirsty, clothing the naked, sheltering the stranger, nursing the sick, visiting the prisoner, and burying the dead).[3]

In spite of the universal system for religious education, religious belief was not uniform. The quality of religious instruction was not always very good, especially in remote parts of the country in parishes served by poorly trained priests. Even those individuals who received the proper education were not merely passive vessels filled with church doctrine. Peasants from the southern French village of Montaillou in the early fourteenth century are known to have reshaped and even rejected church teachings in formulating their own personal systems of belief, and the same could easily have been true of England, even though no English village is as well documented as Montaillou. It is difficult to generalize about religious belief, but one could probably say that while most inhabitants of England in this period genuinely held some form of

---

The Apostles' Creed (Credo)

Credo in Deum Patrem omnipotentem	I beleve in God, Fader almyghty,
Creatorem coeli et terrae	Makere of heven and erthe,
Et in Jesum Christum Filium eius unicum	And in Ihesu Crist, his onely sone
Dominum nostrum	oure Lorde
Qui conceptus est de	that is conceyved
Spiritu Sancto	by the Holy Gost,
Natus ex Maria Virgine	born of the Mayden Marye
Passus sub Pontio Pilato,	suffred under Pounce Pylate,
crucifixus	crucyfied,
Mortuus, et sepultus	ded, and beryed;
Descendit ad inferna	descendid to helle;
Tertia die resurrexit a mortuis	the thridde day he aros fro dethes
Ascendit ad coelos	styed [rose] up to hevene
Sedet ad dexteram Dei Patris omnipotentis	sitte on his Fader half [side];
Inde venturus judicare	schal come to deme [judge]
vivos et mortuos	the quick and dede.
Credo in Spiritum Sanctum,	I beleue in the Holy Gost,
Sanctam Ecclesiam Catholicam,	holy Chirche,
	that is alle that schulle be saved,
Sanctorum communionem	and in communion of hem,
Remissionem peccatorum	remissioun of synnes,
Carnis ressurectionem	risyng of flesch,
Et vitam aeternam. Amen.	and everlastynge lyf. Amen.

Christian belief, official doctrine was in many cases reformulated under the influence of folk tradition and personal inclination.[4]

The only organized alternative to church orthodoxy in Chaucer's England was the movement known as Lollardy. The Lollards had arisen in part as a result of general anti-clerical feeling in England. The obvious failings of the priests, monks, and friars of the official church made many doubt whether such men had any power to bring people closer to God, and the sorry spectacle of two rival popes did little to enhance the prestige of the papacy. At the same time, the Lollards espoused a new set of doctrines. They minimized the importance of traditional church rituals, offices, and customs, and emphasized the personal relationship of the individual with God, especially as achieved by reading the Bible. To promote this goal they undertook the first full translation of the Bible from Latin into English, a project completed in the 1380s. The leader of the Lollard movement was an Oxford scholar and priest named John Wycliffe. The movement was only a tiny minority, vigorously opposed by the Church and apparently mistrusted by most people, but it had some powerful supporters and was not finally forced underground until the beginning of the fifteenth century.

The focal point of religious observance was the ceremony of the Mass, celebrated every Sunday in every parish church. At the heart of the Mass was the sacrament of Communion, the ceremony by which the sacred wafer and wine were turned into the body and blood of Christ and received by the communicants. The bread and wine were usually received only by the priest himself: it was considered sufficient for the parishioners to participate vicariously. Mass was not always accompanied by a sermon: sermons were required only four times a year, when the priest was expected to preach on the fundamental points of the faith. The frequency of preaching probably varied with the locality. More heavily populated and prosperous areas had better trained priests and were more likely to receive sermons. During the service the parishioners were supposed to kneel on the floor, although they stood during the reading of the Gospel—the pew was a later development.[5]

A priest in his robes for celebrating mass [Clinch].

Most people received Communion only once a year, at Easter. The laity generally received Communion only in the form of the bread, except on very special occasions such as a coronation. Current doctrine held that the body and blood of Christ were present in both the bread and the wine. Prior to Communion, the communicant was expected to confess his or her sins to the priest, who would assign some form of penance. This process was known as the sacrament of Confession, or Penance, and was intended to ensure that the communicant would receive Christ's body in a state of spiritual cleanliness. Confession was supposed to take place with the confessant kneeling at the altar. There was no confessional booth: the priest merely pulled his hood down over his eyes. He was especially enjoined to avert his glance if the confessant was a woman. Many believed that Confession and Absolution should be in the hands of the parish priest—parish priests most especially were of this persuasion—but since the previous century the mendicant orders of Franciscan and Dominican friars had also enjoyed this privilege, and many worshippers resorted to them instead. As part of the ritual of Confession, the priest would examine the penitent on the Credo, Ave Maria, and Pater Noster; additional penance was assigned to those who failed this annual test. Penance for ordinary sins might be an imposed almsgiving, prayers, additional attendance at church, a pilgrimage, or abstinence from food or sex. From the time of the Fourth Lateran Council in 1215 all Christians were required to confess annually, although this rule was not always observed.[6]

There was no significant Jewish presence in fourteenth-century England because the Jews had been expelled from the country in 1290. However, a few may have trickled into the country from time to time, since additional measures were taken to remove them in 1358 and 1376. The culture of medieval England, as of the rest of Christian Europe at the time, was intensely anti-Semitic, although almost no Englishmen of Chaucer's day had met a Jew or had any real understanding of Judaism aside from what they knew of the Old Testament. Medieval society in general did not tolerate religious diversity, and in the eyes of medieval Christians, Jews bore the guilt for the crucifixion of Christ, so Jews were regarded at best with suspicion, at worst with the most brutal hostility.

THE MEDIEVAL COSMOS

According to medieval thought, God in His Heaven at once lay at the center of the created universe and encompassed it. As a physical entity, the universe was envisioned as a series of spheres nested within one another. At the outside was the sphere of heaven. Just inside was the *primum mobile*, the first mobile sphere. The *primum mobile* was turned by God and imparted its motion to the spheres within. After the *primum mobile* came the sphere in which the fixed stars were lodged. Inside this were the seven spheres of the planets. These were, in descending order, Saturn, Jupiter, Mars, the Sun, Venus, Mercury, and the Moon. Within the sphere of the Moon was the sphere of the Earth itself, which lay at the center of the physical universe. This was itself divided into concentric spheres for each of the four basic elements of matter, in descending order, Fire, Air, Water, and Earth.

Anyone who had any education knew that Earth, like all the spheres above it, was round. However, it was thought that the ocean encompassing the known continents of Europe, Africa, and Asia was too broad to be crossed, and that the heat of the equatorial regions made them impassable. These three continents, comprising only a quarter of the actual earth, were all that humans would ever be able to see. Most medieval maps offer a schematized view of the known portion of the world—they are intended as diagrams rather than as maps in the modern sense.[7]

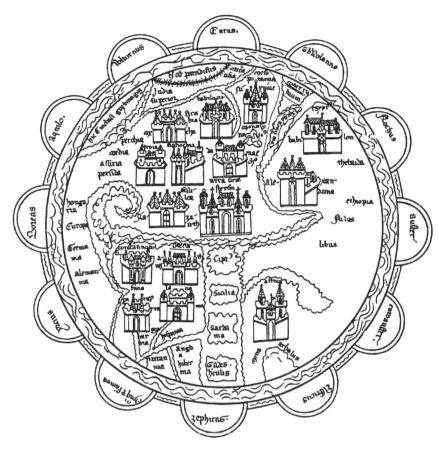

A map of the world, made between 1364 and 1372; the text is in Latin. East is at the top, as is usual with medieval maps. The lobes around the edges represent the winds—each had its own name depending on the direction from which it came. Within these is the encircling ring of the ocean. The upper portion of the map represents Asia, with Paradise at the top, and Jerusalem at the center. Africa is on the right, separated from Asia by the Nile. At the lower left is Europe, separated from Africa by the Mediterranean Sea and from Asia by the Black Sea; the cities of Constantinople, Athens, Rome, and Paris are shown. England is at the bottom and slightly to the left, marked "Anglia" [Santarem].

WORK AND THE ECONOMY

Most people in medieval England derived their living from the land. The basis of late medieval land cultivation was what is now called the three-field system. The lands   **Agriculture** under cultivation would be divided into three: in any given agricultural year (which began in October), one field would be planted in October-November with a "winter crop" of wheat and rye; one in February-March with a "spring crop" of oats, barley, peas, and beans; and one would lie fallow. The next October, the fallow field would be planted with the winter crop; in the spring, the winter field would be planted with the spring crop, and the field planted the previous spring would lie fallow. This system allowed the land to renew its nutrients to maximize productivity.

Wool   Although the traditional feudal system had been geared towards agriculture, pastoralism was playing an ever-growing part in England's economy. Wool was a better cash crop than grain: it was relatively easy to produce, it traveled well, and there was a constant demand for this staple fabric of medieval clothing—especially since English sheep yielded particularly fine wool. Sheep-raising provided relatively little employment on the land itself: a single shepherd could tend the sheep in land which would require many people for tending crops. However, the wool trade stimulated secondary economic activity. Threadmaking was a major cottage industry. Peasant women spent a great deal of time carding wool and often carried a spindle as they did their work around the house, to devote idle moments to the easy but time-consuming task of spinning thread. The thread was sold to the growing cloth industry, which was one of the most mechanized parts of the English economy: cloth was woven on sophisticated horizontal hand-looms and "fulled" (cleansed and thickened) in water-driven fulling mills. Clothmaking was still only a domestic industry in England—exported wool was invariably raw, bound for foreign looms, especially those of Flanders—but English weavers were gaining in skill and over the next few centuries would come to dominate the trade in woolen cloth.

Crafts and Trades   Agriculture was the staple of the rural English economy, but a wide variety of other occupations existed. In most places the principal specialists were the smith and the miller—it is no coincidence that these are two of the commonest surnames in the English-speaking world. The smith was a vital part of every community, as only he had the skills and equipment for producing and repairing iron goods. Iron was quite expensive, and still used sparingly, yet the smith's services were necessary for repairing tools and equipment. The miller's job also required expensive, specialized equipment. He had to own a mill, in which grain could be ground into flour; the mill might be powered by a waterwheel, or it might be a windmill.

In the towns, a full range of crafts and trades were represented. Particularly numerous were those involved in preparing and selling foodstuffs, such as bakers, cooks, fishmongers, butchers, brewers, and innkeepers. The other principal clustering of trades involved the making of apparel, including weavers, dyers, tailors, skinners, tanners, leatherworkers, glovers, furriers and shoemakers. Other common trades included barbers, carpenters, coopers (barrelmakers), masons, potters, and tilers. In addition, the maritime occupations of fishing and overseas trade were both expanding significantly in this period.

It is important to recall that a very large number of people were employed in domestic service—some 20% to 30% of the urban population of England may have been servants. Labor was relatively cheap, and even an urban craftsman might have one or more servants.

Buying turnips from an itinerant vendor. Italian, c. 1390 (TS Paris, f. 43) [McLean].

The labor of women played a vital part in the medieval economy. We can gain an idea of medieval women's occupations by considering the professions ending in "-ster," which originally designated a female worker. The "spinster" spun woolen or flaxen thread, which might be woven by a "webster" and sewed by a "seamster." The "baxster" baked bread, and the "brewster" brewed ale, which might be poured from the tap by a "tapster." In a peasant family, the woman was responsible for all sorts of domestic work. This meant not only cooking and cleaning but also caring for livestock, attending to the dairy, cultivating the garden, and selling produce at the market. In addition, the housewife would spend a fair bit of time carding wool and spinning it into thread. Because of the constant demand for thread for weaving cloth, this craft was certain to bring extra revenue into the home.

Standards of Living

Overall, the economy and standard of living in fourteenth-century England had more in common with the modern Third World than with modern Europe. Discrepancies in income were comparable to those in industrialized countries today, but a much higher portion of the population was poor. Although an industrial base was growing during this period, industry—in the sense of mass mechanized production—was practically nonexistent. Anything that is now mass-produced by machine was much more expensive than it is today. For example, plain russet wool, suitable for the clothes of a respectable peasant, at a shilling per yard would cost a laborer three days' wages for a single yard. On the other hand, because wages were low, anything requiring more labor than materials today was relatively inexpensive—domestic service is an important example.

At the same time, the economic upheavals of the fourteenth century were generally favorable to the commons. The ravages of the Black Plague left many bereft of friends and family, yet survivors found themselves in an economy where labor had become more scarce and valuable. In spite of governmental attempts to fix wages at pre-plague levels, laborers were able to negotiate better terms and there is evidence of a rising standard of living for working people during this period.

Fourteenth-century English coins (both sides, actual size). Top, l-r: noble, quarter-florin (both gold). Bottom, l-r: groat, penny, farthing (all silver) [Ruding].

Money, Wages, and Prices

As a rule, all money took the form of coins, and coinage was all of silver or gold. For this reason even the smallest coin was relatively valuable, and many transactions were conducted in goods rather than in money. The design of silver coins was generally the same regardless of date or denomination: on the front was a stylized face of the king, and the reverse bore the image of a cross; the only variations were the name of the king (that of the king reigning when it was minted) and the size of the coin. Gold coins were more diverse and quite valuable: the smallest was equivalent to a laborer's wages for an entire week.

The value of a coin varied according to the actual amount of silver or gold it contained. All coinage was alloyed to a greater or lesser extent, but English coins were generally of good and consistent quality during this period. By contrast, the French kings had fallen into the bad habit of mixing more base metal into the coinage whenever they needed to make their money stretch further. This simultaneously produced a dramatic surge in the apparent wealth of the French crown and instant inflation.

To complicate matters further, prices, particularly of staples, fluctuated greatly from year to year. Poor transportation and storage made it difficult to deal with local shortages. Grain prices might double or halve from one year to the next. Because random fluctuations in food prices around a fairly constant mean could mean widespread starvation and death, there was an understandable desire to legislate prices, particularly of staples. Basic foodstuffs, particularly bread and ale, were

Table 2.2: Relative Values of Fourteenth-Century Money

	Denomination	Monetary Value	Purchase Value	Rough $ Equivalent
Silver Coins	farthing (q.)	1/4 of a penny	1 loaf of bread	$1
	halfpenny (ob.)	1/2 of a penny	1 gallon of small ale	$2
	penny (d.)	20 (1/24 oz.) grams of 90% pure silver	1 lb. of butter	$4
	half-groat	2d. (2 pence)	1 day's earnings for an unskilled laborer	$8
	groat	4d. (4 pence)	1 day's earnings for a skilled laborer	$15
	shilling (s.)	12d. (12 pence)	1 day's earnings for a gentleman	$50
Gold Coins	quarter-noble, quarter-florin	1s. 8d.	1 lb. sugar or spice	$75
	half-noble, half-florin	3s. 4d.	1 year's rent for a floor in a townhouse	$150
	noble, florin	6s. 8d.	1 day's earnings for a lord	$300
Moneys of Account	mark (marc.)	13s. 4d., or 2/3 of a pound		$700
	pound (li.)	20s.	1 carthorse	$1,000

subject to precise price regulations, although they were not always successfully enforced.

Money was most often reckoned in pounds, shillings, and pence. Some denominations, such as the mark and pound, existed only as moneys of account, that is, for convenience of reckoning rather than as actual coins. Table 2.2 offers an idea of the relative value of the various denominations, but the modern equivalents should be taken as magnitudes rather than values: the differences between modern and fourteenth-century price structures make it impossible to derive a universally valid equivalence.

A clearer idea of the value of money can be had by comparing wages and prices. In Table 2.3, the column on the left represents pay in military service to the king, that on the right the income of civilian craftsmen and laborers.[8]

Table 2.3: Sample Daily Wages

Bishop or Earl	6s. 8d.	Clerk	1s.
Baron or Banneret	4s.	Mason	$5^1/_2$d.
Knight	2s.	Carpenter	$4^1/_2$d.
Squire, Chaplain	1s.	Thatcher	4d.
Mounted Archer	6-8d.	Thatcher's Assistant	$2^1/_4$d.
Archer	3-6d.	Agricultural Laborer	8d. at harvest, 3-4d. at other seasons
Page	2d.	Female Agricultural Laborer	2d.

Laborers' wages were also subject to seasonal variation: they were paid more in the summer, when demand for labor was high and the extra daylight permitted longer hours of work. Wages were not always based entirely on money: sometimes the employer would provide food or lodging as part of the remuneration. Of course, many people were not paid wages at all: landowners, landholders and independent tradesmen made whatever money their lands or professions yielded. Table 2.4 shows sample annual incomes for such people.[9]

Table 2.4: Sample Yearly Incomes

Duke of Lancaster	£10,000	Petty Merchant	£10
Knight	£40 or more	Craftsman	£5
Yeoman	£10	Husbandman	£4
Cottar	£1 from land	Laborer	£2

To gain an idea of the purchasing power of these incomes, one may compare the sample prices in Table 2.5.[10] Bear in mind that prices could vary drastically according to time and place (for example, city prices might be $1^1/_3$ to 2 times as high as those elsewhere). Another important factor was the heavy reliance on secondhand wares. Most ordinary people could not afford to buy major items new, so used goods (especially clothing) constituted quite a large portion of the economy. Quality was also a factor: it is normally impossible to tell from the context what quality of item the price represents.

Goods might be purchased from an itinerant vendor, a market stall, or a shop. Produce was generally sold at market stalls; manufactured goods were more likely to be found in a shop.

Table 2.5: Sample Prices of Goods and Services

Cow	9s.	Cart horse	20s.
Horse	40s.-70s.	Pig	3s. 2d.
Sheep	1s. 6d.	Hen	$1^3/_4$d.
Ale, best quality (1 gal.)	$1^1/_2$d.	Small ale (1 gal.)	$^1/_2$d.
Loaf of bread	$^1/_4$-1d.	Butter (1 lb.)	1d.
Roast pig	8d.	Roast hen	4d.
Eggs (10)	1d.	Leg of pork	4d.
Herrings (6-10)	1d.	Wine (1 gal.)	8-10d.
Pepper (1 lb.)	1s. 4d.	Oil (1 gal.)	1s. 4d.
Sugar (1 lb.)	1s. 7d.	Almonds (1 lb.)	3d.
Ginger (1 lb.)	2s. 3d.	Saffron (1 lb.)	14s.
Canvas (12 ells)	3s. $9^1/_2$d.	Linen (1 yd)	6d.
Wool, fine (1 yd.)	4s.	Wool, 2nd grade (1 yd.)	2s.
Breech	1d.	Gown	4-5s.
Russet gown	9d.	Kirtle and hood	1s. 4d.
Surcoat	2s.	Hose	20d.
Hood	4d.	Straw hat	6d.
Cap	7d.	Fustian shoes	6d.
Wax candles (1 lb.)	1s.	Tallow candles (1 lb.)	2d.
Eyeglasses	$^1/_2$d.	Stool	6d.
Knife	$1^1/_4$d.	Wooden comb	1d.
Bible	£1-3	Ordinary book	2s.
Peasant house	£2-£7	Castle tower	£400
Rent for a craftsman's townhouse	20s.	Rent for 1 acre (villeinage tenure)	3-9d.
Rent for 1-2 rooms	3-4s./year	Hire courier from London to Oxford	10d.

[Note: The price of a loaf of bread was fixed: the weight varied according to the price of wheat.]

3

The Course of Life

The basic biological facts of birth in the fourteenth century were of course much the same then as now, but the human context was **Birth** rather different. A useful glimpse is offered by John of Trevisa's late fourteenth-century translation of the thirteenth-century encyclopedia *De Proprietatibus Rerum* by Bartholomeus Anglicus:

> A midwife is a woman that has the craft to help a woman that labors with child, that she may bear and bring forth her child with less woe and sorrow. And so that the child should be born with the less labor and woe she anoints and balms the mother's womb, and helps and comforts her in that manner. Also she takes the child out of the womb, and knots his navel four inches long. With water she washes away the blood of the child, and balms him with salt and honey to dry up the humors and to comfort his limbs and members, and swathes him in cloths.[1]

As Trevisa suggests, birth was in the hands not of a physician but of a midwife. A physician would not be involved unless there was a pathological complication. The setting was also different, since childbirth almost invariably took place at home. Hospitals in this period were principally a place for long-term care of the infirm poor, rather than for short-term intervention in acute medical circumstances.

Another difference was the degree of risk to the mother. We have no accurate figures for childbirth deaths in England during this period, but they were certainly higher than they are now. Some historians have suggested as high as 20%, but this is a gross overestimation—England would soon have been empty at so catastrophic a rate of maternal death, and the evidence of wills suggests that a majority of women survived their husbands rather than vice versa. No certain data exist for England during this period, but in fifteenth-century Florence the rate of maternal mortality was 14.4 in 1,000, which is probably nearer the mark. This would still be very high by modern standards: Nigeria in 1988 was reported to have a rate of 8 in 1,000, which was unusually high even for the Third World.[2]

Childbirth—a representation of the birth of the Virgin Mary in a fourteenth-century home. North Italian, c. 1385 (Bibliothèque Nationale MS Lat. 757, f. 351v) [McLean].

The Newborn   The first formal event in the newborn's life was the ceremony of baptism, or "christening." This was the single most vital of the rituals administered by the Church, for without it one could never enter heaven. Baptism was so important that everyone was encouraged to learn the basic words of the ritual, even if only in English, so as to be able to pronounce them at need; in a doubtful birth, midwives were urged to baptize the infant as soon as its head appeared. The formula was quite simple: *Ego baptizo te in nomine Patris et Filii et Spiritus Sancti. Amen*; or in Middle English, *I crystene the [thee] in the nome of the Fader, and the Son and the Holy Gost. Amen.*

If the infant survived the birth, the christening could take place within the week—the degree of haste would depend on the health of the child. When the time came, the godparents were summoned and the family proceeded to the church, where the ceremony was celebrated by the parish priest. Ironically, the mother would probably not be present, since it was the custom for her not to enter the church prior to her own ceremony of "purification" or "churching," which was supposed to cleanse her from the spiritual stain of childbirth—although some people felt this restriction was not a proper part of Christian observance.

The child would have two godparents of the same sex and one of the opposite. The bond between the infant and the godparents was a significant one. They were expected to play a role in the religious instruction of the child, and people who were related by godparentage were forbidden to marry each other. The word "gossip," or "god-sib," originally meant someone related by godparentage—a "god-sibling." It later came to mean "an intimate friend," and is now applied to the kinds of discussions people have with close friends.[3]

A baptismal procession. French, late fourteenth century (TBH, p. 262) [McLean].

Baptism marked the child as a part of the Christian church; because church and society were considered equivalent, this also meant bringing the child into society. It was through this ceremony that the child received the most important symbol of its public identity: a name. As a rule, the child was supposed to be baptized with the name of its principal godparent of the same sex. For boys, this generally meant either a saint's name or a name of French origin. The single most common masculine name fell into the first category: perhaps a third to a half of the male population of England was named John. Other common saints' names included Matthew, Thomas, Andrew, James, Simon, Pierce (Peter), Stephen, Nicholas, Bartholomew, Edward, and Edmund. Names from the Old Testament were less common: Adam, Joseph (also a New Testament name), David, and Daniel were the only ones widely used. French names had become fashionable as a result of the Norman Conquest in 1066, the most common being Robert and William; other popular names in this class included Roger, Richard, Walter, Henry, Hugh, and Philip. In the north of England there was a slightly greater diversity, including the occasional Alexander (perhaps from Scottish influence), Alan, Brian, and Conan (names imported by Breton participants in the Norman Conquest), and even Tristan (a name from Arthurian legend).

The trends in girls' names were quite different. A few saints' names were common, notably Katherine, Julian, Cecily, Lucy, Christine, Elizabeth, Annice or Agnes, and Margaret (with its variant, Margery), although none dominated in the way John did among men. Of Old Testament names, only Sarah was common. Joan was also common, as were Isabel, Alice, Lettice, Emma, Maud (Matilda), Rose, and Beatrice. Some women even bore names from legend, such as Isold or Sibil. A distinctive feature of English names in this period is the nearly complete absence of Mary or Martha.

Among the lower classes, these names might be reduced to an abbreviated or diminutive form. Richard might be called "Dick" or "Hick"; Roger "Dodge" or "Hodge"; Robert "Dob," "Hob," or "Robin"; John "Jack"; Nicholas "Coll"; Gilbert "Gib"; Thomas "Tom"; David "Daw"; William "Will"; Walter "Wat"; Catherine "Kit"; Cecily "Cis." Diminutive versions of a name were often formed with the suffix "-kin," such as "Jankin" for John, "Perkin" for Pierce, "Simkin" for Simon, "Malkin" for Maud, or "Watkin" and "Wilkin" for Wat and Will.

In previous centuries, individuals of a given name had been distinguished from each other by second names. These were usually one of three types: patronymics designating the person's father (such as Robertson, Roberts, Robinson, Robins, Dobson, Hobson, and Hobbes, which originally meant "the son of Robert"), place-names designating the individual's place of origin (such as "of Lincoln," later "Lincoln"), or professional names indicating the person's trade ("the Smith," later "Smith"). In London it had become customary for children to inherit their father's second name as a surname by the mid-fourteenth century; and by the end of the century surnames were almost universal, although names continued fluctuate as late as the sixteenth century. The shift towards surnames was slightly slower in the countryside than in the towns.[4]

Infancy

From the outset, the shape of the infant's life depended on its social background. All medieval babies were breast-fed for the first two or three years, but while most women nursed their own children, the babies of privileged families were often given to a wet-nurse. Trevisa's description of the infant's world seems familiar in most respects:

> Nurses rock children in cradles to promote natural heat with gentle and moderate moving. . . . Also they sing lullabies and other cradle songs to please the wits of the child. . . .
> A nurse . . . takes him up if he falls, and gives him suck if he weeps, and kisses him if he is still . . . and cleans and washes him if he fouls himself, and feeds him with her fingers against his own will. And because he cannot speak, the nurse pronounces the words childishly, the more easily to teach the child that cannot speak. And she uses medicines to bring the child to suitable state

if he is sick. And she heaves him up, now on her shoulders, now in her hands, now on her knees and lap; and so she heaves him up and down if he squeals and weeps. And she puts food in her own mouth and makes it ready for the toothless child, that he may the more easily swallow that food.

Children might also be fed a mixture of milk and grain as a kind of pap. One major difference between medieval and modern methods of infant care was the practice of "swaddling":

Because of tenderness of the limbs, the child may easily and quickly twist and bend and take diverse shapes, and therefore children's limbs are bound with strips of cloth and other suitable bonds so that they will not be crooked or ill shaped.[5]

In addition to its supposed virtue of making the infant's limbs grow straight, swaddling kept it warm and out of trouble. The baby was not always confined in this way but would be unwrapped at times so that it might crawl about.

During the first years of life, there was surprisingly little differentiation between boys and girls. Whether male or female, the child was almost exclusively in female care, either of its mother or a nurse. However, girls seem to have had a higher mortality rate, which may indicate that more attention was lavished on a son's well-being.

Childhood in the Middle Ages was a time of enormous danger, due primarily to the ever-present risk of illness and disease. Accidental death was also a problem, especially in poorer families where the requirements of household labor sometimes meant that the child was left unattended. The risk was highest just after birth. In the latter half of the fourteenth century, nearly 300 of 1,000 children died in their first year (by comparison, even among the poorest Third World nations today an infant mortality rate of 125 in 1,000 is exceptionally high). After 10 years, only 500 of the 1,000 would still be living, and only 300 would survive to age 20.[6] Of course, these figures were extreme even by medieval standards, as Chaucer's lifetime corresponds to the worst ravages of the Black Plague.

The early life of children was mostly a combination of learning and play. For most children, the only formal education was their religious instruction. This was seen primarily as a familial responsibility, especially that of the godparents, who were expected to ensure that by the age of 5 or 7 the child knew the basic elements of Christian belief and observance. Children would also learn good manners. They were taught not to pick their nose, or scratch or rub themselves, or swear, and were expected to learn to keep their hands and faces clean and to pare and clean their nails.[7] Some children may even have been taught letters as early as age 3, 4, or 5, at least in aristocratic families.

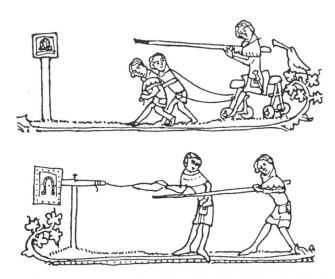

Boys playing at the quintain. Flemish, 1338-1344 (RA, f. 82v) [McLean].

In laboring-class families, a child of 4 or 5 might be set to do small tasks about the house, such as fetching water or minding a younger sibling. However, the bulk of a child's time in these early years was probably given to play and to exploration of the world around them. Most of what we know about the early life of children comes from the records of coroners' investigations into accidental deaths, so we tend to see rather a grim side of children's play: a child tries to fetch a white feather out of a brook and falls in, a 2-year-old girl tries to follow older children across a stream and drowns, a 3-year-old girl wanders out into a London street and is run down by a rider who has lost control of his horse.[8]

It is a popular myth that medieval parents responded to the high rate of child mortality by investing little emotion in their children, but contemporary evidence suggests otherwise. Trevisa's description of a mother's devotion to her child is amply supported by other contemporary sources:

> The mother conceives with pleasure, and labors and brings forth her child with sorrow and with woe, and she loves the child tenderly, and hugs and kisses him and feeds him and nurtures attentively.

Medieval theory expected the father to be less emotional, but not less loving:

> A man loves his child, and feeds and nurtures him, and sets him at his own table when he is weaned, and teaches him in his youth with speech and with words, and chastises him with beating, and sets him to learning under ward and keeping of wardens and tutors. And the father shows him no glad cheer

lest he become proud. And he . . . gives to his children clothing and food as their age requires, and acquires land and heritage for his children constantly and makes it greater and greater, and improves his acquisition, and leaves it to his heirs.[9]

One of the first and most important things a child learned was its mother tongue. In previous centuries, this would have been French for an aristocrat and English for a commoner. The **Language** Norman Conquest of 1066 had placed French-speaking Normans in charge of England, and for several centuries French remained the language of government and aristocratic life. By the fourteenth century this situation had changed substantially. By the early part of the century, aristocrats no longer necessarily spoke French as their native tongue, and by the end of the century the scholar John Trevisa remarked that the English aristocracy knew "no more French than their left heel." A few years later two English ambassadors to France—a knight and a lawyer— had to confess that they were as ignorant of French as of Hebrew. French continued to enjoy considerable prestige, being extensively used among the most cultured Englishmen as well as in the legal system, but its use was now purely artificial.

English gained ground as French lost it. In 1353 the law courts of London abandoned the requirement that proceedings be conducted in French, and the rest of the courts in the country followed suit soon after. In 1363 the Chancellor opened Parliament in English. The latter half of the fourteenth century witnessed the re-emergence of English as a fully developed language of literature and learning. In the 1360s a London clerk of northwestern origin named William Langland produced *Piers Plowman*, the first major work in the new literary tradition. Around this time Geoffrey Chaucer was beginning his own poetic career, which was to culminate in the *Canterbury Tales*, composed between about 1380 and 1400. It was also during these years that the school of religious reformers known as Lollards wrote the first complete translation of the Bible in English; John Trevisa's late fourteenth-century translations of the encyclopedia *De Proprietatibus Rerum* and the massive history *Polychronicon* marked the entry of English into the world of learning. For the first time in three centuries, it was no longer necessary to know Latin or French in order to participate in the learned or literary culture of the day.

To a modern English speaker, fourteenth-century spoken English would be extremely difficult to understand. For a start, the long vowels sounded more like their equivalents in Spanish or German, and final -*e* was pronounced: *have* would sound (roughly) as if it rhymed with "lava," *be* with "say"; *liking* would sound like "leaking," *moon* like "moan," and *town* like "toon." Some consonants that are silent today were pronounced, such as the *k* in *knight*, the *g* in *gnat*, and the *gh* in *light* (which resembled a rough *h* sound). The grammar was different too. For example, "thou" was used as a familiar form of "you"—people might call their close friends or family "thou" ("thee" was used for "thou" in exactly the same ways we use "him" for "he"). For a sample of fourteenth-century English, see the prayers and creed in Chapter 2.

A man and boy, after a contemporary Italian painting—the boy is dressed in a smaller version of an adult's gown. Italian, c. 1385 (Altichiero, "The Beheading of St. George) [McLean].

Childhood According to medieval ideas of child development, infancy, as the first stage of life, ended by age 7 or so. At this point the child began to be integrated more directly into society. John Trevisa offers a convincing description of these years:

> A child that is between seven years and fourteen . . . is able to receive chastising and learning, and then he is put and set to learn under tutors and compelled to receive learning and chastising. . . . Such children . . . are able and light to move, clever to learn ditties, and without industriousness, and they lead their lives without care and industriousness and are interested only in mirth and pleasure, and dread no peril more than beating with a stick; and they love an apple more than gold. . . . When they are praised or blamed they set little thereby. . . . For tenderness of body they are easily hurt and injured, and they cannot well endure hard work. . . . Since small children often have evil manners and faults, and think only about things that are and care not for things that will be, they love playings and games and vanities. . . . When they

are washed of filth and dirt they soon dirty themselves again. When the mother washes and combs them they kick and prance and push with feet and hands, and resist with all their might and strength. They think only of the pleasure of the stomach, and know not the measure of their own stomach. They covet and desire to eat and drink all the time. With difficulty they rise out of their bed, and they ask for food at once.[10]

By the age of 5 or 7, having learned the elements of religious belief, the child would receive the sacrament of Confirmation, a ceremony administered by the bishop to mark the child's full entry into the Christian community.[11] Somewhere around the age of 7, the child would begin to be actively oriented towards his or her future place in society, and from this age the process of sexual differentiation began in earnest. Religious counselors recommended separating the sleeping arrangements for boys and girls at this age.[12]

Girls continued to live in the female sphere of the home, where they learned domestic skills appropriate to their station in life. For an aristocrat, this might mean the skills necessary for household management, as well as embroidery, music, and other adorning accomplishments; for a commoner, cooking, spinning, sewing, laundry, healing, and other needful domestic skills. Boys meanwhile began to operate in the world of men. The sons of ordinary commoners might be set to fishing, herding, or caring for the larger livestock, while boys of the privileged classes would be given to the care of male tutors or teachers. Among other skills, a gentleman's son would learn the aristocratic arts of riding and hunting, and perhaps the rudiments of combat.

Formal education was much rarer in the Middle Ages than it is today: in general, it was the preserve of a tiny privileged **Education** fraction of society consisting mostly of the aristocracy, the clergy, and the more prosperous townsfolk. Children who were destined for a full education would begin studying by age seven or so. Those who were to be taught only basic literacy might begin later. There were several ways a child might receive an elementary education. The most privileged children had private tutors. Children of less wealthy families might be sent to a commercial school in a town or a school attached to a religious institution. The poorest children were unlikely to receive any education at all, except for boys who were marked for a career in the church: such boys might be sent to a religious school, with the costs paid for by some form of scholarship.

The first stage in a formal education was learning how to read. Literacy was a relatively rare skill in the fourteenth century, although it was becoming more widespread. Just how rare it was depends on how one defines it. There is a broad gray zone between total literacy and total illiteracy, and many medieval people lived within it.

a cursive form
of batarde:

a b c d e f g h i
j k l m n o p q r
s t u v w x y z

LETTER HEIGHT
4-6 PEN
WIDTHS
HIGH.

PEN AT 45° ANGLE

ALTERNATE CONSTRUCTION
OF ASCENDERS FOR GREATER SPEED

LETTERS WRITTEN
WITH ROTRING L9

KDW

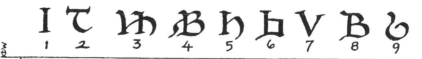

1 2 3 4 5 6 7 8 9

—NUMERALS WERE OCCASIONALLY REVERSED OR TURNED 90° OR 180°.
—O OCCASIONALLY APPEARED IN MODERN FORM OR SPACE WAS FILLED WITH
A + OR — SIGN OR A DIAGONAL STROKE.

(DROGIN, P. 170)

Fourteenth-century letters [Weatherbee].

Fourteenth-century capital letters [Weatherbee].

Some could read but not write. Ordinarily, the medieval student would be taught reading first; only when he had mastered that would he be taught how to write. Some never got beyond the ability to read, and some learned only the bare rudiments of writing.

Some could read but not understand what they read. Most of the business of the church and royal administration was still conducted in Latin or French. The priest of a remote parish might be able to read familiar phrases of ritual but not be able to understand the Latin very well.

Some could read and write but chose not to. Many people of gentle birth preferred to employ scribes to read and write for them, even though some were perfectly capable of writing for themselves when necessary— much as a modern executive dictates letters to a secretary.

Fragment of a letter written in 1419, actual size. The hand is a rapid and informal cursive typical of ordinary correspondence. The text reads "Furthremore I wole that ye . . . of northumbrelond and my . . . northmarches and specialy . . ." [Warner].

Overall, male literacy at the end of the fifteenth century may have been around 10%. It was certainly lower in the fourteenth century, although there is little information on which to base a precise figure. The most literate men were scholars and the professional clerks that carried out the business of royal and church administration. They needed to be able to read, write, and express themselves in Latin, French, or English. Many, but not all, were clerics, and not all clerics were men of letters in this sense.

Among the aristocracy, most could read and write, at least in English. Yet there were exceptions. The squire who commanded the La Rochelle garrison in 1372 was easily tricked by the pro-French mayor of the town because he could not read. When the mayor showed him a letter from the King of England, the squire recognized the king's seal but was entirely unable to read the letter. This allowed the mayor to pretend to have the letter read aloud, but he actually gave a fabricated message that led to the capture and betrayal of the entire garrison. Even in the seventeenth century there were still illiterate men among the aristocracy.

Literacy tended to be higher in the city than in the country. The richer merchants could read and write as a matter of course. Many of the poorer merchants and shopkeepers could read and write as well, and some of their bills and accounts from this period have been preserved. Among craftsmen, practitioners of well-paid sedentary crafts like limners (manuscript painters) or goldsmiths might well be literate, while tanners and smiths were probably not. By the late fifteenth century, many urban guilds expected their members to be able to read and write.

At all levels of society, women were less literate than men. At the close of the Middle Ages, female literacy appears to have been about one-tenth that of men. As among men, female literacy was most common among the aristocracy and the richer merchant families. A wealthy citizen such as the one who wrote the *Goodman of Paris* [*Le Ménagier de Paris*], a collection of instructions for running an urban household, expected that a prosperous townsman's wife would be able to read letters from her husband and perhaps "answer them in your own hand, if you know how."

Few husbandmen were literate, and even fewer poor laborers. Most rural folk had little opportunity or incentive to learn to read and write. Not all were completely illiterate, however. Two of the seven husbandmen called in to witness John Fastolf's will in 1466 signed their names, and as early as the thirteenth century manuals were being written on the office of the "reeve." The reeve was almost always a villein, although usually a substantial one. He had an important role in the running of the village and was often responsible for keeping manorial accounts. Such a man would find literacy valuable, as would any husbandman who did not want to be utterly at the mercy of others in dealing with a lease or a will or financial accounts. Apparently literacy was common enough among the lower orders that the revolutionary priest John Ball could circulate subversive letters during the Peasants' Revolt of 1381 and expect them to find readers.

In addition to basic literacy, elementary education might include the study of Latin, especially for boys destined for a career in the church. If the child was headed for a life in the urban elite, education would almost certainly include "ciphering," or using Arabic numerals. Children of privileged families would also learn French, which remained the distinctive language of upper-class culture.

Advanced education began in the teens and took one of two forms. A boy headed for a career in the church or as a physician might go to university—Oxford, Cambridge, or a university on the Continent. University teaching was always in Latin. The course of study for the Baccalaureate degree concentrated on Grammar, Logic, Rhetoric, Geometry, Arithmetic, Astronomy, and Music. Advanced degrees were available in Canon Law (that is, church law), Philosophy, and Medicine. A more secular form of education was available at the Inns of Court in

London. These were institutions where young men could gain an introduction to the workings of English law.

Adolescence By age 14, children were becoming integrated as subordinate participants in the world of adults and specializing for their role in the society and economy. At age 14 a child was subject to the national poll tax that was instituted in 1377. Aristocratic youths at this age continued in a manner similar to that of younger years, the primary difference being that a boy of 14 was considered old enough to be learning the arts of war in earnest.

A peasant girl by this age would be engaged in exactly the same sorts of work as her mother, such as carding wool, spinning thread, cooking, cleaning the home, tending to the garden and dairy, and looking after the younger children. For boys, however, the process was slightly slower. At age 14 they had not yet achieved a physical development sufficient to handle the heaviest agricultural tasks, but as they matured through their teenage years their work patterns assimilated to those of their elders; by the time they attained legal majority at 21, they were performing the same work as the rest of the men, although it might be years before they actually inherited their own holding.

Urban adolescents, or those whose families had urban connections, might be apprenticed to a craft or trade at this point. Apprenticeship was a privileged position, since completion of apprenticeship entitled the youth to membership in the guild and concomitant citizenship in the town. For this reason there seem to have been two tracks, one for full apprentices and another for those who were not to be fully admitted to the craft. The apprentice lived with his master, perhaps along with one or more other apprentices. Apprenticeship traditionally lasted 7 years, although it could last longer. Girls as well as boys might be apprenticed; their choices were more limited, principally such crafts as embroidery and dressmaking, and their apprenticeships were not expected to last as long, since they were regarded as an interim measure prior to marriage. Girls' apprenticeships did not lead to membership in the guild.[13]

Those in both town and country who had no expectations of advancement through inheritance or family connections were more or less already in their lifetime economic roles by the age of 14 or so. For people in this position the usual route was selling one's labor, whether in domestic service, in agriculture, or in a craft or trade.[14]

Coming of Age For the duration of his teens, a boy remained a subordinate participant in the society and economy of adults. This transition from a subordinate to an independent position varied from class to class. In theory, people came of age at 21, the official age of inheritance, but this was not necessarily significant in practice. The age of 21 was most likely to be significant for a male aristocrat, since his family might have the means to set him up in some sort of independent position. A youth who had been apprenticed as a part of the guild system remained under tutelage until the end of his apprenticeship, at which point he might set up as an independent master, if he could afford it, or become a journeyman and sell his labor to others. A peasant remained in a semi-dependent position until he inherited a holding, until which time he continued to work on his family's holding. For laborers or servants, coming of age would not be a very meaningful event: they would have been fully participating members of the work force since their early teens and would probably remain in a semi-dependent state for the remainder of their lives.

For women these professional considerations were of less importance. Women were essentially treated as adolescents until they were married (unless they entered religious life), at which point they exchanged subordination to family or employer for subordination to husband. Girls might inherit property at age 16 if they were married and their husbands were age 21 or older.

For both men and women, marriage was probably the most important step in the transition to independence. Marriage was **Marriage** a religious rather than a civil procedure, and it fell under the jurisdiction of the Church. Canon law prohibited marriage before the age of 12 for girls, or 14 for boys. In reality, such child marriages were practically unknown. As it was unusual for two couples to live in a single house, marriage was delayed until the prospective couple had some sort of household slot to occupy, whether by inheritance or by economic or professional advancement. This meant that most commoners married rather late: men in their late twenties, women in their mid-twenties. Aristocrats, whose economic opportunities were less restricted, usually married younger: the men in their early twenties, the women in their late teens. The urban elite tended to marry at ages similar to that of the aristocracy.[15]

Marriage in the Middle Ages was a fairly involved process. It began with an arrangement between the two families, so that each would know what property was being settled on the prospective spouses. Once these matters were accomplished, a betrothal took place. Prior to the actual ceremony, the "banns," or marriage announcement, had to be read publicly in church on three successive Sundays, announcing the planned wedding. The theoretical purpose of the banns was to allow anyone who knew of any impediment to the marriage to come forward—doubtless this could have been a problem in the insular agrarian communities of the medieval world, where the couple could easily be related to each other. The wedding itself was celebrated at the door of the church, but might be followed by a nuptial Mass within.[16] The bride might wear a garland on her head, and the man gave his bride a ring as part of the ceremony, which was followed by a feast.

Such was the ideal. In fact, according to custom, a promise of marriage followed by sexual consummation was also reckoned to be a legally valid marriage. Such clandestine marriages were frowned on, but since there was as yet no official requirement of witnesses, they were inevitably a part of life. This made for substantial problems: in the event of sexual consummation one partner might claim marriage on the grounds of a prior promise, and the other might deny that such a promise had been made.

A husband and wife [Ashdown].

Once the marriage was made, it was generally considered permanently binding. Divorce had been a part of European practice earlier in the Middle Ages, but by the fourteenth century the Church had succeeded in suppressing it. However, a marriage might be annulled if it were found to have been invalid in the first place. An annulment might be procured if a prior family relationship existed between the couple (whether by blood or marriage), if either partner had been coerced into the marriage, or if the man was found to be sexually impotent, to name just a few possible reasons.

Once a person reached adulthood, the prospects of living a full life increased dramatically. Life expectancy at birth was only 17 years, but this figure is distorted by the extremely high rate of child mortality. Even in this **Aging and Life Expectancy** century of plague, a 20-year-old had a total life expectancy of 45 years, a 30-year-old of 50, and a 40-year-old of 60.[17]

These figures seem all the more remarkable in light of medieval medical practice. As with other aspects of medieval life, medieval medicine was highly stratified. At **Sickness and Medicine** the top of the profession was the physician, who was primarily a theorist, educated at a university faculty of medicine. He was expected to have mastered the physiological learning passed down from the ancients about the workings of the body in sickness and health and the efficacy of diverse substances against specific illnesses. His primary skills were in diagnosis and in prescription of remedies. One of the physician's principal skills was "uroscopy," the art of diagnosing patients' conditions from the appearance, scent, and even taste of their urine—at once reminiscent of modern urine analysis, but very unlike it!

Under the circumstances, it is hardly surprising that the physician's medical practice tended to be bookish. Like other mainstream intellectuals of the period, he favored authority over experience: medical learning was acquired by reading the works of Galen rather than by devising new interpretations of observed phenomena. Human physiology was based on the Four Humors: Blood (hot and moist), Phlegm (cold and moist), Choler (cold and dry), and Melancholy (hot and dry). An individual's personality was thought to be based on the mix of humors in their body. Illness was typically attributed to an imbalance of humors, so the remedy was to be found by administration of substances that would restore the balance. The Four Humors corresponded to the Four Elements of which the material world was thought to consist, and there was an elaborate scheme of correspondences between both of these and other aspects of the material universe and the human body, as laid out in Table 3.1.

Manual work was considered beneath the dignity of a physician: any procedure that we would consider an "operation" was left to the surgeon. In fact, the surgeon's title derived ultimately from the Greek words for "manual worker." Whereas the physician enjoyed the gentlemanly status of the professional, the surgeon was classed with artisans: instead of studying at the university, he learned his craft in apprenticeship to a master surgeon. All physical aspects of physiological care were the responsibility of the surgeon: this included not just surgery, but dentistry as well. The work of the surgeon was more practically oriented than that of a physician: as a craftsman the surgeon had to learn by experience, and in any case there were not many ancient authorities on surgery. Ironically, the less prestigious profession seems to have been more effective in healing and more fruitful in contributing to the understanding of human physiology. The distinguished English surgeon John Arderne successfully operated on certain kinds of cancerous tumors, and a number of ground-breaking surgical treatises were written in this period. Comparable in status to the surgeon was the apothecary, who concocted the medications prescribed by the physician and who belonged to the powerful and wealthy guild of grocers.

Surgeons and apothecaries occupied a position at the highest end of the artisanal spectrum: they were literate (even in Latin) and sometimes acquired considerable prestige and wealth. The same was not true of the next lower grade of medical practitioner, the barber-surgeons. These belonged to the barbers' guild; they were less educated than the surgeon, although they performed the same sorts of procedures. They might also offer haircuts and shaves. In spite of their lower status, barber-surgeons were sometimes quite competent medical practitioners. Ordinary barbers (called "barber-tonsors") also performed surgical procedures, particularly the simple ones such as pulling teeth or letting blood. In token of their surgical activities, the barbers had a red-and-white striped pole as their professional emblem. Finally, there were various part-time healers. Country folk might rely on "leeches," people who practiced folk medicine in addition to their principal occupation. Many women were part-time practitioners too, and for most families the housewife was the primary source of medical care.[18]

Access to medical care varied enormously. Most of the professional practitioners were in London. In other large towns there might be a few physicians and surgeons, but medicine was primarily in the hands of the barber-surgeons and barber-tonsors. The countryside was served only by part-time healers, unless a patient was wealthy enough to import the services of a professional. Treatment by a highly skilled practitioner could be very expensive: Arderne recommended a fee of 100 marks for a great person, £40 for lesser people, and £5 as a minimum. In principle, medical practitioners were supposed to treat the poor free of charge, but it is unlikely that they devoted much of their valuable time to such charity.

In a society that was generally poor, with a relatively primitive standard of living and very little understanding of the causes of illness, sickness and disease were never far away. The situation was worst in the cities because of overcrowding and inadequate sanitation. The surgeon Arderne estimated post-operative infection to be as high as 50%. Remains of villagers found by archeologists have shown evidence of rheumatic diseases and gallstones. On the other hand, the rate of dental cavities among these villagers was relatively low—not surprising, given the near total absence of white sugar. The average height was 5' 5"—slightly short

Table 3.1: Humors, Elements, and Correspondences

Humor	Element	Qualities	Wind	Celestial Quarter	Time of Day / Gender	Zodiacal Sign	Part of Body	Planet
Blood	Air	Hot-Moist	South	West	Day / Male	Gemini Libra Aquarius	Shoulders, Arms, Hands Lower Belly, Navel Shins	Mercury Venus Saturn
Choler (Yellow Bile)	Fire	Hot-Dry	East	East		Aries Leo Sagittarius	Head, Face Stomach, Muscles, Heart Thighs	Mars Sun Jupiter
Melancholy (Black Bile)	Earth	Cold-Dry	North	South	Night / Female	Taurus Virgo Capricorn	Neck / Throat Belly / Guts Knees	Venus Mercury Saturn
Phlegm	Water	Cold-Moist	West	North		Cancer Scorpio Pisces	Breast, Ribs, Lungs Genitals Feet	Moon Mars Jupiter

This table illustrates the system of correspondences between various aspects of the physical universe as understood by medieval science. The humors are the four substances which compose the human body; the elements are the substances which compose the physical world. Each of the humors and elements is defined by two pairs of opposing qualities (cold/hot and moist/dry). All of these substances and properties are integrated into an orderly scheme of associations, as show above. For example, the Sun was said to govern the human stomach, and was associated with the zodiacal sign Leo, with daytime and the male gender, with the East, and with Choler and Fire.

by modern standards, but much taller than the stunted peasants we sometimes imagine today.

Health conditions were rendered even worse by the omnipresence of vermin: rats were common, and fleas and lice a perennial source of discomfort. Rats and fleas contributed disastrously to the spread of the greatest health risk of Chaucer's day—the Plague, or Black Death. This disease came to Europe from the Crimea in 1348 and reached England in 1349. The disease took two principal forms. Initially, it is carried by the flea *Xenopsylla cheopis*, which lives primarily on rats. If the flea transfers to a human host there is the possibility of an outbreak of bubonic plague, which has a mortality rate of about 50%. If the disease enters the pulmonary system, it can become pneumonic plague, an even more deadly and virulent form of the disease that can be transmitted directly from person to person, and has a mortality rate near 100%.

The effects were devastating: within a few years the disease wiped out a third of England's population, and local mortality was sometimes much higher. After its first visitation the plague returned in several lesser outbreaks during the rest of the century, and it remained a health problem in England long after the end of the Middle Ages. It did not truly subside until the late seventeenth century, and it is still present in some parts of the world today.

Fourteenth-century Englishmen usually referred to the plague as "the Pestilence" or "murrain." Both of these were fairly vague terms that might be applied to any epidemic. It can be difficult to diagnose medieval sicknesses across the centuries—the characteristics we use to identify an illness today are not necessarily the same ones noticed in the Middle Ages. Among the ailments that afflicted fourteenth-century people, many were skin diseases—which is not surprising given the infrequency of bathing. Leprosy was one of these, although medieval people used the term for a broad and poorly defined spectrum of skin ailments; they also used the word "measle" for the same sorts of sicknesses, although for us "measles" has a much more precise and different meaning. The "falling evil" was another affliction, probably corresponding to what we would call epilepsy or apoplexy. There were various sorts of tumors and cancerous phenomena, known by such names as "apostemes," "fistula," "cancer," and "blains." Many afflictions were simply known as fever—the "quotidian" fever that occurred daily, the "tertian" fever that recurred on alternate days, and the "quartan" fever that recurred on every third day. At the most ordinary level, medieval people were also subject to the head cold, known to them as a "pose."

Old Age and Death   There is a popular notion that medieval people were considered aged at 40. In fact, old age was most often reckoned to begin at 60, and a fair number of people reached this age—it has been estimated that at any given time some 10% of the population were over 60. In Verona in 1425 some 15% of the population were over age 60, and 6% over 70. Retirement did not exist as an official institution, but when people became too feeble to work, they often made an arrangement to transfer their property to a younger person (usually their own children, if possible) in exchange for a perpetual allowance of food and lodging for the remainder of their lives.

Many wives, perhaps even most, outlived their husbands; indeed, a woman was not infrequently widowed at a relatively young age. Widowhood could be a uniquely independent state for a woman. If her husband left her with sufficient property or a viable business, she could continue to hold it in her own right and even take over the business in person. By this means some women managed to enter professions otherwise barred to them. Under these circumstances a woman enjoyed considerable freedom and might remarry or not as she pleased.

When death was imminent, a priest was summoned to administer the last rites. This involved hearing a last confession, administering Communion, and anointing the feet with holy oil. Those who had not done so were encouraged to make a will for the disposal of their property; even illiterate paupers sometimes had written wills. After death a wake was often held—to the disapproval of moralists, who saw them as an occasion for drunkenness and riotous behavior. The corpse was buried to the sound of the churchbell, and funerals were commonly occasions for the distribution of alms for the benefit of the deceased's soul. Ordinary people were buried in the churchyard, while important people were buried in the church itself, sometimes with ornamental brass or stone effigies. Friends and relatives grieved, yet death was a familiar occurrence. Corpses were by no means a rare sight, and, barring unforeseen accident, death, like birth, probably happened at home: this too was a part of ordinary life.

The sacrament of Extreme Unction. French, late fourteenth century (TBH, p. 178) [McLean].

4

Cycles of Time

The passage of time for people in the fourteenth century was not nearly as finely marked as it is in the modern world. The rural **Time** majority most often reckoned time by the daily cycle of natural events: the time of day was perceived in relationship to cockcrow, dawn, sunrise, midday, sunset, dusk or twilight, and midnight. For such people, the closest thing to a clock would be the bells of the village church, so if some precision was needed, time would be reckoned according to the "canonical hours," the traditional schedule of the monastic cycle of daily prayer: Prime, Terce, Sexte, None, Vespers, and Compline. Each of these hours referred both to the time at which that period of prayer began, and to the space of time from that hour to the next; thus, "Prime" could mean either 6 a.m., or the period from 6 to 9. The canonical hour could also be subdivided: "half Prime" was halfway though Prime (roughly 7:30 a.m.), "whole" or "high Prime" the latter end of Prime. The system was

---

The Canonical Hours

Matins (Midnight)

Lauds (around 3 a.m.)

Prime: 6-9 a. m. (sunrise and early morning)

Underne (Terce): 9-12 a.m. (morning)

Sexte: 12-3 p.m. (afternoon)

None: 3-6 p. m. (late afternoon) or noon

Vespers (Evensong): 6-9 p.m. (evening)

Compline: 9 p.m. (roughly the time of curfew)

complicated by the fact that Sexte had largely fallen into disuse, so None moved forward to cover midday as well as mid-afternoon, whence our modern word "noon." The canonical hours divided the daylight period into equal parts, so the hours varied from 30 minutes in midwinter to 90 minutes in midsummer.

Town-dwellers were likely to reckon time by the equal hours used today, since there was a chance of a clock tower being nearby or at least a bell ringing the hours. Other devices for the precise reckoning of time included hourglasses and sundials, some of which were made portable for personal use. In principle, time could also be divided into minutes and seconds, but these were little used—even a clock did not normally have a minute hand, let alone a second hand. In practice, the half or quarter hour was the minimum duration of reckoned time—shorter durations might be reckoned as "the time it takes to recite three Pater Nosters."

The Day For those who had to earn a living, the working day began a bit before dawn—artificial light was expensive and relatively weak, so it was important to make the most of the sun. It was common to begin the morning with a prayer and by washing one's face and hands. Another important activity in the early morning was stoking the fire from the previous night's coals, so there would be warmth and a source of hot water for the rest of the day. Some people ate breakfast upon rising, although others may have waited until a few hours into their workday. Morning labor began promptly: city folk often did their marketing when markets opened at sunrise, and farmers were already in the fields at this time.[1]

Laborers pause for a meal. Italian, c. 1395 (TS Vienna, f. 64) [McLean].

Work lasted all day, with breaks for meals and refreshments. The midday meal was usually called "dinner," and the evening meal "supper." Those who could not take a break for a full meal might have a lighter repast at noon or afterwards called a "noon-shench" ("noon-drink"), later "nuncheon," the ultimate source of our word "lunch." One guild in the fifteenth century specified the working hours as 4 a.m. to 8 p.m. in the summer, and 6 a.m. to 6 p.m. in the winter; total time off during this workday was probably two hours or less. Rural hours of work likewise depended on the season, since they ran from dawn to dusk. As is often the case when people are subjected to lengthy hours of work, the actual intensity of labor was not necessarily very high, especially among wage laborers. This may have been less true of landholders, and certainly there were seasons in the year when landholders had to work very hard to complete the necessary labor in time.[2]

At the end of the day, hearth fires were extinguished or banked and lights as a precaution against the hazard of fire. One might recite a prayer in the evening before retiring. People slept in nightgowns, shirts, or nothing at all—although those who slept naked might opt for some sort of head covering, as nights became chilly once the fires were out. In towns, there was generally a curfew around 9 p.m., and the taverns and town gates closed at about that time. After curfew, only the town watch and reputable people carrying lights and going about legitimate business were supposed to be on the streets, although in reality revelers were often known to cause disturbances late at night.[3]

Buying wine from a vendor. Italian, c. 1385 (TS Liège, f. 57) [McLean].

Then as now, the work week began on Monday. Those who owed labor services might have to spend one or more **The Week** days working on the lord's land—sometimes as many as five in harvest season. Friday was set aside as a day of religious penance, observed especially by fasting: no one was supposed to eat meat other than fish. Saturdays and Wednesdays might also be observed in the same fashion. Saturday was often a half-holiday, theoretically in preparation for the Sabbath—workers might be let off in the afternoon, sometimes as early as midday. Markets took place on regular days of the week, so shopping also followed a weekly schedule.[4]

Sunday   For people who worked from dawn to dusk for five and a half to six days a week, the break in labor on Sunday must have been especially important. This was a day of enforced leisure when noone was supposed to work. Shopkeepers in London were permitted to sell on Sundays, since laboring people found it difficult to shop on working days, but no wares were to be placed out in the streets.[5]

A bishop preaches [Wright].

Sunday morning was reserved for religious observances. It began for the devout with Matins at dawn, followed by Mass from early morning until midday, which everyone was supposed to attend. Once Mass was over, the rest of Sunday was free for a variety of secular entertainments. Strict moralists believed that games and carousal were inappropriate activities for the Sabbath, but time-honored custom entitled people to spend Sunday afternoon feasting, drinking, playing, or otherwise making merry.[6]

The Year   The life of the country dweller was dominated by the cycle of the seasons. Even in towns, where the natural cycle was of less importance, the shape of the year played a crucial role in the ceremonial life of the community. The cycle of the rural year is evoked in this late medieval poem:

January	By this fire I warm my hands;
February	And with my spade I delve my lands.
March	Here I set my things to spring;
April	And here I hear the fowls sing.
May	I am as light as bird in bough;
June	And I weed my grain well enow.
July	With my scythe my mead I mow;
August	And here I shear my grain full low.
September	With my flail I earn my bread;
October	And here I sow my wheat so red.
November	At Martinmas I kill my swine;
December	And at Christmas I drink red wine.[7]

There were two distinct systems for dividing the year into seasons, one astronomical, the other agricultural. The astronomical year was essentially the system of solstices and equinoxes known to us today. Following the system that Europe had inherited from the Romans, January 1 was said to be New Year's Day, but in reckoning years, the number actually changed on March 25, the Feast of the Annunciation. All of Europe was still on the Julian calendar, originally established by Julius Caesar. The Julian calendar reckoned leap years, but this made the Julian year slightly longer than the solar year, so that the seasons were inching their way earlier on the calendar. England had accumulated an 11-day discrepancy by the time it adopted the modern Gregorian calendar in 1752 (on the Gregorian calendar, three out of four years ending in -00 are not leap years, which reduces the difference between the calendar year and the solar year to a negligible amount).[8]

The agricultural year was quite different. For the medieval peasant, Winter was the first season. It ran from Michaelmas (September 29) to Christmas. Christmas was reckoned to last the full twelve days from Christmas Day until Epiphany (January 6). The next season, from Epiphany to Easter, was called Lent. "Lent" derived from the Anglo-Saxon word for Spring, so named from the "lengthening" of the days. The term was later adopted by the Church to designate the season of religious penance from Ash Wednesday until Easter. The term "Spring" did not come into common use until the Protestant Reformation of the sixteenth century did away with Lent. Easter lasted from Easter Sunday until Hocktide, which fell on the Monday and Tuesday a week after Easter. Afterwards came Summer, which lasted from Hocktide until Lammas (August 1). The final season of the year was called Harvest; it ran from Lammas until Michaelmas. The terms "Fall" and "Autumn" came into use in the sixteenth century, probably owing to the waning influence of agricultural life. Sometimes the year was simply thought of as consisting of two seasons: Winter, from September to February, and Summer, from March to August.

In addition to the seasons, the year was shaped by the cycle of holidays and festival seasons. In the Middle Ages every official holiday was theoretically religious—literally a "holy day"—although even religious festivals had secular aspects. In addition to the holidays familiar to us today, like Christmas and Easter, there were many commemorative days that are less well known. In particular, there was a multitude of saint's days commemorating the various saints and other holy figures; these were sometimes called feasts or feast days—the term "feast" was originally another word for "festival." Feast days were occasions for conviviality and plentiful food and drink, which is how the word acquired its modern sense. A few particularly important saints had two or more feast days, commemorating different events in their lives. These commemorative days were extremely numerous, and only the most important days were actually observed as official holidays. These were observed in a similar manner to Sundays, with church services in the morning and leisure in the afternoon. The afternoon before a holy day might be a half-holiday and was supposed to be observed by abstaining from meat.

Reckoning Dates Individual days were reckoned much as they are today, for example, "xi November" or "xi of November."

Similarly, one might identify a day as "the last day in July." A more learned way was to use the Roman system. This method reckoned days in relation to the Kalends ("kl.": the first of every month), the Nones ("N.": the 5th, but the 7th in March, May, July, and October), and the Ides ("Id.": the 13th, but the 15th in March, May, July, and October). The date was determined by counting forward to the next of these three days, including the day being reckoned. Thus, "xi November" could also be "iii Id. Nov."; "xv November" could be "xvii kl. Dec."; "i December" would simply be "kl. Dec."

Another popular means of reckoning was according to feast days. The Feast of St. Martin was November 11. The "Vigil" or "Eve" of the Feast of St. Martin was November 10. The "Morrow" or "Second Day" of the Feast of St. Martin was November 12. The Third of St. Martin was November 13, and so on. Alternatively, a day might be identified as "Monday next after Martinmas," "the Tuesday before the Feast of St. Martin," and so on.

The reckoning of years may have been important in urban and aristocratic circles, but it was less important for the lower reaches of society—the poorer commons may indeed have had only a rough idea of their own age at any given point. There were two principal means of reckoning years. One was by Anno Domini, which differed from the modern system only in that it considered the new year to begin on April 25. The other common means of reckoning, particularly in legal contexts, was by regnal year: Edward III came to the throne in 1327, so that 1350 would be called "the 24th year of the reign of Edward III" (1327 being the first year of his reign).

A MEDIEVAL CALENDAR

On the following calendar, major feasts are listed in **boldface**: these are the days that people would most likely have as holidays, although customs and terms of employment varied from place to place.[9] In addition to the fixed feasts listed here there were two important holidays that varied from community to community. The first was the Dedication Day of the parish church (that is, the day of the saint to whom the church was dedicated), the other was Fair Day, since many communities had a certain day or days in the year when they were permitted to hold a fair. Fairs were most often held during the summer, but some took place during the winter months. Not every saint's day is listed in this calendar, and some that are listed were not necessarily very familiar outside of ecclesiastical circles.

JANUARY

January was a month of relative leisure: the winter planting was over, and the spring planting had not yet begun. Such tasks as were done in January had little time constraint, and fell into the category of maintenance: repair of home buildings, hedging and ditching around fields to keep animals out, and so on.

1   **The Circumcision of Christ** (*New Year*).
5   *Edward the Confessor.*
6   **Epiphany** (*Twelfth Day*). This was the Twelfth Day after Christmas, and the end of the Christmas season. It commemorated the occasion on which the Three Kings brought their gifts to the infant Jesus. The evening before Twelfth Day was called Twelfth Night, and was an occasion for riotous merrymaking.
13   *St. Hilary the Bishop.*
15   *St. Maure the Abbot.*
16   *St. Marcel Pope and Martyr.*
17   *St. Supplis the Bishop and St. Anthony.*
18   *St. Prisce the Virgin.*
19   *St. Wolston the Bishop.*
20   *Sts. Fabian and Sebastian.* St. Sebastian had been put to death by archers and was therefore the patron saint of archers.
21   *St. Annice (Agnes) the Virgin.*
22   *St. Vincent the Martyr.*
24   *St. Timothy.*
25   *The Conversion of St. Paul.* This feast commemorated the occasion on which Paul, originally a persecutor of Christians, was converted to Christianity.
27   *St. Julian the Bishop.*
30   *St. Batilde the Queen.*
31   *St. Ignace the Bishop and Martyr.*

FEBRUARY

At this time the ground was soft enough to allow plowing to resume in preparation for the Spring, or Lenten, crop of oats, barley, peas, and beans, which had to be sown by the end of March or so. For this purpose, cattle were driven out of the previous year's fallow fields; they were also put out of the meadows to make way for the new year's hay.

The land was first plowed. This involved hitching a plow to one or more horses or oxen, which would pull it up and down the fields. The plow had a knife-like "coulter" projecting downwards that cut through the ground, creating a trench called a furrow. The plow also had an angled "mouldboard" that cast dirt up sideways out of the furrow. Afterwards, the husbandman would sow the crops, walking through the fields with a box of seeds and casting them into the furrows. Finally, the ground was harrowed: a large wooden frame was hitched to a horse and dragged over the fields; this pulled the loose dirt into the furrows to cover up the seeds.

Plowing [Ashdown].

 1 *St. Bride (Bridget) the Virgin.*
 2 **The Purification of Mary** (*Candlemas*). This feast commemorated the churching of Mary after the birth of Christ. Churching was a ritual observed by women after childbirth in which they bore a candle to church. This day was therefore observed by the bearing of candles, and was also known as Candlemas.
 3 *St. Blase Bishop and Martyr.*
 4 *St. Agatha the Virgin.*
 5 *Sts. Vedast and Amande the Bishops.*
10 *St. Scholaste the Virgin.*
14 *St. Valentine.* In Chaucer's day as today, this day was associated with love and romance. One of Chaucer's poems hints that there may have been a custom of "choosing one's Valentine" as was done in later centuries.
16 *St. Julian the Virgin.*
22 *The Cathedration of St. Peter.* This holy day commemorated St. Peter's establishment as the Bishop of Antioch.
24 **St. Matthie** (Matthias) **the Apostle.**

29   *St. Oswald the Bishop and Confessor.*

—*Shrove Tuesday*: This day was one of the movable feasts, being dependent on the date of Easter. It fell six weeks and five days before Easter, between February 3 and March 9. Shrove Tuesday was the last day before Lent.

—*Ash Wednesday*: This was the day after Shrove Tuesday and the first day of Lent, which lasted until Easter. Lent was a season of religious penance: all Christians were supposed to abstain from eating meat and having sexual contact for the duration of Lent. The day was named from the custom of placing ashes on one's head as a sign of penance. The following Wednesday, Friday, and Saturday were "Ember Days," days of particular fasting and penance.

MARCH

The work of planting the Lenten crops continued in this month; they were to be sown by Annunciation or Easter. Warfare tended to begin in March or April after the harsh winter weather had subsided. At about Easter time, the sheep were put out to their pastures once again.

1   *St. David.*
7   *Sts. Perpetua and Felice the Virgins.*
12   *St. Gregory.*
17   *St. Patrick.*
18   **St. Edward the King and Confessor.**
20   *St. Cuthbert the Bishop and Confessor.*
21   *St. Benet (Benedict) the Abbot and Confessor.*
25   **The Annunciation** (*Feast of Our Lady in Lent*). In England the number of the year changed on this day.

—**Palm Sunday:** This day was one week before Easter. It commemorated the arrival of Christ into Jerusalem just before the Crucifixion: the parishioners would bear rushes or willow wands into church (palm leaves being rare in England).

—*Shere Thursday*: The Thursday before Easter. This was traditionally a day for almsgiving.

—*Good Friday*: The Friday before Easter.

—*Holy Saturday*: The day before Easter.

—**Easter:** The date of Easter is variable because it is based on the Jewish calendar. This calendar follows the cycles of the moon rather than the solar year of the standard calendar we inherited from the Romans. Easter falls on the first Sunday after the first full moon on or after 21 March; if the full moon is on a Sunday, Easter is the next Sunday. This means that Easter comes between March 22 and April 25. Easter marks the end of Lent. It was commonly a quarter-day, on which one quarter of the annual rent for a landholding was due.

—*Hocktide*: Hocktide consisted of Hock Monday (also called Rope Monday), Hock Tuesday (also called Hockday), and Hock Wednesday, the three days a week after Easter. Hocktide was apparently celebrated, as in later centuries, by the young men and maidens of the village catching people in the street with a rope and forcing them to pay a small ransom.

APRIL

By about this time the spring planting was complete, allowing the farmer to turn to the task of preparing the fallow fields for the next year's crop; the fields were plowed two or three times before harvest time. At about this time the woman of the house began her dairy work, as the cows had calved by now and were producing milk.

2   *St. Mary the Egyptian.*
3   *St. Richard the Bishop and Confessor.*
4   *St. Ambrose the Bishop and Confessor.*
6   *St. Sixtus.*
13 *St. Eufemie.*
14 *Sts. Tiburce and Valerian.*
19 *St. Alphege Bishop and Martyr.*
23 **St. George the Martyr.** St. George, famous for having slain a dragon, was also the patron saint of soldiers and of England.
25 **St. Mark the Evangelist.**
26 *St. Clete the Pope and Martyr.*
28 *St. Vital the Martyr.*

Milking the sheep. English, before 1340 (LP, f. 163v) [Bateson].

MAY

This was traditionally regarded as the first month of summer. In this season, the time pressures of agricultural work were somewhat diminished until the hay harvest began. At some point in this season, typically May Day, Ascension, or Whitsun, there would be a festival to welcome the arrival of summer. The festival often involved gathering branches and flowers to decorate the village, and choosing a Summer Lord and Lady to preside over the festivities.

1   **Sts. Philip and Jacob the Apostles** (*May Day*).
3   **The Discovery of the Cross** (*Holy Rood Day in May, Crouchmass*).
6   *St. John at Port Latin.* This commemorated the occasion when the Emperor Domitian attempted unsuccessfully to have John the Evangelist boiled in oil at the Porta Latina in Rome.
10   *Sts. Gordian and Epimache.*
12   *Sts. Nere Achille and Pancras.*
19   *St. Dunstan the Bishop and Confessor.*
25   *Sts. Urban and Aldhelm the Bishops.*
26   **St. Austin** (Augustine) **the Bishop and Confessor.**
28   *St. Germain the Bishop and Confessor.*
31   *St. Purnel the Virgin.*

—*Rogation Sunday*: This day fell five weeks after Easter, between April 26 and May 30.
—*Rogation Days* (*Gang Days*): This was the Monday to Wednesday between Rogation Sunday and Ascension Day. The Rogation Days were an occasion for asking divine forgiveness of sins. On these days the parishioners would process around the boundaries of the parish, bearing a cross and banners to the sound of the church bells.
—**Ascension Day** (*Holy Thursday*): This was the Thursday after Rogation Sunday, between April 30 and June 3.
—**Whitsunday** (*Pentecost*): This fell on the Sunday ten days after Ascension, between May 10 and June 13. The Monday, Tuesday, and Wednesday following could also be holidays. The Wednesday, Friday, and Saturday following were all "Ember Days," to be observed with fasting and penance.

JUNE

This was the month for sheepshearing. After a year of poor harvests, hard times would tend to set in around June and last until October, when the next harvest came in. Traditionally, the hay harvest began after Midsummer Day.

1   *St. Nichomede the Martyr.*
2   *Sts. Marcelin and Peter.*
5   *St. Boniface the Bishop.*
8   *Sts. Medard and Gildard.*
11 *St. Barnabas the Apostle.*
14 *St. Basil the Bishop and Confessor.*
15 *St. Vitus.*
16 *St. Cyriac.*
17 *St. Botulf.*
18 *Sts. Mark and Marcellian.*
19 *St. Gervase.*
22 *St. Alban the Martyr.*
23 *St. Etheldred the Virgin and Martyr.*
24 **The Nativity of St. John the Baptist** (*Midsummer*). The holiday would be celebrated with gathering of greenery and with dancing, perhaps also with bonfires. This festival was often an important civic occasion marked by a variety of festivities and displays of communal identity. It was commonly a quarter-day on which quarterly rents came due.
26 *Sts. John and Paul.*
28 *St. Leo the Pope and Confessor.*
29 **Sts. Peter and Paul the Apostles.**
30 *Commemoration of St. Paul the Apostle.*

—**Trinity Sunday**: This fell one week after Whitsun, between May 17 and June 20.
—**Corpus Christi Day**: This was the Thursday after Trinity Sunday, between May 21 and June 24. It was instituted in honor of the sacrament of Communion. In towns this day was often celebrated with major civic festivities, including elaborate religious plays.

JULY

This month was dominated by the hay harvest. The grass in the meadows had been allowed to grow long; then the men would go out and cut it down with scythes, lay it out in the sun to dry, stack it, and cart it indoors for storage. Hay was of great economic importance, as it would provide the fodder on which animals were kept during the following winter.

2   *St. Swithun.*
7   **The Translation of St. Thomas the Martyr.** This day commemorated the occasion when Thomas à Becket's bones were removed from their

burial place to a holy shrine. Thomas, the Archbishop of Canterbury, had been assassinated in 1170 and was England's most venerated saint.

14 *St. Metheldred the Virgin and Martyr.*
17 *St. Kenelm the King.*
18 *St. Arnulf the King.*
20 *St. Margaret the Virgin and Martyr.*
22 **St. Mary Magdalene.**
23 *St. Appolinar the Martyr.*
24 *St. Christine the Virgin and Martyr.*
25 **St. James the Apostle;** *St. Christopher.*
26 *St. Ann.*
27 *Feast of the Seven Sleepers.* The sleepers were seven young Christian men who, according to legend, were walled up alive in a cave and found alive when the wall was opened 112 years later.
28 *St. Sampson.*
29 *Sts. Felix, Simplis, and Faustin.*
31 *St. Neot.*

AUGUST

The arrival of August marked the end of the hay harvest and the beginning of the harvest of grain. The grain was cut, bound into sheaves, stacked, and carted indoors for storage. It was harvested with a sickle rather than a scythe and was cut relatively high, leaving a long stem of straw. The straw was later cut with scythes to provide material for thatching, making hats and baskets, strewing on floors, stuffing beds, and other uses. This was the most demanding season of the year for the farmer. Temporary workers were often hired, and women and children commonly helped with binding and stacking, in order to get the crops in by Michaelmas. August and September were the worst months for the plague.

1 **St. Peter ad Vincula** (*Lammas*). This holy day was named in commemoration of miracles performed by the chains (*vincula* in Latin) in which Peter had been bound while imprisoned in Rome.
2 *St. Stephen the Pope.*
4 *St. Dominic.*
5 *St. Oswald the King and Martyr.*
7 *St. Donate.*
8 *St. Cyriac.*
9 *St. Roman the Martyr.*
10 **St. Lawrence the Martyr.**
11 *St. Tyburce the Martyr.*

13 *St. Hypolite.*
15 **The Assumption of Our Lady.**
20 *St. Oswin the King.*
23 *St. Timothy.*
24 **St. Bartholomew.**
25 *St. Louis.*
28 *St. Austin the Bishop (Augustine of Hippo).*
29 *Beheading of St. John the Baptist.*
31 *St. Cuthburg the Virgin.*

Reaping grain. Italian, c. 1400 (TS Casanatense, f. lxxxvi) [McLean].

SEPTEMBER

In this month the harvest would be finished. When the weather began to get wetter, more days might be spent indoors threshing the grain—beating it with flails to crack open the husks. The husks, or chaff, were then separated from the grain by winnowing, either fanning the grain to blow away the chaff or tossing it up in a basket. The grain was stored and could later be boiled in a broth or ground in a mill to make flour. September and October were also the time for gathering fruit. Warfare tended to diminish in September or October, as the armies sought their winter quarters.

1   *St. Giles.*
5   *St. Bertin.*
8   **Nativity of Our Lady** (*Our Lady Day in Harvest*).
14   **Exaltation of the Cross** (*Holy Rood Day in Harvest*). The following Wednesday, Friday, and Saturday were "Ember Days," observed with fasting and penance.
16   *St. Edith the Virgin.*
17   *St. Lambert.*
20   *St. Eustace.*
21   **St. Matthew the Apostle.**
22   *St. Maurice.*
26   *Sts. Justin and Cyprian.*
29   **St. Michael the Archangel** (*Michaelmas*). This day marked the end of the agricultural year, at which time the annual accounts were cast up; it was also a quarter-day on which the last installment of rent came due.
30   *St. Jerome.*

Threshing grain. Italian, c. 1400 (TS Casanatense, f. lxxxvii) [McLean].

OCTOBER

During this month husbandmen began to plow in preparation for the winter planting of wheat and rye.

1   *St. Remigius.*
2   *St. Leodegar the Bishop and Confessor.*
4   *St. Francis the Confessor.*
6   *St. Faith the Virgin and Martyr.*
9   *St. Dennis.*
15   *St. Wolfran the Bishop and Confessor.*

18 **St. Luke the Evangelist.**
21 *Feast of the 11,000 Virgins.* According to legend, these pious Christian virgins had been martyred in Cologne.
25 *Sts. Crispin and Crispianus.*
28 **Sts. Simon and Jude the Apostles.**
31 *St. Quentin the Martyr.*

NOVEMBER

The winter seed was supposed to be planted by All Hallows, or by Martinmas at the latest. Martinmas traditionally marked the beginning of the slaughter and preserving of extra livestock for the winter; the remaining livestock were housed for the winter.

1   **All Hallows (Hallowmas).** This holy day was dedicated to all the holy people of the Christian religion—"hallow" was another word for a saint.
2   **All Souls.** On this day people were supposed to pray for the souls of the dead, to help speed their way through their time of penance in Purgatory.
6   *St. Leonard the Abbot and Confessor.*
11 *St. Martin the Bishop and Confessor (Martinmas).*
13 *St. Brice the Bishop.*
16 *St. Edmund the Archbishop.*
17 *St. Hugh the Bishop.*
20 **St. Edmund the King and Martyr.**
22 *St. Cecily the Virgin and Martyr.*
23 *St. Clement the Pope.*
25 **St. Katherine the Virgin and Martyr.**
30 **St. Andrew.**

—*Advent*: This began on the fourth Sunday before Christmas and lasted until Christmas eve. The truly pious might observe a fast from meat during this season.

DECEMBER

This was one of the more leisurely months in the agricultural year: the livestock had been housed, all planting was over, and people could look forward to the celebrations of Christmas.

4   *St. Barbara.*
6   **St. Nicholas the Bishop and Confessor.**
7   *St. Ambrose.*

8   **Feast of the Conception of Our Lady.**
13 *St. Lucy the Virgin and Martyr.* The following Wednesday, Friday, and
    Saturday were "Ember Days," obverved with particular fasting and
    penance.
21 **St. Thomas the Apostle.**
25 **Christmas.** Christmas was a time for celebrations, including games,
    dancing, plays, and colorful decorations. It was also a quarter-day
    when quarterly rents came due.
26 *St. Stephen the Martyr.*
27 *St. John the Apostle and Evangelist.*
28 *Feast of the Holy Innocents (Childermas).* This feast commemorated the
    children slaughtered by King Herod in his attempt to slay the infant
    Jesus.
29 **St. Thomas the Archbishop and Martyr.**
31 *St. Silvester the Pope and Confessor.*[10]

5

The Living Environment

BUILDINGS AND INTERIORS

Medieval dwellings varied enormously, from the manorial complexes of the nobility to the hovels of the poor; yet to a modern observer even the most luxurious medieval home, however sumptuous, would probably seem short on comfort and convenience.

At the lower end of the social scale, the typical peasant house had very few rooms—probably just one to three—and consisted of two or three bays, or framed construction units, measuring about 15' x 15' each. In some cases the structure sheltered not just the family but its livestock as well, albeit in the far end from the human occupants. The frame of the peasant house was of joined timber, and the walls were commonly filled in with wattle and daub. In this technique, the spaces between the posts and beams were filled with wattling: long stakes fixed upright between lateral beams, with flexible sticks woven densely between them. The surface thus created was covered on both sides with daub: clay or loam mixed with straw or some similar fiber for strength. Alternatively, the walls might be made of turf (peat cuttings), cob (unbaked clay), or even stone, although this was beyond the means of the peasant except in places where stone was locally abundant. The roof was thatched with straw or reeds, although wood shingles, tiles, or slate might be used if these were plentiful in the area. The house normally had a packed dirt floor and only one story; boards might be laid across the overhead beams to create lofts for additional space.

The Peasant Home

Pillaging a house. Late fourteenth century (British Library MS Royal 20.C.VII, f. 417) [McLean].

The ground on which the house was built was called a toft, and might include a cobblestone courtyard and a few additional outbuildings for storage and housing for domestic animals—cows, sheep, goats, pigs, geese, chickens, and the like. Behind the toft was usually a croft, a small garden for herbs, vegetables, and other household plants.

The Village In areas of woodland settlement, where land was held in compact units, the peasant house might stand alone in the middle of the holding; but in champion lands a couple dozen or more tofts might cluster together as a village, usually with a parish church among them and perhaps a green or the local lord's manor house. Surrounding the village were fields and meadows, and beyond them lay the uncultivated ground, often forested or marshy lands. In champion lands the landholdings were not actual blocks of land but a share in the land surrounding the village. This land was divided at each new planting into multiple strips of land, each holder receiving a number of scattered strips commensurate to the size of his holding. Villages were mostly of 400 to 600 people or less. Water was an important factor in making settlement possible, so most villages tended to have a well or stream nearby.[1]

Homes of the Aristocracy The dwellings of the medieval aristocracy varied as enormously as their incomes, but certain patterns were generally common to them all. Stone was the preferred material of construction, although the lesser aristocracy might have to be content with brick or even with a superior version of wattle and daub. The ideal roof was made of slate or tile, although floors and rafters were always made of wood.

The largest room of the aristocratic home was the hall, the most public space of the house. Here the members of the household interacted with each other and with the outside world: it was a place for transacting public business, for holding entertainments, and especially for eating formal meals. It was usually the largest room in the building and was often high as well, with no ceiling but open to the roof. The hall had a "high" and a "low" end demarcated by a raised dais. The area below the dais pertained to the servants and to ordinary guests. At the low end a wooden partition cut down on drafts; behind it were the main door to the outside and the doors to the service wing of the manor (kitchen, larder, and other areas used by the household staff).

Tickenham Court, a manor house of c. 1400 [Parker].

At the high end, on the dais, sat the family itself with its favored guests. From here there was access to the solar (a private room for the family) and other private chambers. These rooms might be located in their own wing of the building or above the hall. Although it was traditional for the family to eat in the hall, aristocrats increasingly chose to have their meals in the private section of the house.

The physical division of the aristocratic home by the hall dais was a major factor in organizing home life. The entire establishment was divided into the "household" (the public section of the house below the dais) and the "chamber" (the private section—the dais and beyond). Even for servants there was a distinction between the prestigious jobs of the chamber and the ordinary ones of the household.

The interior of the great hall at Nurstead Court (mid-fourteenth century) [Parker].

Depending on the wealth of the owner, the manor house would sit at the center of a greater or lesser number of buildings grouped in a complex, often surrounded by a wall and perhaps a ditch. The complex included all the specialized facilities needed by the aristocratic household, such as bakery, brewery, stables, barns, cowshed, dovecotes, and granary. A large manor might also have decorative gardens and peacocks to grace its grounds.

The Townhouse   Different from both peasant and aristocratic dwellings was the townhouse. In construction the ordinary townhouse resembled the timber-framed peasant dwelling, commonly measuring about 12' by 20' with a garden of comparable size behind. Unlike the peasant house, it was two or three stories high and was more likely to have a floor and a cellar as well as a wooden, tile, or slate roof (many towns tried to forbid thatched roofs because of their extreme vulnerability to fire).

If the house belonged to a craftsman or tradesman, the front door would lead into the shop. This shop might extend into the street during the day: wares were placed on display out front, and some tradesmen (notably butchers) actually did their work there. The family lived in a room behind the shop or above it; upper floors could also be used for servants, apprentices, or tenants. The upper floors were accessible by stairs or ladders and sometimes projected over the street to make maximum use of limited urban space. Most urban families probably lived in two rooms and a kitchen or less. Richer city-dwellers tended to have complexes comparable to aristocratic manors, consisting of several specialized buildings grouped around a courtyard, with a gateway leading to the street.[2]

Townhouses were packed much closer together than peasant homes or manors; some were actually built as a solid   **The Town** row. With multiple occupancy of a single building, urban density could be quite high. A large provincial town like Winchester had 29 people per acre within its walls and as many as 81 per acre in the center, greater than that of modern British cities. The largest town was London, with a pre-plague population of between 40,000 and 60,000. By 1375 this number had dropped to 35,000. The next largest towns were Bristol with 9,500, York with 7,000, and Norwich with 6,000. Other towns all had less than 3,000 inhabitants.

The best streets were cobbled, often with a gutter running down the center. Lesser streets might be only of dirt and became very muddy in bad weather.

Water was piped into towns from nearby streams and stored in cisterns and water towers. Town-dwellers might collect water from public fountains, purchase it from a professional water carrier (saving them the trouble of collecting it themselves), or, for a fee, have it piped directly to their homes—this was only possible for those who lived close to the water pipes.

Sanitation was a constant problem in spite of earnest efforts by town governments to regulate waste disposal. Numerous ordinances sought to restrict the dumping of rubbish in the streets, and official "rakers" had the job of carting rubbish and cleaning the streets; but these efforts were never enough to deal with the mass of waste produced in a medieval city. Consequently, the streets were often foul-smelling and littered with various sorts of waste.

Animals were another hazard. The animal population of a town was high, including both horses for transportation and livestock for meat and dairy production. Pigs were a handy animal in a city, since they could feed on refuse, but they could also be downright hazardous: babies were occasionally bitten to death when a pig wandered into an unsupervised home.

Since many or most townhouses had gardens, there was a great deal of green space within a city. In addition, the division between a town and the country outside was not very great: even London measured only about half a mile by a mile and a half, and beyond its walls were fields. It was never a very far walk to the countryside. Many English towns were surrounded by walls, but by no means all—the custom was more common on the Continent, where the danger of war was always more imminent.[3]

Domestic Interiors
All types of houses had windows to make use of daylight. The wealthy had windows made of paned glass, but the poor made do with mere shutters; some windows were constructed with glass in the upper part and shutters below. At night people relied on candles. The finest were made of beeswax, but most people had to be content with tallow, made of processed animal fat. Tallow was much cheaper than wax, as it was a by-product of meat consumption, but it burned less brightly and less cleanly. Candlesticks might be made of silver or of cheaper materials such as pewter, brass, or wood. Some were simple sockets on an angled spike, designed to be jammed into the timbers of the house. Candles were more complex to use than they are today: the wicks were not designed to burn up their own excess, as in a modern candle, so they had to be trimmed as they burned. Other sources of light included the rushlight—a rush steeped in fat and set alight—and the oil lamp, also generally fueled with animal fats. Lanterns were made with glass or ox horn windows, or pierced with many small holes.[4]

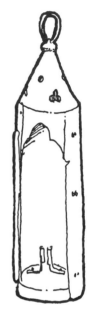

A fourteenth-century lantern. It is about 8 1/2" high, made of a copper alloy (the door is missing) [McLean, after a photograph in Woods].

Fires were another essential element in every house, since without them people could neither cook nor keep warm. Aristocratic and urban houses had fireplaces with chimneys, while peasant homes had only a raised firepit in the center of the room with a hole in the roof to let out smoke. Firewood was an important commodity for any household, although Londoners usually used charcoal. Mined coal was mostly restricted to industrial use, since its foul smoke makes it ill-suited for use on an open fire. At night, fires had to be either extinguished or banked—allowing the coals to smolder slowly so the fire could be easily relit in the morning, preferably without causing a house fire in the interval. Banking was made easier by use of a perforated ceramic lid placed over the coals. If the fire went out, it had to be rekindled with tinder and flint, or perhaps with hot coals from a neighbor's hearth.

Walls were plastered and whitewashed. Those who could afford them adorned their rooms with wall hangings, which served the double purpose of decoration and insulation. The very rich used tapestries for this purpose, but others contented themselves with painted cloths. Alternatively, decoration might be provided by wall paintings. The floor could be covered with woven rush-mats or with straw; the wealthy often strewed the floor with sweet-smelling herbs and flowers. People used besom-style brooms made of birch or broom; even peasants swept their earthen floors, replacing the dirty straw with fresh. On the whole, a medieval room would seem chilly, dim, and smoky to a modern observer.

A lantern mounted on a staff. After 1380 (TBH, p. 181) [McLean].

Personal property for most people was very limited. A surviving inventory from a thirteenth-century butcher in **Furnishings** Colchester lists a trestle table, two silver spoons, a cup, a tablecloth, two towels, a brass cauldron, a brass dish, a wash basin and ewer, a trivet, an iron candlestick, two beds, two gowns, a mantle, and two barrels, the total valued at £2 5s. 5d (this inventory was probably not entirely complete: since the butcher had a table, he probably also owned some benches or stools, and probably a lockable chest or coffer for his valuable silver spoons).[5]

By contrast, the inventory of a knight in 1374 lists the following items in the various parts of the manor:

Chamber: 7 full beds, 4 mattresses, a selection of blankets and bedspreads, a white coffer, two basins and a laver, a full set of plate armor for a man and war-gear for a horse, 3 habergeons, 4 ordinary helmets, a cloth sack and a leather sack.

Pantry and Buttery: Several silver bowls, a silver ewer, a collection of tablecloths, napkins, and towels, 3 canvas cloths, 12 barrels, 4 brass candlesticks, 2 tubs, 4 bottles, 4 leather pots.

Hall: 3 tables with benches, 2 basins with a laver, a brazier and a fire-fork.

Kitchen: Vessels and plates of pewter, brass bowls and plates, 3 iron spits, 1 cob-iron, a griddle and frying pan, a trivet, 2 hooks, a grater, 2 knives for the dressing board, 2 brass mortars and pestles.

Larder: a salting-trough, 30 pigs, 3 oxen, a salt-box, a table.
Bakehouse: a brewing vat, 3 leaden pots, 2 kneading troughs, a pail.
Lord's Chapel: a complete vestment with chalice, book, altarcloth.
Lord's Stable: 4 horses.
Cart Stable: 5 horses, 2 carts.
Cowshed: 12 oxen, 5 plows, 2 bulls, 19 cows, 10 steers and heifers, 5 calves, 1 cart, 78 pigs with boars
Various Granges: 30 quarters wheat, 60 quarters barley, 90 quarters peas, 8 quarters rye, 40 quarters mixed grain and oats.[6]

The list is substantial yet still limited in comparison to a modern counterpart of such an aristocrat; any amount of property was much more expensive in relative terms. Again, the inventory is not complete—no spoons or clothing are mentioned, for example.

Well-dressed people at a very simple table. Italian, c. 1395 (TS Vienna, f. 45) [McLean].

The commonest item of furniture for storage was the chest; for greater usefulness, it might have removable shelves inside, a lock on the outside, or a small locked till inside at one end. Commoners relied on chests because they were simple, versatile, and relatively inexpensive. Aristocrats used them because their lives often involved a great deal of travel, especially from one manor to another, and chests could be readily transported. Storage was also provided by sacks and bags made of leather, linen, canvas, or wool. For seating, benches and stools were more common than chairs. Tables were typically boards set up on trestles, and could be taken down for transport or to open up floor space.

Naturally, one item of furniture in almost every house was **The Chamber** the bed. A fully appointed bed had as its base a wooden bedstead, which might be hung about with curtains to keep out the chilly night air. On this was placed a mattress made of canvas or linen stuffed with wool or cotton and stitched to hold its contents in place. Next came a featherbed, which was another mattress (probably of linen) waxed on the inside and stuffed with feathers. Both mattress and featherbed might be white or colored—for example blue or red. Striped ticking was probably also used. Across the head of the bed was a long bolster, probably stuffed canvas or linen, covered with a headsheet of linen, and topped with feather pillows in pillowcases. The person sleeping lay between two white linen sheets, covered by blankets or quilts, and perhaps a decorative coverlet. From the waist down, the sleeper lay flat on the bed, with his or her back up on the bolster and the head almost vertical on the pillow. A more economical style of bed had a mattress but no featherbed. A poor person would at best have a simple pallet on the ground, equivalent to a mattress but smaller and stuffed with straw or hay; others might use a straw pallet underneath a finer mattress.

A domestic scene. Italian, c. 1400 (TS Casanatense, f. cxliv) [McLean].

The ordinary wash involved pouring water from a water jug (called a "ewer" or "laver") over the hands into a basin; a **Hygiene** towel of linen or silk could be used for drying. Ordinary or "French" soap consisted of two-thirds lye and one-third sheep's tallow; more expensive was "Saracen" soap, which was made with olive oil instead of tallow and might be scented as well. Medieval people seem to have been fairly conscientious about keeping their hands and faces clean, and it was customary to wash one's hands before beginning a meal, or after defecating. Washing the entire body occurred less frequently. This does not mean that cleanliness was not valued. In fact, there was a very real risk of illness, even death, in a cold climate and drafty home. The substantial effort involved in drawing and heating water was probably a factor as well. However, the pleasant medieval custom of eating and drinking during a bath, and the various comforts afforded by the public bathhouses (some of which were essentially brothels) afforded incentives to cleanliness. People bathed in wooden tubs, using water heated over a fire. Hair could be washed using lye and water.[7]

Bathing [Gay].

For urinating or defecating, people used metal or ceramic chamber-pots, known as jordans, which could be used as needed and emptied when convenient. A slightly more substantial device was the "night-chair" or "close-stool," which enclosed the chamber-pot in an actual seat. Permanent "privies" were also in use, so called because they were actual rooms that afforded genuine privacy. In the town, several houses might share a common privy; there were even public privies in London.

Both urban and rural privies usually emptied into a cesspit, which had to be cleaned out from time to time. On a peasant farm this was done by the householders, and the refuse was carted out to the fields as fertilizer. In the city there were professional "gong farmers" ("gong" being the word for a cesspit) who cleaned cesspits for a fee. The best cesspits were lined with stone to facilitate cleaning and prevent leakage. Privies were sometimes located on an upper floor and might sit above an unused plot of ground or have a pipe leading to the cesspit. For toilet paper people used a piece of cloth of cheap wool, cotton, or linen, or an "arsewisp," which appears to have been a small bundle of straw or some similar material.[8]

TRAVEL

Most people spent the bulk of their time in their own town or village, but in an increasingly market-oriented economy there were growing incentives to travel, if only to sell produce at a nearby market. People were also increasingly traveling on pilgrimage, whether to visit a local saint's shrine, a major national shrine such as that of Saint Thomas à Becket at Canterbury, or an international site such as Rome or Jerusalem. The theoretical purpose of pilgrimage was its spiritual value, but in many respects it shaded into the medieval equivalent of tourism.

Buying sour milk from a vendor. Italian, c. 1395 (TS Vienna, f. 59v) [McLean].

Mobility was limited by the technology available. The simplest means of travel was on foot, which, as contemporaries reckoned, would be about a mile in 20 minutes during the summer or 30 minutes in winter. A person traveling on foot could expect to cover 10 to 20 miles in a day, a merchant train 15 to 18, and a household or army on the move, with carts and pack animals, about 10 to 12. The fastest mode of travel was on horseback, a method used by both men and women across a wide social spectrum. Horses were quite plentiful: even a peasant might own one for agricultural work. Horses could also be rented, much as people rent cars today. A rider might typically cover 40 miles in a day. A mounted courier could cover some 60 miles on a good road, half as much over rough country. A rider traveling by post (that is, with pre-arranged changes of horses) might cover as much as 100 or 120 miles in a day. In addition to carts and wagons for transporting goods, there were special covered wagons for people. Noblewomen were particularly likely to use these, although the ride was far from comfortable, since these vehicles had only rudimentary systems for shock absorption.

A wagon. Flemish, 1338-1344 (RA) [Bateson].

In practice, rates of travel varied enormously. English roads in Chaucer's day were rather a problematic affair. Few had any foundations and none were paved, so they became pools of mud in bad weather. As if this were not enough, the traveler had to face the ever present threat of ambush by robbers. Poor communications made law enforcement difficult, so the traveler was always at risk.

A wheelbarrow [Bateson].

Water was an important factor in travel, whether as a hindrance or a medium. The routes of overland travel were governed by the availability of bridges, fords, and ferries. A ship of 60 to 80 tons with a crew of 15 sailors was considered large; by comparison, a modern harbor tug can be as large as 250 tons. A ship could sail at about 5 to 6 knots under favorable conditions, or some 75 to 100 miles a day. The rate of travel varied enormously with the weather. The voyage from London to Bordeaux in southwestern France could take as little as 10 to 12 days or as much as a month.

In most of the country, travelers had to make arrangements to lodge in private homes, but in a town they could make use of an inn. The workings of a fourteenth-century inn are illustrated by the testimony in a case regarding the theft of two small chests containing 40 marks and miscellaneous documents from an inn in Southwark in 1381:

The said John [the innkeeper] . . . says that on the said Monday about the second hour after noon the said William [the Sheriff of Somerset and Dorset] entered his inn to be lodged there, and at once when he entered, the same John assigned to the said William a certain chamber being in that inn, fitting for his rank, with a door and a lock affixed to the same door with sufficient nails, so that he should lie there and put and keep his things there, and delivered to the said William the key to the door of the said chamber. . . .

William says that . . . when the said John had delivered to him the said chamber and key as above, the same William, being occupied about divers businesses to be done in the city of London, went out from the said inn into the city to expedite the said businesses and handed over the key of the door to a certain servant of the said William to take care of it meantime, ordering the servant to remain in the inn meanwhile and to take care of his horses there; and afterwards, when night was falling, the same William being in the city and the key still in the keeping of the said servant, the wife of the said John called unto her into her hall the said servant who had the key, giving him food and drink with a merry countenance and asking him divers questions and occupying him thus for a long time, until the staple of the lock of the door aforesaid was thrust on one side out of its right place and the door of the chamber was thereby opened, and his goods, being in the inn of the said John, were taken and carried off by the said malefactors. . . .

The said John says . . . [that] the said servant came into the said hall and asked his wife for bread and ale and other necessaries to be brought into the said chamber of his master.[9]

Tents. Italian, c. 1360 [McLean].

In towns there were established businesses for housing and victualing travelers, but in the country these services were provided on a less professional basis. Here a traveler would often have to make arrangements to stay in a private home. There were alehouses in the country, but these were less likely to be a permanent establishment than a temporary arrangement whereby one of the local women who had just finished brewing a batch of ale would put out the "ale-stake" (a bush or broom that hung outside the house—very possibly the same one which had just been used to scoop the scum off the new batch of ale). Anyone who wished might come and purchase a drink—ale did not keep well, and any given batch was likely to be more than the household could consume. Finally, some travelers brought their own accommodations: tradesmen at a fair might have simple tents made of wood and canvas, while aristocrats in an army or a tournament might erect pavilions made of the same materials but brightly painted—the ordinary soldier billeted where best he could.

6

Clothing and Accessories

The latter half of the fourteenth century was a period of rapidly changing techniques and fashions in clothing. Prior to Chaucer's **Fashion** lifetime, clothing fashions had been fairly static for centuries. Garments were generally cut on straight lines, which severely limited the possibility for variation. The fourteenth century witnessed the true emergence of the tailor's craft as clothesmakers began to experiment with curved seams, allowing garments to be more fully shaped. At the same time, buttons began to be used to allow a closer fit—in previous centuries garments had to be loose enough to be pulled over the torso. The history of costume was precipitated into the age of fashion, which has continued ever since.

In Chaucer's *Canterbury Tales*, the Parson comments bitingly on the new trends:

> Superfluity of clothing . . . makes it most expensive, to harm of the people; not only the cost of embroidering, the elaborate notching of edges or ornamenting with strips, undulating and vertical stripes, folding or bordering, and similar waste of cloth in vanity; but there is also costly furring in their gowns, so much piercing with blades to make holes, so much slitting with shears, along the superfluity in length of the aforesaid gowns, trailing in the dung and in the mire. . . .
>
> Upon the other side, to speak of the horrible disordinate scantiness of clothing, as be these "cutted slops," or "hainselins," that through their shortness cover not the shameful members of man, to wicked intent . . . and eke the buttocks of them fare as it were the hinder part of a she-ape in the full of the moon. And moreover . . . in dividing of their hose in white and red, it seems that half their shameful privy members were flain. And if so be that they divide their hose in other colors, as in white and black, or white and blue, or black and red, and so forth, then seems it, as by variance of color, that half the part of their privy members were corrupt by the fire of Saint Antony, or by cancer, or by other such mischance.[1]

Of course, rapidly changing fashion mostly affected the aristocracy and wealthy townsfolk. The clothes of poorer people seem to have been simple in construction and were sometimes fifty years behind the current styles. Indeed, as medieval garments were generally quite durable, there was a thriving trade in used clothing.

A man and woman in conservative but rich clothes of the mid-fourteenth century. The man affords a rare example of a mustache [Ashdown].

Fabrics The staple fabric of medieval clothing was wool. Woolen fabrics are versatile, durable, and elastic. They take dye well, resist water, and have good insulating properties. For all these reasons, wool was the most popular material for the visible layers of the medieval wardrobe—even among the aristocracy, most of whom relied on wool for everyday use. Raw wool was England's principal source of commercial wealth. Some woolen cloth was produced domestically, but the best woolen cloths were manufactured on the Continent, especially in the Low Countries.

Although outer clothes were generally made of wool, most people wore linen next to the skin. Linen derives from the fibers of the flax plant. It is easy to wash and quick to dry and is much more pleasant on the skin than wool. It takes dye poorly, but white linen can be washed to quite a brilliance. For these reasons, linen was favored for undergarments of various sorts and was also used to line garments (in fact, the word "lining" derives from the same root as "linen"). Flax was grown in

England to make linen cloth, but the best linens came from the Low Countries and northeastern France.

A woman in a close-fitting kirtle with pocket slits and sleeve-tippets (c. 1380) [Ashdown].

Another relatively common fabric was canvas, a heavy and coarse material made from flax or hemp. Canvas was most often found as lining in garments that needed extra strength. Cotton, which had to be imported from the Mediterranean regions, was less common. Pure cotton cloth was rare, but cotton was sometimes used as stuffing and as a component in the relatively common fabric known as fustian, a blend of cotton and linen. Fustian was especially used in military undergarments such as doublets. Both linen and canvas were sometimes treated with beeswax to enhance their resistance to water.

The finest fabrics were all made from silk. These were imported and very expensive. Fancy shirts were made of silken cloth. Rich fabrics such as satin, velvet, and taffeta were always made of silk.[2]

The weave of most fabrics was of two principal sorts, plain and twill. In plain-woven fabrics, the threads alternate over and under in every direction. Plain weave was used for wool and linen. Plain-weave wool is very durable and sheds water well, so it was especially common among the lower classes. It was often heavily fulled and felted, which made it warmer and more resistant to water as well as resistant to fraying. In twill fabrics, the threads pass over and under two or more other threads at a time, giving twills their characteristic diagonal look. Twill weave was used for woolen fabrics and was particularly favored for fashionable garments, as it drapes more gracefully than plain-weave. There is also some evidence of knitting in England at this time, at least for gloves and caps.[3]

The outer layers of clothing, such as mantles, gowns, hoods, gloves, and surcoats, were occasionally lined with fur for extra warmth or display. Many of the finest furs came from animals of the weasel family, notably marten, sable (which is dark brown to the point of black), and ermine (the winter coat of the stoat, which is snowy white save for a spot of black at the tip of the tail). Some fine furs came from various species of squirrel. Such quality furs were often imported from Scandinavia or Russia, where the cold climate caused especially rich pelts. Less expensive furs included fox, rabbit, lamb, and even cat.

Colors and Dyes The colors of fashionable clothes tended to be bold and bright; ordinary people's clothes were diverse in color but generally muted in tone. All dyes derived from natural sources, usually plants. Blue was derived from the native plant woad and from indigo imported from the East. The native plant madder produced a warm brick-red, while imported kermes (made from a Mediterranean insect) dyed a rich scarlet. The plant weld was used for yellow, while other plant sources were used for purple and brown. Dyes could be combined to produce other colors—blue was overdyed with yellow to produce green, for example. Black was difficult to achieve with dyes of the period and was therefore expensive, although not beyond the means of a prosperous gentleman. Coloration could also be provided by the wool itself. Some wools are naturally pigmented black, although they tend to produce a coarse fabric. Other wools are naturally brown or gray. Earth tones and natural tones were the least expensive and were generally worn only by the poor. Bold and long-lasting dyes were generally costly, whereas the cheaper dyes tended to fade fairly quickly.[4]

Construction Some garments were lined, but many seem to have been unlined except for silk, linen, or wool facing around the buttonholes. In many surviving unlined garments, neck and wrist openings are faced with a narrow linen or silk strip to cut down on chafing. Often the edges of wool garments were left unfinished, since the heavily felted wool resisted fraying. Raw edges of cuffs and collars were sometimes finished by tablet-weaving a fine braid directly onto the cloth, probably using a weft thread on a needle. Many rough openings that were not faced or finished with tablet-woven edging were turned back and trimmed with a narrow silk or linen ribbon folded over the edge. All these finishes helped prolong the life of the garment by protecting the areas that received the most wear. Silk and linen thread were the most common materials for sewing garments, with silk usually being

Women in simple but elegant kirtles. Italian, c. 1365 (Giovanni da Milano, "The Birth of the Virgin") [McLean].

used for buttonholes and finishing stitches on quality garments (although its use also seems to have been common among the lower middle classes).

Decorative fabric finishes were quite fashionable. The most common was probably the "notching of edges," or dagging, that Chaucer's Parson found so distasteful. In this technique the edge of the garment was cut into decorative shapes. On well-fulled wool, the cut edge could be left unfinished; on other fabrics, a contrasting lining added to the decorative effect. Such dagging might be found on the lower edge of a coathardie, hood, or mantle, or on the voluminous cuffs of a houppelande (all described later in this chapter).

The outer layers of clothing, made of wool or silken fabric, did not generally wash well and were likely to be brushed instead. Ideally, linen underclothes were to be washed once a week. Wrinkles might be pressed out with a heavy flat-sided object called a "sleek-stone"—like nineteenth-century irons, it may have been heated in a fire.

Medieval people had different ideas than we do of what it was to be properly dressed. The public was more likely to see **The Outfit** a man's underpants than his naked elbows. In part this was because clothing was so expensive. When most people could only afford one or two complete outfits to serve them throughout the year, they didn't invest in specialized clothing they could only wear for a short season. By layering and other strategies, they tried to get as much use as possible out of a limited set of garments.

Imagine one of Chaucer's contemporaries getting dressed on a chilly spring morning. Over breeches (underwear), hose, and shirt he might pull a kirtle (the basic form of outer garment), over-kirtle, and hood. If his over-kirtle had short sleeves, whatever he wore under it would certainly have had long ones. Aside from a change or two of shirt and breeches, this might well be the only outfit he owned. As the day warmed he might put aside his over-kirtle. Warmer still, and he might fiddle with his hood. Hoods are wonderfully versatile garments, and whether they are worn as a hood, a cowl pushed back onto the neck, a hat, or slung over the shoulder makes a surprising difference in warmth. Warmer still, and he would unlace his hose and roll them down over his garters, or remove them entirely. Laborers in the fields in summer often stripped to their shirt and breeches. Aristocrats did not need to sweat as often, but even young gentlemen playing at swords or handball might roll their hose down, revealing their breeches below their short doublets.

Women also wore several layers for comfort and versatility, although they had fewer options without offending against contemporary standards of decency. A complete outfit might include headgear, an over-kirtle (possibly short-sleeved), a kirtle, a shirt, and short hose. The over-kirtle might come off for warm weather or housework. Sometimes women would hike the skirts of their garments for convenience and comfort. Like the men, farm women in the fields at harvest time sometimes stripped to their shirts, but you would not have seen naked elbows outside the bathhouses. Except under exceptional circumstances, decent dress involved a shirt and one other layer, at least one of which had long sleeves.

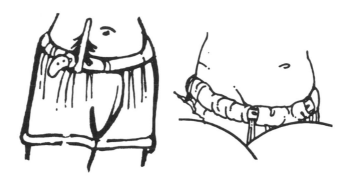

Breeches. The example on the left is from a woodcut of c. 1410-20; the belt is clearly visible (Anonymous Bavarian Master, "The Martyrdom of St. Sebastian"). The breech on the right is from a painted cloth of c. 1375. Note the cords attaching the hose to the belt within the casing of the breech. ("Le Parement de Narbonne") [McLean].

Underwear:
Breech and Shirt
The first layer of a man's clothes was a pair of loose shorts, known as a "breech," which served the double purpose of helping to concealing his private parts (if he was wearing one of the fashionably short garments of the age) and providing support for his leggings. The clearest illustrations show breeches held up by belts, which may have passed through a channel in the top of the breech, or the tops may simply have been folded around the belt; alternatively, they might have been held up by a drawstring, particularly if a doublet supported the hose. The belt sometimes supported a purse—it was, after all, a relatively secure location for one's money. Breeches were normally made of white linen.

Women did not wear breeches. Evidence regarding women's supporting garments is predictably scarce, but a few texts of the period refer to a "breast-girdle" or "breast-band," which may have been some sort of linen band that served the function of a modern bra.[5]

The next garment for a man, and the first for a woman, was the shirt, again typically made of white linen. The shirt was considered underwear. People were not normally seen in public wearing nothing over their shirts unless they were engaged in particularly strenuous labor or exercise. In fact, a person wearing only a shirt was said to be "naked." The medieval shirt was characteristically cut with straight seams and was pulled over the head.

The pattern shown here is that of the thirteenth-century shirt preserved at Notre Dame cathedral in Paris and reputed to have belonged to Saint Louis. It may be the only surviving medieval European shirt. It

illustrates the value of fabric in the Middle Ages: the design of the shirt is such as to keep waste to an absolute minimum. The cut of this shirt is long, designed for the long kirtles of the thirteenth century. In the fifteenth century, 3 yards of fabric were reckoned enough to make a shirt, some 2' less than the St. Louis shirt.[6] The triangular gores inserted at front and back allowed greater ease of movement. Shorter shirts in the fourteenth century might achieve the same effect with open side seams from the waist down. Shirts had necklines roughly congruent with those used on the outer garments: the triangular neckline on the St. Louis shirt is again a thirteenth-century feature.

The female equivalent to the man's shirt was called a smock. It is possible that, as in later centuries, the smock was distinguished by having the gores inserted into the side seam rather than in front and back. A smock could be decorated with embroidery about the collar.

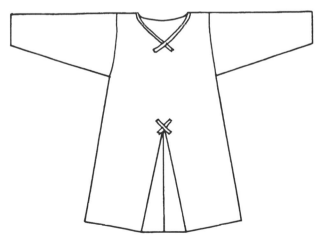

The St. Louis Shirt (thirteenth century). It is shown above inside-out, revealing its reinforcing tapes. The cutting pattern on the left illustrates how carefully the fabric is used [McLean, after Burnham].

ORIGINAL   CONJECTURED   RAGGED   FALSE   WARP
EDGE   EDGE   EDGE   SEAM   FOLD   DIRECTION

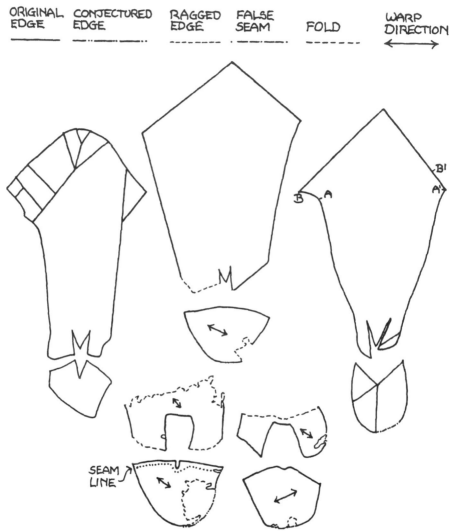

Hose. Top, l-r: Hose from Bremen (thirteenth century), Boksten (1300-1350), Herjolfsnes (probably 1350-1400). Bottom: Late fourteenth-century hose fragments from London—the heel and foot on the right are probably not from the same hose. All are for the right foot except the Herjolfsnes hose (uncertain) and the London foot piece at bottom right (probably left, but reversed here for easier comparison). The complete hose all have a triangular extension of the leg over the instep, overlapping the foot piece in the case of the Boksten hose. The overlap at the top of the Herjolfsnes hose reduces the strain on the seam. The piecing probably served to economize on fabric. Leather straps to hold up the hose were attached at three points at the top of each leg of the Boksten hose [McLean: Bremen and Boksten hose after Lundwall, Herjolfsnes hose after Norlund, London fragments after Unwin].

To cover their legs, both men and women wore a pair of cloth leggings known as hose. These were typically made of wool, cut **Hose** on the bias (diagonally) for extra elasticity. Still, being of woven cloth rather than knitted, they tended to be baggy (unlike the tights we see in today's movies). Medieval hose were often brightly colored, striped, or even of contrasting colors for each leg. Sometimes they were lined with plain white linen. Hose could also be made of leather; sometimes just the soles were made of leather, so the hose could be worn without shoes.

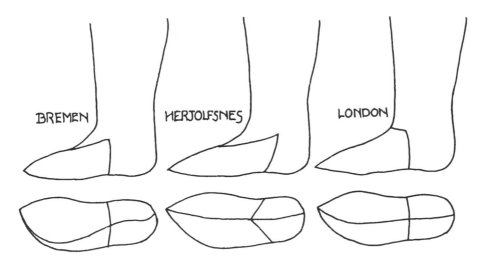

Assembled hose. Note how the seam on the bottom curves to avoid the ball of the foot [McLean].

The length of the hose was determined by the length of the upper-body garment. Men's hose covered the entire leg and had cords or laces called "points" attached to the top, with which the hose were secured to the breeches-belt, breeches, or doublet. Since women's legs were already covered by their kirtles, their hose reached only to the knee, where they were secured with garters. Men might also wear short hose with longer garments. Sometimes they rolled their long hose down to their knees in hot weather.

More fashionable men's hose were cut high enough to lace to a short upper-body garment (called a doublet or pourpoint) at front, side and back. This restricted the wearer's range of motion, and contemporary illustrations often show the rear and/or side points unlaced to allow extra freedom of movement for difficult tasks.

The usual form of outer clothing for ordinary people was the kirtle, a garment worn over the shirt, usually of wool, **Kirtles** occasionally of linen. In its simplest form it was similar in cut to a shirt: the body was made of a single piece, with gores in the front and back or sides (usually both), and straight-cut sleeves. A kirtle of this sort was found in a bog at Boksten in Sweden. Kirtles reached to the knee or calf for men; for women they were cut longer, stretching to the ankle or foot. A kirtle could be lined and might be adorned with braided lacing, which also served to bind loose edges. Several layers of kirtles might be worn, and men's over-kirtles sometimes had slits in front for riding.

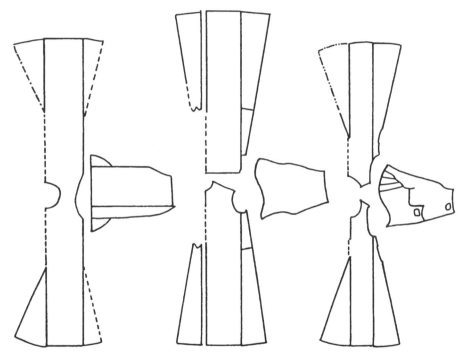

Kirtles illustrating the development of tailoring techniques (left half, 1/30 scale): Boksten (c. 1300-50), Moselund (?c. 1350), Herjolfsnes no. 43 (?c. 1340-1400) [McLean].

The fourteenth century witnessed a turning point in the history of costume, with the introduction of curved seams, which allow garments to be more fully shaped. This development significantly changed the design of kirtles. A transitional style is found in the Moselund kirtle, another Scandinavian bog-find. It is partially tailored and probably somewhat later in date than the Boksten kirtle: most of the seams are straight, but the front and back pieces are separate, the top of the front piece is angled to fit the shoulders better, the side gores extend to the armholes, and the armhole edge of the sleeves is curved in essentially the same shape as a modern sleeve.

Loosely fitted kirtles from Herjolfsnes (nos. 33 and 45, right half and left sleeve, 1/30 scale) [Norlund].

The next development from this type of garment was the fully tailored kirtle, of which quite a few have been excavated from graves at Herjolfsnes in Greenland. The shoulder seams are angled in both the front and back. The side gores, stretching right up to the armholes, have become fully tailored pieces rather than simple triangles. In several cases they are shaped to give a very narrow waist and a broadly flaring skirt. The necks are often close-fitting, with a slash to allow them to be pulled over the head, and are fastened with buttons, a lace, or a brooch. In some cases the sleeves are quite tight, and are designed to be fastened with buttons or sewn up at each wearing. The Herjolfsnes kirtles show the highly pieced construction that is typical of medieval garments, by which the makers conserved precious fabric. Several have pocket slits, probably giving access to a purse worn underneath.

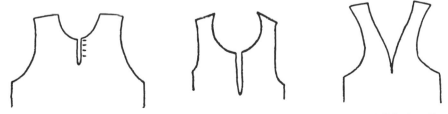

Additional necklines from Herjolfsnes (nos. 60, 43, and 58, 1/15 scale) [Norlund].

Women's kirtles were not substantially different from those of men, save that they were cut longer. Two examples have been identified from Herjolfsnes.

Closely fitted kirtles from Herjolfsnes (nos. 38, 41, and 39, left half and left sleeve, 1/30 scale). Nos. 38 and 39 have been identified as women's kirtles on the basis of their length: their cut does not differ from those of male kirtles [Norlund].

By the latter half of the fourteenth century, the kirtle was considered an ordinary sort of garment and by no means particularly fashionable.

Tailored kirtles fitted better than their straight-cut predecessors, but they still had to be pulled over the head and could not be very closely fitted. The fourteenth century witnessed another major development with the use of buttons to allow a closer fit. A garment that buttoned in front did not have to be pulled over the head, and could be tailored more closely to the body. In fact, the truly fashionable styles for the first half of Chaucer's lifetime were extremely tight-fitting.

The characteristically tight-fitting garment of the period is known today as the coathardie, although it is uncertain that contemporary terminology would have been so precise. Such garments were worn by both men and women. They were closely fitted about the waist, and sometimes about the hips too, although they might have a flaring skirt. On men they were shorter than a kirtle, sometimes reaching as far as the tops of the knees but often only to the upper thighs. The female version was probably still known as a kirtle: like more old-fashioned kirtles, it reached to the ankles or feet. The sleeves might be embellished with decorative strips of cloth hanging from the upper arms.

The distinctive feature of these garments was the opening for putting them on. The male version usually opened from neck to hem in front, buttoning all or most of the way. Occasionally the front opening laced shut. Some pictures of quite tightly fitted male coathardies show no signs of a front opening; these may have laced under the arm. The female version usually opened to the waist in front and was secured with buttons or lacing; alternatively, it might lace up the side under the arm. The coathardie might also have buttons at the lower sleeves to allow for a very tight fit. Buttons were small and might be unevenly distributed, with more buttons at points of greater strain such as the midriff. Coathardies became less fashionable in the latter part of the century, when they were likely to be covered by looser outer garments.

Close relatives of the coathardie were the doublet (a sort of under-jacket for extra warmth) and the pourpoint (a stuffed and quilted doublet, worn for warmth or under armor for additional protection). One of the essential purposes of these garments was to hold up hose (hose returned the favor by keeping the doublet from riding up). By fitting as tightly as a belt at the natural waist level, the doublet or pourpoint could anchor the hose to the waist just as a belt does for modern trousers. Although it had to fit snugly at the waist, a doublet could fit more loosely above that point. Such garments might well be loose from the bottom of the ribs on up. The difference in fit might be emphasized by using larger buttons above this point or buttons above and laces below. The wasp-waist effect could also be emphasized by padding. A pourpoint worn beneath armor was padded most heavily on the shoulders. Garments worn over the doublet or pourpoint, such as the coathardie, often followed the same cut.

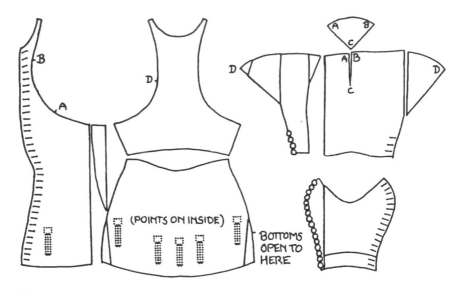

The Charles of Blois doublet. For a reconstruction, see the chapter on Arms and Armor. [McLean, after Zylstra-Zweens]

Perhaps the only surviving garment of this sort is the pourpoint associated with Charles of Blois, dating to 1360-1400. It is elaborately tailored, fitting closely at the waist and hips and more broadly at the chest. It has very large armholes, with a seam across the elbow; it would theoretically have been worn under armor, so the design is intended for maximum flexibility and a good fit. Again, the highly pieced construction illustrates how precious fabric was, even for a nobleman like Charles of Blois. The pourpoint is made of ivory-colored silk brocaded with gold, lined with fine linen canvas, and interlined with cotton wadding; it is quilted with horizontal rows spaced at 1 $^1/_2$". There are points (laces) sewn in for attaching hose. The points are of linen, except for those at the center back, which are of kid leather. The separate triangular piece shown for the sleeve seems to have been added last, to allow for precise fitting. The cut of the arms provides for ample arm movement, suggesting military use, but other characteristics make this unlikely. The buttons, especially those up the length of the arms, are large enough to interfere with any sort of armor, there are no attachment points for arm harness, and the fabric seems too delicate (and well preserved) to have been worn under mail or plate. It might have been worn *over* armor, but its very tight tailoring suggests it was not. It is more likely a top-quality coathardie, although a more robust version of the same garment would serve well as an arming doublet.

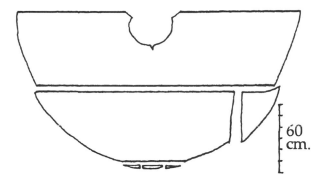

The Boksten mantle [McLean, after Lundwall].

England had never been an especially warm country, and the climate of the fourteenth century was, **Outer Garments** if anything, probably a bit cooler than it is today. For this reason, and for reasons of fashion, people usually wore several layers of clothing. A variety of outer garments were in use. The simplest of these was the mantle, of which an example was found in a bog at Boksten in Sweden. The right shoulder is sewn together rather than buttoned, and the neck opening is large enough to go over the head. It is cut with a dart over the left shoulder for a better fit. This style of mantle, opening on the side, seems to have been a male fashion; women's mantles (as well as many for men) opened at the center front. The mantle might fasten with a brooch or with buttons. A mantle might have a lining, which could be shorter than the outer shell and not sewn directly to it at the bottom—like the lining of a modern raincoat, the design kept water from collecting in the hem.

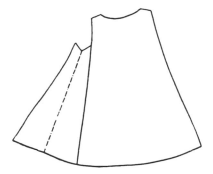

Incomplete garment, perhaps a surcoat, from Herjolfsnes (1/30 scale) [Norlund].

Over a close-fitting garment people often wore a sleeveless surcoat. The fashionable woman's version of this garment was distinguished by deeply cut arm-holes, which allowed the kirtle underneath to be seen, showing off the shape of the body.

The Herjolfsnes gown (1/20 scale) [Norlund].

An even warmer overgarment was the gown. One of these was among the archeological finds at Herjolfsnes in Greenland. This loose garment covered most of the body and was open at the front, fastening with buttons.

Man and woman in fashionable houppelandes from the end of the century [Ashdown].

The latter part of the century saw the emergence of the houppelande as the most fashionable garment for both men and women. The houppelande was a loose gown made to fit only at the shoulders. It might be belted—above the waist on women and below the waist on men. It was usually quite long and ostentatious in its liberal use of fabric, although men's houppelandes were sometimes cut short to show off the legs. The sleeves, long and loose, were frequently cut with dags and lined with fur or silk. Sometimes the full sleeves narrowed to a cuff at the wrist. The collar came up to the middle of the back of the head and buttoned up to the chin at the front. Often the collar was turned down, leaving the top few buttons undone. Men's long houppelandes were generally open from the hem to the knee.

The characteristic headgear for a fourteenth-century man was the hood, of which many original examples survive. Like other outer garments, the hood was normally made of wool. The typical hood sported a **Hoods, Hats, and Other Headgear** tippet, or tail, at the back, which could be quite long on fashionable hoods—young gallants sometimes used it for storing knickknacks. The Herjolfsnes hoods also have a slight peak at the top of the face opening, improving the fit when the hood was folded back away from the face. Some fancy hoods had elaborate dagging cut into the hem of the cape.

There were two distinct styles of hood. One form had a small shoulder cape, with a gusset inserted into the shoulder. The other had a larger cape with a gusset inserted at the front, and sometimes one at the back as well. The front gusset allowed the selvage of the fabric to run along the edge of the face opening, permitting a more durable and easier finish for that edge, which was not always hemmed or lined. No lining survives on any of these hoods, but paintings of the period often show contrasting linings.

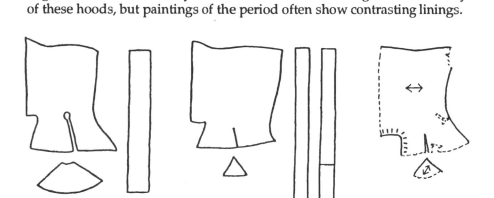

Side-gusset hoods (1/15 scale): two from Herjolfsnes, one from London [Left and center: Norlund; right: McLean, after Unwin].

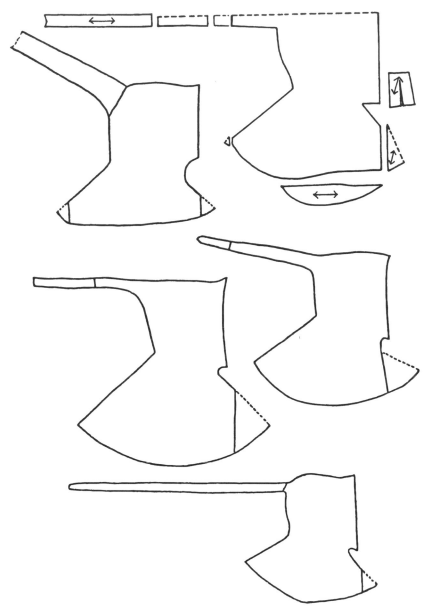

Front-gusset hoods (1/15 scale): the one in the upper right is from Boksten (Sweden), the others are from Herjolfsnes (Greenland) [Upper right: McLean; others: Norlund].

One fashionable way to wear the hood was as a hat, with the face opening going over the head and the cape and tippet draped to the side or back. The edge of the face opening could be rolled back to control the fit, and sometimes the tippet was wrapped around the head and tucked into itself to secure the hood in place.

Women could also wear hoods; theirs typically buttoned or tied under the chin. Illustrations often show women's hoods with a relatively short shoulder cape, and frequently worn unbuttoned. Sometimes these hoods appear to be designed so as not to close at all; they only vestigially preserve the shape of a hood that could be buttoned. Other illustrations show women wearing hoods with shoulder capes that almost reach to their elbows, worn with the hood thrown back. A few seem to show hoods worn as hats in the masculine style, with the top of the head inserted into the face opening.

Woman in open-style headdress, showing the arrangement of the headbands.
[Ashdown]

For women, the characteristic headdress of the early fourteenth century was the veil and wimple. The veil was typically a rectangle of white linen or silk worn draped over the head, trailing in back. The wimple was a similar piece of fabric arranged to fall in folds under the chin and around the neck—some wimples only covered the front, others surrounded the neck completely. Both veils and wimples were held in place with straight pins, anchored to a headband.

Later in the century, fashionable women ceased to cover the neck and chin, preferring only the veil. These veils were often fastened to a narrow fillet that circled the brow. The fillet also served to support the hair, which was braided, made into two bundles at the side of the face, and wired into place. The fillet might be tablet-woven or of more expensive jeweler's work. The veil might have a frilled edge, and it was often folded so that several layers of frilling framed the face and hair.

Older women, as well as the less fashionable, wore the plainer veil. Servants, peasants, and those performing arduous tasks often wore a simple veil or cloth tied about the head in some fashion to keep it from shifting and to keep the hair covered and out of the way.

Woman in veil and wimple. [Ashdown]

In addition to their hoods, men often wore a coif made of linen or leather; this could be padded for military use. Hats were also popular. Ordinary hats were probably made of wool felt. They might be broad-brimmed with a low round crown or high-crowned with a small brim; the brim was sometimes folded up in front or in back. Men's hats were occasionally adorned with a hatband and feathers. Both men and women wore straw hats in hot weather. Some hats were fitted with laces so they could hang from the neck. Unlike other head coverings for women, hats seem only to have been worn for outdoor pursuits, and they were often worn over a veil and wimple.

Fashionable women and men might adorn their hair with chaplets—wreathes made from flowers or greenery, or fabric cut to imitate those ephemeral materials, or from jeweler's work. At the end of the century thick, padded rolls of fabric began to appear on fashionable heads; these were to become very popular in the fifteenth century for both sexes.

Some women wore their hair uncovered, particularly if
they were young and unmarried.   Various arrangements of   **Hair and**
braids were typical, or the hair might be worn in long tresses   **Grooming**
or gathered behind. Hairnets, which had gone out of fashion
during the middle of the century, re-appeared towards the end with a
more open and conspicuous mesh. Uncovered and undressed hair is
sometimes seen in contemporary illustrations, but it was unusual. Most
often women's hair was cut rather long, but a few contemporary
illustrations show modern-looking cuts no longer than neck-length.

Men wore their hair fairly long—to or past the collar, though not long
enough to braid. Beards were common, except for churchmen, who were
obliged to be clean-shaven. Moustaches had fallen out of fashion after the
Norman Conquest, and were very rare at this time, although not wholly
unknown. Shaving involved a straight razor and basin, in a manner that
remained essentially unchanged until the rise of the safety razor in the
present century; the process is tricky, not to say dangerous, and gave
employment to a legion of professional barbers.

Hair was groomed with a comb—brushes were apparently used only
for clothes. Medieval combs had two sets of teeth, one broad to deal with
the larger tangles, the other fine to finish up. Ordinary combs were made
of wood or horn; expensive ones were made of ivory. Then as now, curly
hair was fashionable among women, who sometimes used curling irons to
achieve this effect. The best mirrors were made of glass; a cheaper version
consisted of polished metal; all were hand-held. Cosmetics were also used
by fashionable women, although moralists condemned the practice as
pure vanity.

Shoes in Chaucer's day were normally made of leather.
The soles were flat, without heels, typically made with heavy   **Shoes and**
"sole leather" to protect the underside of the feet. In some   **Pattens**
cases the need for shoes was circumvented by using leather for
the soles of one's hose.

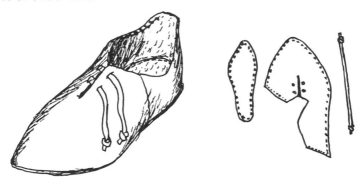

Low shoe. [Vernier, after Mitford]

A variety of shoe types were in use. Archeological evidence from London suggests that most were cut below the ankle, fastening either with a buckle, a latchet (a split leather strap passed through a pair of holes), or a leather lace. The next most common appears to have been ankle shoes, extending up to the ankle or a bit beyond. The least common were boots. Both ankle shoes and boots typically fastened up the front with laces. In the middle of the fourteenth century a round toe was favored, but by the later part there was a definite trend toward pointed shoes. Side-laced, front-laced, or ankle shoes had modest points, and were probably everyday wear or working-class shoes. Shoes with longer points, known as "poulaines" or "cracows" ("Polish" or "Krakow" shoes), were cut low over the instep and had an ankle strap secured with a buckle or latchet. The point on these fashionable shoes could reach 4", but most were shorter. Such shoes could be stuffed with moss or hair to retain their shape. Buckled shoes seem to have been worn by men, whereas front latchets and laces were worn equally by both sexes.[7]

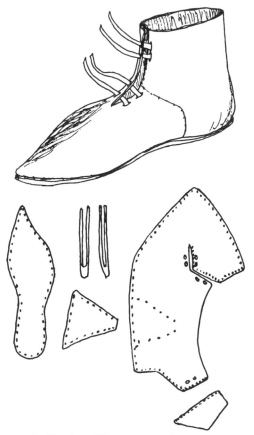

Ankle shoe [Vernier, after Mitford].

An older method for making shoes involved a one-piece upper, with the seam on the inside of the foot. This method remained in use in the later fourteenth century, but poulaines, which required more leather, were usually made with two-piece uppers consisting of a "vamp" (front) and "quarters" (rear). The soles of poulaines were often of two pieces as well, joined at the arch of the foot.

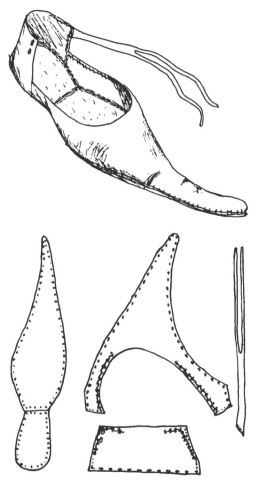

Poulaine [Vernier, after Mitford].

Shoes for ordinary use were plain, but others might be decorated. One style of ornamentation was openwork, in which small holes were punched out of the leather in a pattern. This could simply be a design around the upper part of the vamp or could cover the entire vamp and quarter. The second style involved engraved lines and shapes cut or scraped on the surface of the leather. Incised latticework or engraved leaf motifs were both popular.

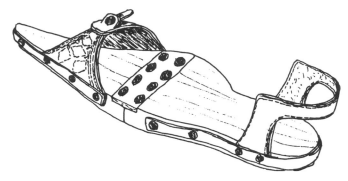

Patten [Vernier].

Because medieval shoes lacked heels and were not particularly durable or waterproof, people often relied on pattens, the medieval equivalent of modern overshoes, for walking in rain and mud. Pattens resembled sandals. The sole was usually made from a soft wood such as alder, poplar, or willow and had leather straps to hold it onto the feet. There were three basic types: the platform patten, the flat patten, and the leather patten. Platform pattens were typically carved from a single piece of wood and held the feet off the ground on "stilts" or wedges. Flat pattens, also of wood, were hinged to follow the movement of the foot. Leather pattens were made by sewing together five to seven layers of thick leather to form the sole. The straps were sometimes adorned with stamped decoration.

Laces, Buttons, and Garters Men's hose were laced to upper garments with laces called "points." The laces might be woven or braided threads, or leather. They had metal ends known as "tags" or "aglets," which made it easier to push them through lacing-eyelets. Points were generally tied in a half-bow.

Most buttons were made of fabric stuffed with fabric scraps. Others were discs or domes of wood or horn, also covered with cloth. Wealthier people could afford metal buttons: either tin, pewter, latten, or brass. The rich might have buttons of silver or gold, or even set with gems. Buttons were essentially of the shank variety rather than pierced like modern shirt-buttons. Examples found in London range from about $1/8$" to about $1\,1/4$" in diameter. Buttons were generally sewn to the garment at the very edge, not set in from the edge as is the modern custom.

Garters were essential to keep up a woman's hose and were sometimes worn by fashionable men as well. They tied just under the knee. The simplest ones were probably plain strips of cloth, but fashionable men and women wore garters of leather with buckles and sometimes painted decorations or mottoes. The most famous example was worn by members of the Order of the Garter; it can still be seen on the British royal coat of arms.

Another important fastener was pins, which were used extensively to hold clothing in place, particularly women's headgear. They were quite expensive, since they had to be made individually. The simplest style involved hammering the end of a piece of wire to make a head, and sharpening the other end. The wiremaking itself was a time-consuming process: a piece of metal had to be first hammered thin, then drawn through a series of successively smaller holes to make it wire-shaped.

Pouch [Gay].

Belts were a most important accessory, used to carry pouches, knives, and other essential items. The belts of the **Accessories** rich might be made of metal plaques hinged together—richly ornamented discs, squares, quatrefoils, or other shapes, often gilt or made of some precious metal. Sometimes the plaques were riveted to leather or fabric belts. More utilitarian belts were made of leather, fastened by a tongued buckle. Those who could afford them wore belts with strap ends, buckle mounts, and grommets of metal, and the strap itself might be decorated with appliqué or with rosettes of tin or brass. Tablet-woven belts were also worn; these were made of wool or linen for ordinary folk, or of silk for the rich.[8]

The belt supported a purse or belt-pouch, a crucial part of everyone's attire, since medieval clothes did not incorporate pockets. This might be a purse made of sturdy leather with a flap and buckle, or a pouch made of supple leather or fabric that closed with a drawstring, sometimes heavily embroidered. Such pouches were also kept inside a belt-purse as a handy way to store coins.

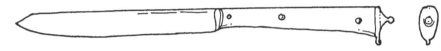

Reconstruction of a fourteenth-century knife from London, about 5 1/2" long, with copper alloy shoulder and butt plates [McLean, after Griffiths].

A knife was another essential item of personal gear—in fact, people were expected to provide their own knives at the table. Knives were carried by all classes of people and were quite different from daggers, being designed for peaceful rather than violent uses. They were smaller than daggers, the blade was sharp on only one side, and there was no cross hilt. The typical knife was of carbon steel with a wooden or bone handle; it might have steel or brass fittings. Often the sheath tied onto the back of a purse.[9]

Both gloves and mittens were used in the fourteenth century; to judge by visual evidence, gloves were generally worn by people of social pretensions, mittens by commoners. As a mark of social status, gloves were as likely to be worn for display as for warmth. Both gloves and mittens had characteristically long gauntlets extending well past the wrist.

Glasses in use [Gay].

Eyeglasses were a relative novelty in Chaucer's day and were used only for reading, being essentially magnifying lenses comparable to modern reading glasses. They were similar to the modern pince-nez style, having no temple-pieces but resting on the nose. They hinged in the middle.

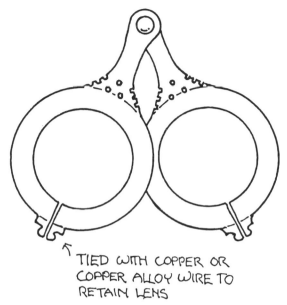

TIED WITH COPPER OR COPPER ALLOY WIRE TO RETAIN LENS

Fifteenth-century glasses, carved from bone (actual size) [McLean].

Handkerchiefs were not unknown, but they were apparently a rarity—doubtless, sleeves suffered for this omission.[10] Travelers often carried drink in leather bottles, gourds, or miniature wooden barrels bound with iron.

The upper classes delighted in jewelry. Brooches were especially fashionable, sometimes in the shape of letters or **Jewelry** bearing mottoes. One example is the brooch worn by Chaucer's Prioress, on which was written *Amor Vincit Omnia*. In many cases brooches were a functional part of people's clothes, being used to fasten a mantle or the neck-opening of a kirtle, or to attach points to the hose. Rings were also popular. They were a common love token, and a man placed a ring on his bride's finger as part of the marriage ceremony. Necklaces made of gold or silver were sometimes worn by both men and women.

Faceted cuts were very rare on fourteenth-century gems, and those few that do exist are much simpler than the faceting on most modern gems. The vast majority of fourteenth-century examples are cut *en cabochon*, that is, shaped like a smoothly rounded pebble. Then as now, imitation gems of glass were used in cheaper jewelry.

For those who wished to look fashionable but could not afford it, there were brooches and rings of pewter, made in imitation of costly jewelry, complete with raised domes where one might expect gems or pearls—these domes may originally have been painted to contribute to the illusion. Pilgrim badges were another form of jewelry that enjoyed wide popularity. These were typically small badges of cast pewter in the shape of an image relating to the holy shrine where they were sold—an early version of the tourist's souvenir.[11]

CLOTHING PATTERNS

The instructions in the following pages are designed to allow you to make a complete set of simple fourteenth-century clothing. Unlike most costuming books, the patterns given here are as close to the originals as possible. Just how far you choose to take the authenticity will depend on the purpose of the clothing you are making. Dedicated living history groups like to be accurate even down to the kinds of stitching used on their garments, but if you are making costumes for a school pageant you won't want to worry about such precision.

By cultivating the characteristically layered look of medieval clothing, you can get the maximum mileage out of a few well-chosen, well-made garments. An ankle-length gown or kirtle is a good first garment for a man, since it can conceal shortcomings in the rest of the outfit. Hoods are versatile garments for both sexes. Linen, silk, and summer-weight wool are good choices if you expect to have to wear your clothes in hot weather. A hat, particularly a broad-brimmed straw one, will add a great deal to your comfort in summer.

The instructions describe each of the garments as being made of linen or wool—whether you actually use these fabrics will depend on your goals. When buying your fabrics, we recommend at least looking at the real linen and wool. Even if you plan to use another fabric, a glance at the real thing will give you some idea of the look the original garments would have had.

Medieval wool was often heavily fulled and therefore quite resistant to fraying. Dagging was often cut into the edge of the fabric without any further finish. This might work well with coat-weight modern wool, or you might try fulling a lighter-weight wool yourself. Do-it-yourself fulling can be accomplished by washing the wool in hot soapy water in the washing machine (this tends to shrink the center of the fabric more than the selvages); toss in a tennis shoe with it, as the pounding action is an essential part of the process. Fulling can also be done by hand in a tub by folding the fabric back and forth on itself and treading or pounding it in the water. The wool may shrink as much as 60%. In the Middle Ages, this shrinkage was moderated by stretching the cloth over wooden "tenter-frames" while it was drying after being fulled. Iron hooks called "tenter-hooks" gripped the fabric.

Choosing the correct colors will greatly enhance the authenticity of any attempt at medieval clothing. Many colors available today—bright purple or vivid lime green, for example—were simply impossible to obtain with medieval dyes. The best way to gain an idea of the colors of medieval clothes would be to look at modern wools left undyed or dyed with natural dyes (a good knitting shop might be a place to try; some of the textile suppliers listed in Appendix C will also provide sample swatches).

Many of the following patterns are simple and geometric and should be easy to scale up. For those that aren't, you can use an enlarging photocopier or lay a grid on the pattern and transfer it to a grid where the squares are larger by the proportion that you want to expand the pattern.

When cutting out any of the clothes described, remember to add an extra $1/2$" as the seam allowance unless otherwise noted. With the more complex patterns, it is advisable to make a mock-up, or fitting, of inexpensive material first—muslin is a good choice. You can make the necessary adjustments to this fitting and proceed to the better fabric when you are satisfied with the fit.

Unless you are determined to make your clothing fully authentic, you will probably want to machine-stitch invisible seams. If you do the finishing stitches by hand, the clothes will still look quite accurate except under the closest scrutiny. Linen or silk thread is the most authentic.

For further information on the techniques of sewing, we suggest you consult an experienced seamster; another useful source is *Singer Sewing Step-by-Step* (Minnetonka MN: Cy de Cosse, 1990), which has brilliant instructions and illustrations to assist the home sewer.

A Note on Gussets

Since medieval tailoring often involved inserting a gusset into a slit, we have included the following set of instructions for dealing with them.

Assume you are using a $1/2$" seam allowance, and want to insert a gusset in the front of a kirtle. The same technique was also used on hoods and sleeves (as in the cases of the side-gore hoods and the Charles of Blois doublet).

Find the spot near the tip of the gusset where it is 1" wide, and put a dot in the middle of that inch (i.e. $1/2$" from either edge). Mark the wrong side at the corresponding point. Still on the wrong side, draw a chalk line on the gusset seamline ($1/2$" from right edge). This line will pass through the point you just marked. Draw another chalk line on the fabric you want to set the gusset into, at the place you want the gusset to go. Don't cut yet.

Pin the gusset to the kirtle, right sides together. The bottom right corner of the gusset should line up with the bottom of the kirtle and the line you drew on it. The gusset itself will be off center with respect to the line. Now sew along the line you drew on the gusset from the dot near the point to the bottom. Be sure to fasten your stitching with a knot or backstitch at the point. Cut along the line drawn on the kirtle until about 3" away from the point. Move the gusset seam allowance out of the way and carefully cut along the line right up to, but not through, the point where you started. Be careful not to cut the stitching at that point. You will see that while the seam allowance on the gusset is $^1/_2$" throughout, on the kirtle it will taper towards the point.

Open out the gusset, flip over the kirtle, and match the unsewn side of the gusset to the other side of the cut line, right sides together. Line up the bottom corners as before, and you will see that once again the kirtle side of the seam allowance tapers towards the point, with the kirtle side on top. You want this seam to look like a mirror image of the last one. Pin in place, and stitch $^1/_2$" from the side of the gusset, sewing from the dot to the bottom, again anchoring your stitching securely at the dot. Be careful not to stitch over the rest of the kirtle or gusset, or anything but the seam.

Breech

Breeches were worn only by men. No medieval examples of breeches survive, so this design is purely conjectural. Original breeches were probably more highly pieced. They would have been made of white linen.

The pattern is scaled to a men's medium, with a $^1/_2$" seam and hem allowance and a $^3/_4$" casing at the top for a drawstring. The waist size should be just enough to put your hips through. Since they are made from inelastic fabric, the correct size will probably look much larger than you might expect, based on your experience with modern underwear.

Cutting: Cut 1 of each piece.
G-F = G'-F' = hip measurement
G-H = G'-H' = waist to upper thigh along outseam
A-E = A'-E' = D-H = D'-H' = half the circumference of the thigh + 2"
A-B = A'-B' = C-D = C'-D' = 1 $^1/_2$"
B-C = $^3/_4$"
B'-C' = 3 $^1/_4$" around the curve

Sewing: Place the two pieces right side together and stitch the side seams together (G-H and E-F). Then stitch A-B to A'-B' and C-D to C'-D'. Ease B'-C' to B-C and stitch, forming a pocket for comfort. Hem the leg cuffs. Hem back 3/4" at the top to make a channel for the drawstring. Make two round or vertical buttonholes at center front, 2" apart, to thread the drawstring through. Make two more holes just below the drawstring, one above the center points of each thigh, to tie your hose to: the points will pass around the drawstring on the outside of the casing.

This design can be adjusted to allow for a belt instead of a drawstring.

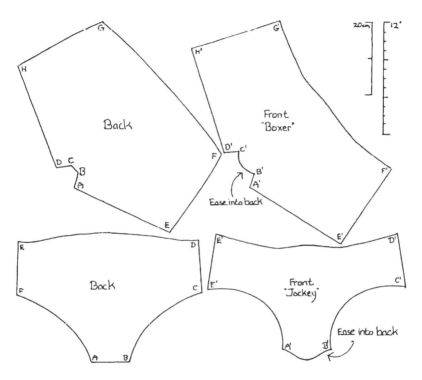

Pattern for breech [McLean, based on a design by Robert MacPherson].

Hose

This pattern is a composite based on the surviving medieval hose shown earlier. It is for the right leg—reverse it for the left. The scale is 1/9 full size for a 6' 2", 210-lb. man with size-13 feet. Note that this pattern includes a 1/2" seam allowance. You will need to adjust for your size, build, and the elasticity of your fabric. You may wish to try a mock-up of inexpensive fabric first. The best final material is wool, since it affords the most stretch. Remember to cut on the bias to allow the hose to stretch.

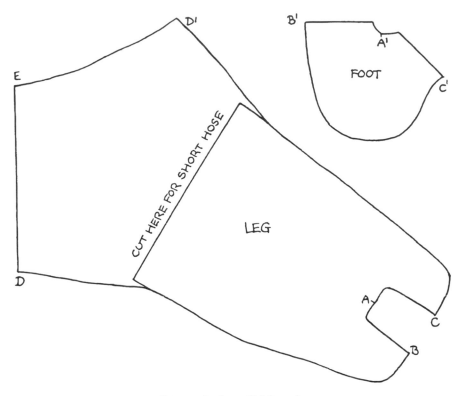

Pattern for hose [McLean].

<u>Cutting</u>:
     Short hose should come just above the knee before you fold the top over your garter. For long hose, **A-E** should be a few inches less than the distance from the top of your instep to your belt to allow for the stretch of the fabric when you tie it up. **D-D'** should equal the circumference of your thigh just below your buttocks, plus 2". For **B'-C'** measure around your foot at the highest point of the instep and under your arch and add 1 $^1/2$". The narrowest point on the ankle should leave you just enough room to force your heel through with your toe pointed. A pair of jeans that fit you well can be a helpful starting point.
     Put right side to right side and sew leg and foot together. You may get the best results by sewing out from the center, sewing from **A** to **B** and then **A** to **C**. Press and finish the seam. Now line **B** up against **C** and sew sole seam forward to the toe. Now sew from **B-C** up the back of the leg to

the top of the hose. **B-C** should fall under the arch of the foot, and the sole seam should curve slightly to avoid the ball of the foot. Press and finish this seam. Finish the top of the hose.

For long hose, you will need to make some arrangement to attach the points. This may be a button sewn to the top, or you may instead reinforce the top with canvas or other fabric and let in holes or slots through which the points can pass. You will need an attachment point at **E**, and you can include additional points at the side.

Shirt

A shirt is an important part of a complete medieval outfit. It adds comfort under wool, absorbs sweat and keeps it away from your outer clothes, and gives you the option of dealing with hot weather, like a medieval person, by stripping off your kirtle. In addition, it enhances the general historical experience to be dressed medievally to the skin.

The design here, for both men and women, is a modified version of the thirteenth-century St. Louis shirt. The normal fabric would be white linen. To assemble the shirt, draft and cut your pieces as shown. Stitch the sleeves to the body, stitch up the side seam and sleeve seam, stitch in the gores in the front and back, hem the cuffs and bottom edge, and either hem back the neck opening or finish it with seam binding, braided lacing, or some similar material.

Cutting:
Width of Body = 1/2 chest measurement + 2" or more.
Length of Body = 2 x distance from shoulder to hem. Men's shirts ranged from crotch-length to mid-thigh. Women's were calf-length or longer.
Gusset Width = about 4/10 height. The gussets can be omitted on a man's shirt. Gussets run from the bottom of the sleeve to the hem.
Sleeve Length = distance from shoulder to first knuckle with elbow bent.
Sleeve Width at Cuff = circumference of fist + 1".
Sleeve Width at Shoulder = 1 2/3 width at cuff.

Sewing:
Stitch sleeve to body. Sew bias edge of gusset to body section so that selvage or warp edge will form a side seam (this is important for the garment to drape properly). Stitch up the sleeve and side seam. If making a man's shirt without gussets, leave the side seam open from hips down. Hem cuffs and bottom edge and finish neck with hem, seam binding, or similar material.

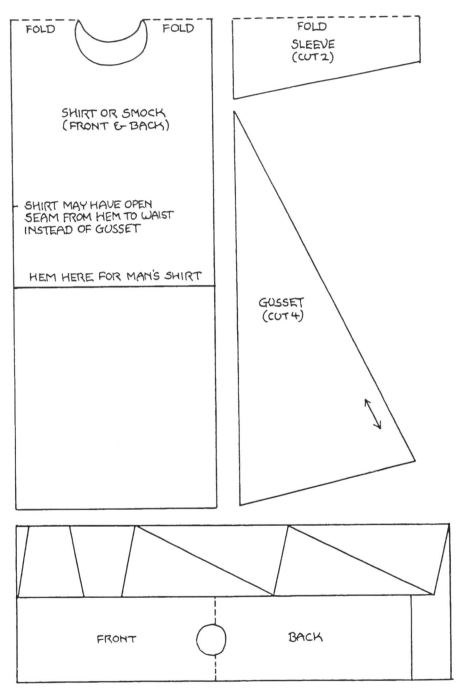

Pattern for a shirt [McLean, based on a design by Daniel Jennings].

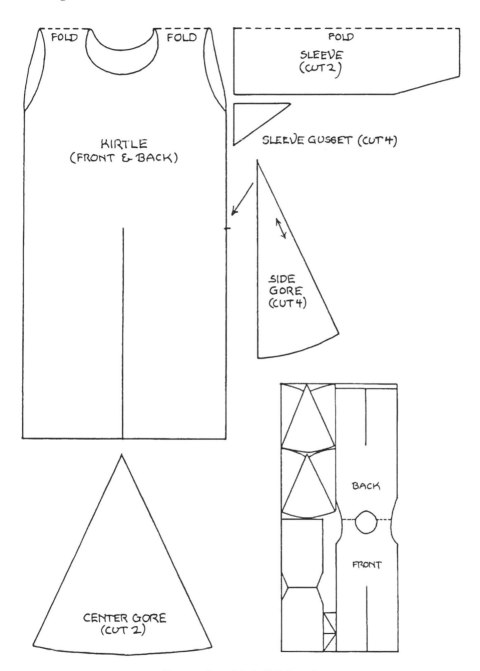

Pattern for a kirtle [McLean].

Kirtle

The simplest kind of male or female overgarment to reproduce is the Boksten-style kirtle. The ideal fabric is wool.

Cutting:
Width of Body = 1/2 chest measurement + 2" or more.
Length of Body = 2 x distance from shoulder to hem. Hems ranged from slightly above the knee to just above the ankle for men, ankle to floor-length for women. The pattern is drafted for a kirtle slightly below the knee.
Slits run from hem to 3" below the sternum.
Center gores are as long as slits and 1/2 to 2/3 as wide as their height.
    Side gores (cut 4) are half as wide as center gores.
Sleeve Length = distance from shoulder to first knuckle with elbow bent.
Sleeve Width at Cuff = circumference of fist + 2".
Sleeve Width at Shoulder = $1\,^1/_3$ x width at cuff.
Sleeve gussets are right triangles measuring about 3" on each leg.

Sewing:
Stitch the sleeve gussets to the sleeves. Stitch the center gores into the slits. Stitch the sleeves to the body. Sew the bias edge of the side gores to the edges of the body section, so that the selvage or warp edge will form the center side seam (as with the shirt, this is important if you want the garment to drape properly). Stitch up the sleeve and side seams. Hem the cuffs and bottom edge and finish the neck as with the shirt.

Men's Headgear

The hood is the distinctive masculine style of headgear, and it is easy to reproduce. The design is based on hood no. 70 from Herjolfsnes. In scaling the pattern to fit, the most critical dimension is the circumference of the neck (at **A-B**), which must be just great enough to go over your head. Scale this pattern up so that **A-B** = 1/2" + 1/2 the circumference of your head (adding your preferred seam allowance).

Wool is the best material for the hood. Cut two of the head piece and the tail, and one gusset. You can eliminate the gusset by extending the shoulder cape as shown, but the gusset saves fabric and lets you put the face opening along the selvage for a simpler, more durable finish.

Placing right side to right side, sew the tail pieces to the head pieces. Sew the gusset to the front of one of the head pieces. Press the seams. Put the two halves together right side to right side and sew them together from the front of the head to the back of the cape. Sew the front seam, working from the face down. Turn right side out. A dowel is useful for pushing the tippet through.

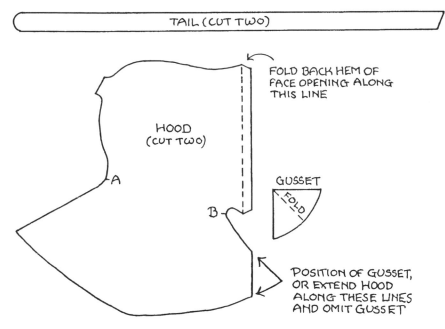

Pattern for a hood [McLean].

You can either finish the seams and hem the cape and face opening, or add a lining. A lining is durable, fashionable, and in many ways no more difficult than hemming and finishing seams, but it is not essential.

Pattern for a coif [McLean].

A man might also wear a coif for additional warmth or protection. Cut two pieces of linen as shown, stitch up the top and back, and add ties at the bottom front. The coif could also be made of leather.

Women's Headgear

The distinctive female headgear of the period is the veil and wimple, and it has the added advantage of being an easy way to cover up a modern hairstyle. The band should be a tightly woven linen that will not stretch, or else a woven band of trim, long enough to reach all the way around your head from the top, under the chin. For the veil, cut a rectangle of very light linen or silk: the long dimension should reach from your forehead across the top of your head to the base of your shoulder blades, the short dimension from shoulder to shoulder across the head (it can be even larger if you like). For the wimple, cut a rectangle of the same fabric and about half the size. Both the veil and wimple will need to be hemmed. Wrap the band under your chin and over the top of your head, pinning it tight. Pin point **a** on the wimple to the band just above your left ear, and pin point **b** just above your right ear. Place the veil on top of your head, and pin it to the band at the sides of your head. Add any additional pins to achieve a drape which pleases you (have a look at the illustrations in this chapter to get an idea of what it might look like).

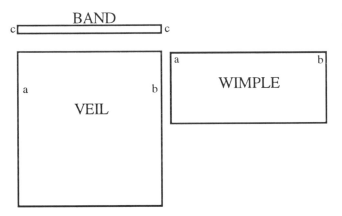

Pattern for a wimple [Singman, based on a design by Karen Walter].

Shoes

An easy ersatz medieval shoe can be had in the form of Tai-Chi slippers, especially the sort with a buckle. However, it is not particularly difficult to make a fourteenth-century turnshoe. The easiest way is to make a paper pattern, cut according to one of the patterns illustrated earlier in this chapter, but fitted to a cobbler's last in your size (if you cannot obtain a last, you can fit the pattern directly to your foot, although the fit will not be as good). Sew up the shoes inside out using an awl or a glover's needle and heavy waxed thread, first assembling the uppers, then attaching the soles. Be sure to leave the tip of the toe loose (the toe will otherwise be very difficult to turn), with long thread ends left on what will become the outside of the toe. Using these threads, turn the shoe inside out, then tighten the toe threads and sew up the toe from the outside. You may wish to glue or sew on an extra sole of thicker leather for heavier use.

Buttons, Holes, Garters

To make a cloth button, cut a 1 ¹/₂" diameter circle, then sew a gathering stitch around it. Gather the stitch to make a kind of purse; flatten the purse into a bulging disk, with the opening in the center of the top; then sew opposite points on the edge of the disk to each other to make the button. An easier, if less authentic, way to reproduce a cloth-covered button is with a kit, which is available at most fabric stores.

To make eyelets, thrust a pointed object through the weave of the fabric, spreading the weave (this will rip fibers, but don't worry about it), or use an eyelet-punch. The eyelet is then stitched in a simple buttonhole stitch, drawing the overcasts tightly to open the hole, with the stitching cast in two layers before moving on to the next eyelet. Medieval buttonholes were constructed similarly to eyelets, the difference being that the buttonhole was first cut into the fabric and was not enlarged appreciably by the subsequent stitching.

To attach buttons, fold the edge of the garment under and secure the buttons by stitching with stout thread through the folded fabric. The loose edge of the fabric can be secured with top stitching.

Garters can be easily made of a strip of fairly elastic fabric about 1" to 2" wide and long enough to tie in a bow just below the knee.

Belt, Purse, and Pouch

For a belt, the ideal would be a leather belt 1" to 2" broad, with a circular buckle and a tongue.

The easiest means of making a pouch is with a piece of leather or cloth roughly 6" x 12". Fold it in half the short way, sew up the two sides, turn it inside out. If using cloth, fold the top edge in and sew it down to make a drawstring channel; open holes into the channel on each side, and thread a drawstring through. If using leather, simply punch holes in it for the drawstring. If the purse is made of fabric, it will be necessary to let in eyelets to avoid fraying.

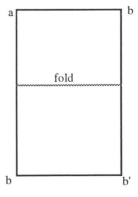

<u>To make a belt purse</u>:

Let **D** = 2 x belt width + 2 x belt thickness + at least $^1/_2$". Size may vary, but 4" high x 7" wide for the main pouch is a good size for carrying essentials, and within the medieval range. Many were smaller.

Fold outside to outside along bottom fold. Stitch vertical seams **B1** to **B2** and **C1** to **C2**, starting at bottom. Turn. Stitch along **A1** through **A3** and **A2** (three layers). Strap may be sewn into **A** seam at center.

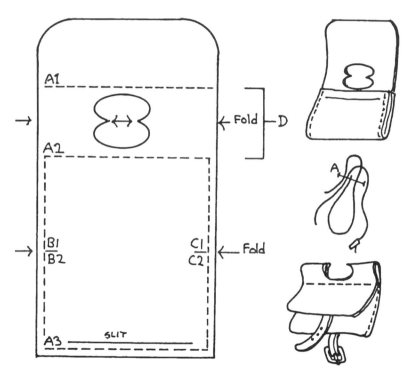

Pattern for a belt purse [McLean, after a design by Robert Charrette].

MAKING A MEDIEVAL LACE

A medieval outfit often involved heavy use of lacing (comparable to modern shoelaces) for such purposes as fastening shoes, holding up hose, or adorning the edges of a kirtle. By a remarkable stroke of luck, a manuscript of the early fifteenth century actually preserves a collection of very clear instructions for making this kind of lace. As these laces are useful in reproducing clothes and are also a fun and easy medieval craft, we have included a sample here. The text in italics is the original, with the language somewhat modernized.[12]

In the manner of making laces, you shall understand that the first finger next the thumb shall be called A, the second finger B, the third C, the fourth D. Also, sometimes you shall take your bows reversed and sometimes unreversed. When you take your bow reversed, you shall take with the one hand the bow of the other hand from without, so that the side that was beneath on the one hand before is above on the other hand. To take unreversed, take with one hand the bow of the other hand from within so that the side that was above on the one hand is above on the other hand. . . . And sometimes you shall raise your bows, and sometimes you shall lower them. To raise them, take bow B and set it on A, and set bow C on B, and set bow D on C. And to lower them, take bow C and set it on D, set bow B on C, and set bow A on B.

To Make a Broad Lace of Five Bows:

Set 2 bows on B and C right, and 3 bows on A, B, and C left. Then shall A right take through bow B of the same hand bow C of the left hand reversed. Then lower the left bows. Then shall A left take through B of the same hand bow C of the right hand reversed. Then lower the right bows, and begin again.

To Make a Round Lace of Five Bows:

Put five bows on your fingers as you did in the broad lace. Then shall A right take through B and C of the same hand bow C of the left hand reversed. Then lower the left bows. Then shall A left take through B and C of the same hand bow C of the right hand reversed. Then lower the right bows, and begin again.

To Make a Baston Lace:

Take five departed bows, that is to say that one side of each bow be of one color and the other side of another color. Set them on your hand as you did with the round lace, so that the color that is above on the right hand is beneath on the left hand, and the work in the manner of the round lace.

To set up, take five pieces of thread, each at least 2' long—embroidery floss works well. Tie each one into a loop. Next you will need a thin but solid handle to attach them to—a drawer handle or something comparable, provided it is not very thick and can be kept motionless. Take one of the loops, pass it around the handle, and then pass one end of the loop through the other. Tighten it around the handle such that the knot is at the handle. Do the same with the other five loops.

Setting up a loop [McLean].

Hold your hands as illustrated in Step 1 of the diagram. To make the broad lace, place one loop on the index finger of the left hand, one on the middle finger, and one on the ring finger; and place one loop on the middle finger of the right hand and one on the ring finger. Pass the index finger of the right hand through the middle loop on the right hand and hook the loop on the ring finger of the left hand, with the index finger pointing in the same direction as the ring finger it takes the loop from (this position is called "reversed") [Step 2 in the diagram]. Take this loop off the ring finger and bring the index finger back to its original position (this will bring the loop through the middle loop of the left hand) [shown on the right hand in Step 3 in the diagram]. Pull the loops to make the lace tight, but not too hard.

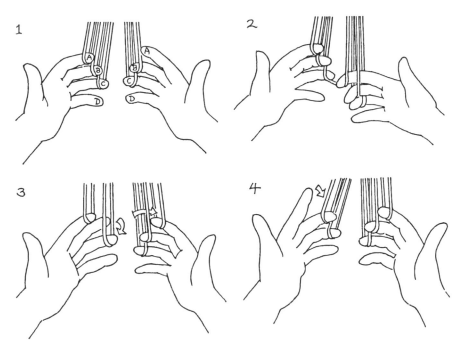

Weaving the lace [McLean].

Now shift all the loops on the left hand down one, the loop on the middle finger going to the ring finger, and the loop on the index finger going to the middle finger [shown on the left hand in Steps 3-4 in the diagram]. Do with your left index finger what you just did with the right, in mirror image, and shift the loops on the right hand as you did on the left. Then start over again. When the loops are too short to go any further, knot the free end to keep it from unraveling, then cut if off the handle and knot that end.

To make the round lace, the index finger passes forward through the first two loops on the same side before hooking the loop from the opposite ring finger; otherwise everything else is the same. The baston lace is the same as the round lace, except that the loops that start on one hand are of one color and the loops on the other hand are of another color.

7

Arms and Armor

THE FOURTEENTH-CENTURY ARMY

England in the fourteenth century was enjoying a period of relative peace. The civil wars of the thirteenth century were far in the past, and the Wars of the Roses of the fifteenth century had only a brief prelude in Henry Bolingbroke's seizure of the throne in 1399. Aside from occasional Scottish incursions in the north and French raids on coastal towns in the south, very few military actions were fought on English soil. Yet warfare was never very far from daily life in the Middle Ages. Many people had either served in person friends or relatives who had served in the wars against Scotland or France. Even men who had stayed home might be liable for service in the militia and were by law supposed to practice the longbow regularly to ensure the king had a ready supply of skilled archers. At a fundamental level, military structures pervaded medieval society—the entire feudal system was theoretically a form of military organization.

The fourteenth-century army consisted of various types of soldiers, with sharp distinctions of class and income among them. At the top of the military hierarchy was the "man-at-arms," a horseman armored from head to toe, who formed the backbone of the English army in the period. The man-at-arms was by definition a man of means. He was expected to provide his own equipment, and this equipment was expensive. A full "harness," or set of armor, cost upwards of £2, as much money as a laborer made in a year. An ordinary warhorse cost £5, and a good one could cost ten times as much. The man-at-arms' pay was correspondingly high—at a shilling a day, his service cost four times as much as that of a common footsoldier.

Men-at-arms in combat on foot, c. 1400, armed with the usual high proportion of axes, spears, and war-hammer [McLean].

The English man-at-arms rode a horse to battle, but he usually fought on foot. Early in the century the English had discovered that they could win battles by dismounting their knights. All other things being equal, in a face-to-face contest properly trained and equipped men on foot have the advantage against an equal number of comparably equipped horsemen. The reason lies in geometry and the psychology of horses. Men on foot can hold a denser formation, outnumbering mounted opponents at the point of impact; and they are, once properly trained, much less likely than horses to whicker nervously and edge away once the yelling and shouting starts. The man-at-arms was by definition a well-equipped, trained warrior, so the only real disadvantage of having such troops fight on foot was the reduced battlefield mobility.

A substantial social gulf separated the man-at-arms from all other sorts of soldiers, who were invariably commoners. The highest paid were mounted archers, at 6 to 8 pence a day; ordinary archers received 3 to 6 pence. Archers were a major component of the English army and could be used very effectively in conjunction with the men-at-arms, weakening the enemy sufficiently for the men-at-arms to break them. Other footmen were armed with weapons for hand-to-hand combat: spears, axes, and other pole-arms. Common soldiers were generally more lightly armored than men-at-arms and therefore relatively vulnerable at close quarters against fully armored opponents, although the man-at-arms was still vulnerable to archers at a distance.

At the base of the military hierarchy were irregular troops called brigands, ribalds, pilars, or coutiliers. Often their only weapon was a long knife. They stayed out of the front lines but generally made themselves useful by foraging, skirmishing, pillaging, and finishing off the wounded. There were also a host of servants whose duties included camp chores and holding the horses of the dismounted men-at-arms. Such servants sometimes made a useful contribution to the fighting—as at Otterburn in 1388, where they defended the Scottish camp as their masters armed themselves. However, they were equally likely to panic and run off with the horses.

In battle, troops of the same type usually fought together; but for purposes of recruitment, muster, and pay they were organized as retinues comprising all these sorts of troops (sometimes containing only a few men), each troop under the command of the man-at-arms that raised them.

ARMOR

The power of the man-at-arms was a direct result of his armor. Surprisingly little medieval armor has actually survived, and hardly any from before 1400. The fighting equipment of the medieval man-at-arms tended to get broken, rusted, or recycled. Almost all the armor seen in museums, which forms the popular image of the medieval knight, is ceremonial or tournament armor from the sixteenth century. It has survived precisely because it was made when armor was losing its importance on the battlefield, so it was less likely to be destroyed in use.

The latter part of the fourteenth century was a time of rapid evolution in armor; it might even be considered the first and last period of major revolution in armor technology. Before 1300, knights were still armored very much like the men who fought for William the Conqueror in 1066, protected primarily by an iron helmet and clad in mail, a fine mesh of small linked iron rings. This was increasingly supplemented by solid plates of iron, steel, or "cuirbouilli" (hardened leather) to offer better protection at critical points such as the joints or vital organs.

Brass effigy of a knight in armor, c. 1380 [Hewitt].

During the course of the fourteenth century, solid steel became the principal component of the best armor. It remained so until armor finally fell out of use in the seventeenth century.[1]

The Suit of Armor   Modern people, who are likely to see armor only from the outside, tend to forget that it was in many ways just an elaborate form of clothing. Like clothing, it was worn in layers, each of which had to be put on and fastened in succession. The following pages offer an idea of what it was like to wear a knight's full set of armor, with some additional information on the sorts of protection that ordinary soldiers might have worn.

The knight preparing for battle wore ordinary civilian clothes as his innermost layer: breech, hose, and shoes. He might also wear a shirt, although a fifteenth-century set of instructions for arming, *How a Man Shall Be Armed*, recommends omitting the shirt. He might also wear a padded coif on his head—this had been common in the thirteenth century, but as the fourteenth century progressed such coifs were less used by aristocratic warriors although they were still worn by more ordinary soldiers.

Man in an arming doublet, a reconstruction based on the Charles de Blois coathardie. To illustrate its use, he is shown with some leg and arm harness attached [Vernier].

Next came the innermost protective garment for the body, variously called a doublet, aketon, gambeson, jupon, or pourpoint (the terms were not fixed; in fact, any of them might also be used to designate a similar garment worn *outside* the armor). The military doublet was essentially a sturdier version of the civilian doublet or coathardie of the period; it was made of a heavy linen or cotton fabric, often fustian, a blend of the two. The doublet helped absorb sweat, and it was padded to provide extra comfort and protection from chafing and impact. It was fitted with lacing holes at the legs and arms for attaching armor. Military doublets commonly laced up the front, giving a tightly trussed fit over the abdomen that helped distribute the weight of the leg harness.

Next the armor itself was strapped and tied on, working from the ground up, an order dictated by the way in which **Leg Harness** the various components overlapped. First came foot pieces called sabatons. These were essentially armor overshoes made of a series of articulating plates, typically pointed at the toe, with another piece wrapping around the heel; they laced to the shoe itself. Less expensive versions were made from hardened leather. Sometimes, however, the man-at-arms wore no additional foot protection beyond his shoes, skimping on protection for a little less encumbrance.

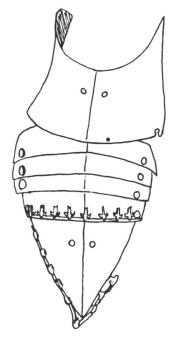

Remains of a sabaton [Vernier].

Next came the shin-guards called greaves. These flared over the foot and at the ankles for ease of motion, arching over the foot to reach close to the ground on each side. The greaves strapped directly to the shins and laced to the sabatons.

Next came the cuisses, which protected the thighs. These might be made of iron plate, but earlier in the period they were more likely to be of leather or fabric with steel splints riveted lengthwise inside. Below the cuisses were knee pieces called poleines, which were half round or slightly pointed in profile, usually with a spade- or kidney-shaped wing on the outside to protect the back of the joint. Below this was suspended a demi-greave, a small piece that protected the upper part of the shin.

The cuisse, poleine, and demi-greave were often a single piece, attaching like contemporary hose by laces to the bottom of the pourpoint. A leather tab with holes was riveted to the top edge of the cuisse for this purpose. An additional strap or two held the cuisse to the thigh; another secured the poleine, and another the demi-greave. The cuisse, poleine, and demi-greave would connect to each other via intermediary lames (comparable to the segments of a lobster's tail), allowing more flexibility than if they were joined directly to each other. The entire leg assembly could flex to a little less than a right angle—enough to kneel in, but not enough to allow a squatting position. Alternatively, the leg might be protected with chausses, entire leg-coverings of mail similar to civilian hose. These were especially common earlier in the century.

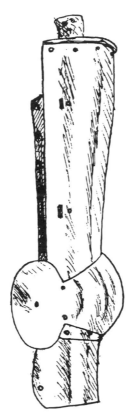

Leg harness consisting of cuisse, poleine, and demi-greave [Vernier].

Torso Armor Next in the process of arming came the main body protection. On top of the doublet was commonly worn a mail shirt called a habergeon or hauberk. The shirt was waisted, and surviving examples show sophisticated tailoring. The tailoring not only addressed the concerns of the fashion-conscious warrior but also made the garment more practical, since the close-waisted design helped distribute some of the shirt's weight to the hips and fit better under the body-armor. The sleeves might be full-length, tailored to a narrow cuff, or—more commonly—half-sleeves ending just above the elbow, this being the practical style to fit over other arm harness. The sleeve and skirt edges were often made with brass links to give the effect of a golden border, and they might be dagged for additional style.

In previous centuries the mail shirt had been considered adequate body protection, but by the fourteenth century it was supplemented with solid iron plates. The move towards plate body armor began with the "coat-of-plates," which fourteenth-century Englishmen probably called a "jack," "plates," or "a pair of plates." There were many variations on the coat of plates, but most were constructed of rectangular iron plates riveted inside a cloth or leather "coat." The coat itself was either sleeveless (opening at the front, back, or sides) or sleeved like a poncho. The plates overlapped, and each plate had rivets only along one edge so that it could work flexibly over the plates below it. Originally simple and tubular in outline, shortly after the middle of the century the coat-of-plates developed a tailored, narrow waist that mirrored civilian fashions.

Knights wearing coats-of-plates. Flemish, 1338-1344 (RA) [Vernier].

Over time, the coat-of-plates evolved in two different directions. On some armors the plates became smaller and more numerous, allowing greater flexibility but sacrificing a degree of protection. References to "brigandine" appear as early as 1368, and it is likely that then, as later, the term referred to this sort of armor. The name came from its popularity among mercenary footsoldiers known as "brigands," although even knights wore this type of protection.

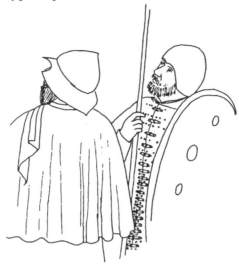

Two footsoldiers. The one on the right apparently wears a brigandine and a "pallet" style helmet; the one on the left wears a kettle-type helmet [Vernier].

Other coats-of-plates developed in the opposite direction. All other things being equal, a large plate spreads the force of a blow better than several small ones and is less likely to catch the point of a weapon. By the middle of the century some coats-of-plates included a large oval plate directly over the chest. By the 1370s this plate commonly cover the entire front of the ribcage.

A breastplate, with v-shaped stop-rib just below the neckline to deflect lance points [Vernier].

The breastplate could be either an integral part of the coat-of-plates or a separate reinforcement. Once it became large enough to protect the entire ribcage it was often worn as a separate defense in its own right, over the habergeon, supported by crossed straps in back. By the 1370s the separate steel breastplate, or "breast," was increasingly common. The breastplate might have v-shaped stop-ribs to deflect lance points from the neck, or a medial ridge to add strength and help deflect blows. Many were fitted with a hook near the right armpit to help support a lance.

The breastplate itself only covered the front of the ribs. Some men-at-arms considered this sufficient supplement to the mail shirt, but by the 1370s it was often worn with tonlets, a short apron of overlapping plates or horizontal hoops that protected the abdomen. Around this time additional plates began to carry the breastplate's protection partway around the back. Evidence for complete backplates appears around 1400.

By this time much of the habergeon's protection was duplicated by plate armor worn over it. From the middle of the century it began to be replaced by separate mail defenses that protected those areas not covered by plate: breeches of mail or a skirt (called a pauncer) to protect the belly and groin, and collars of mail called pisans or standards. With pisan, pauncer, and plate armor, the only place where a habergeon offered additional coverage was at the armpit and inside of the elbow; and by no later than 1420 gussets of mail were sewn to the doublet at these points to make the habergeon unnecessary.

A figure in fully evolved breastplate with a
lance-rest and tonlets, 1403 [Vernier].

The shoulder was the most difficult joint to protect. It is a ball-and-socket joint with greater range of motion than any other major joint, and its mobility was crucial in combat. Plate shoulder armor was by no means universal even by the end of the century. The earliest and virtually the only surviving specimens from the fourteenth century are from graves from the Battle of Wisby (1361). They are simple spade-shaped or oval plates lightly hollowed, hinged to the shoulders of the coat-of-plates. A more developed sort of protection appeared in the 1340s: the "spaulder" or "pauldron," consisting of a shoulder cap with several narrow overlapping lames descending below it over the edge of the shoulder, attached to leather strips underneath for flexibility. The pauldron either connected directly to the rerebrace or, later in the century, was strapped down over it.

A French coat-armor of c. 1380 [Vernier].

In many cases the torso armor was covered by a decorative cloth over-garment, often padded for extra protection. During the reign of Edward III the characteristic garment of this type was a tight-fitting surcoat, but by the end of the century there was a trend towards the loose and unbelted tabard and the "coat-armor," which was typically quilted and had voluminous sleeves covering the arm armor. In some instances the coat-armor was worn under the breastplate. Common soldiers may have relied on a long and loose quilted coat as the sole body protection.

The next step was to put on the arm harness. At the top was
Arm Harness the rerebrace, which covered the upper arm. Like the
cuisses, it often had a leather strip riveted to the top edge, with holes through which laces secured it to the doublet. The rerebrace did not always extend all the way around: some examples covered only the back of the arm. Full rerebraces enclosed the entire upper arm, with a hinge to allow them to be opened and straps and buckles to fasten them shut.

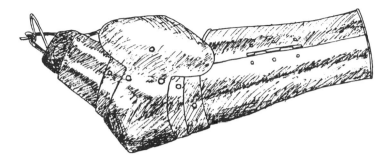

Arm harness consisting of couter and vambrace [Vernier].

Below the rerebrace was the elbow piece called a couter. The couter was small and conical, often shaped to a point, with a wing on the outer side as on the poleine, and with buckled straps to secure the arm harness snugly to the arm. At the bottom of the arm was the vambrace, which protected the forearm and was hinged and buckled like a rerebrace.

The best rerebraces and vambraces were made of plate; but as with the leg harness, splint was a common alternative. In fact, many men-at-arms wore only mail on their arms almost to the end of the century. The rerebrace, couter, and vambrace might all be attached to each other by articulated joints, with extra lames in between to allow more flexibility; or they might all be separate pieces, lacing to each other or to the doublet.

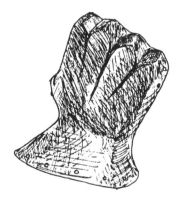

An Italian gauntlet of c. 1370 [Vernier].

Finally, the man-at-arms donned gauntlets and helmet. Iron gauntlets in this period had a distinctive hourglass shape, **Gauntlets** with a narrow wrist and flaring cuff to protect the wrist while allowing it to move freely. The knuckles were sometimes equipped with metal spikes known as gadlings; on the Black Prince's gauntlets the gadlings were cast in the shape of small lions. Usually the finger lames were attached to a leather strip running down the finger; the entire gauntlet assembly was stitched to a glove of leather or fabric. Less expensive gauntlets were made of leather or fabric reinforced with whalebone or iron plates.

Helmets By far the most characteristic style of helmet in the fourteenth century was the bascinet. It resembled a kind of steel hood, with a point somewhere above the crown of the head; it covered the entire head above the neck, except for the face. The bascinet evolved from a hemispherical skull cap worn in the thirteenth century and was already well developed by the 1320s. Towards the end of the century the point became more pronounced. Typically a light crest ran up the front to the point, continuing about one-third of the way down the back; as with the breastplate, this was designed to help deflect blows.

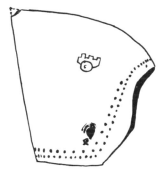

A bascinet of c. 1390-1400. The large hole at the cheek was for a handle—this helmet was discovered in use as a well-bucket in this century. Still visible are the stitching and vervelle holes around the lower edge, and the pivot and fragmentary hinge for the visor [Vernier].

For extra protection, the face opening could be fitted with a visor. The most characteristic form of visor was the so-called "hounskull," characterized by its pointed snout; others had a more rounded face. The visor most often pivoted on bolts at the temples, although some had a single hinge at the forehead. Visors were usually attached to the side pivots by a hinge-and-pin arrangement that allowed the visor to be removed.

In addition to its distinctive snout, the hounskull visor had eye slits and an angular mouth slit. In the later part of the century, the mouth was fashionably cut in vertical slits suggesting teeth. Breathing holes were usually pierced on the right side only, and additional holes were often put around the mouth opening. The vision and ventilation afforded by this style of visor left something to be desired, and many contemporary illustrations show soldiers fighting with the visor open.

A great helm placed over a bascinet, after an Italian manuscript of c. 1380 [Vernier].

To protect the neck, the bascinet was fitted with a mail skirt, or "aventail." This was stitched to a leather strap pierced with holes. The holes fitted over eyes, or "vervelles," protruding around the lower edge of the bascinet. The aventail was held in place by a heavy cord passing through the vervelles. The bascinet also had a row of closely spaced holes around the edge to which a lining was stitched. The lining was stuffed with wool or hair to provide extra protection for the head; surviving linings are cut into scallops at the top, through which a cord is drawn to adjust for size. Bascinets do not appear to have been fitted with chin straps. A common means of securing helmets was a strap hanging down the back of the helmet that buckled to the wearer's backplate or coat-armor between the shoulder blades.

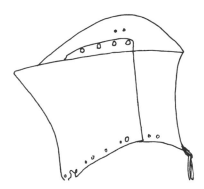

A "frog-mouth" style great helm [Vernier].

In the early part of the century the bascinet was often worn under a "great helm," a less fitted form of helmet that had evolved from the barrel-shaped helms of the thirteenth century. As the century progressed, the great helm was less used on the battlefield but gave rise to a specialized jousting helmet, the "frog-mouth" jousting helm. This specialized helm was fully developed by the end of the century.

A soldier in a "kettle" style helmet, apparently covered with straw [Vernier].

Light helmets were also common in the late fourteenth century, especially for the ordinary footsoldier. One style was the "kettle hat," so called from its vague resemblance to a medieval pot turned upside-down. In the fourteenth century it was typically pointed like the bascinet, with a brim generally not too broad and often pointed at the front. The brim helped to deflect descending arrows and weapon blows without impairing visibility or ventilation. This highly practical helmet was worn by knights and even by kings, although it was particularly popular among footsoldiers. Such helmets might be equipped with chin straps.

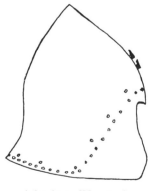

A barbuta [Vernier].

The "barbuta" was also common during this period, particularly in Italy. It was pointed like the bascinet, though the point was more or less centered on the top of the head. This style was distinguished by its narrow face opening and long sides, which were deep enough to protect the neck without an aventail.

The simplest helmets were rounded, covered little more than the top of the skull, and were apparently known as pallets. Light helmets were often worn over a mail hood.

A man-at-arms in bascinet, coat-armor, and breastplate, displaying a "heater" style shield and wearing a fashionable plaque belt (Swiss, c. 1386) [Vernier].

Most surviving armor of the fourteenth century is fairly plain and utilitarian, but armor was a status symbol as well as **Decoration** a tool and was often embellished for display and delight. Brass borders, sometimes engraved, were one of the more common sorts of adornment. The surface of the armor might be finished in one of several ways. Often it was covered with cloth—almost every part of the armor might be treated in this way except the knees, elbows, and visor. Alternatively, the plates might be painted. Towards the end of the century it was becoming fashionable to leave the armor uncovered and highly polished, a style known as "white" armor that was to dominate the fifteenth century.

Surcoats, tabards, and coat-armors were decorative as well as practical. Indeed, exaggerated sleeves and dagging sometimes diminished the garment's practicality. Sir John Chandos, one of the great captains of the Hundred Years War, came to an untimely end when he tripped over his long surcoat and pitched forward onto a French spear. Such garments might be decorated with a single large representation of the wearer's coat-of-arms, or a small badge or device might be repeated over the entire garment. On top of the armor or surcoat the aristocratic warrior often wore the distinctive plaque belt that was fashionable in civilian use.

A soldier on horseback, with helmet strap showing [Vernier].

Encumbrance and Maintenance Armor was somewhat less encumbering than is commonly supposed. Surviving fighting harnesses from before the seventeenth century weighed between 45 and 70 lbs. for a complete suit of armor, and the weight was well distributed. Modern stories about unsaddled knights being unable to lift themselves from the ground are not to be trusted (although on a wet battlefield, with the ground churned into a sea of mud by the horses' hooves and strewn with bodies and debris, this could become a problem). In fact, an ordinary man in full armor can lie down, get up, and do squat thrusts if he wants to. Medieval knights in good physical condition would show off by vaulting into the saddle without using the stirrups or by scaling ladders with only their hands, all while dressed in full armor.

This is not to say that wearing full armor is like wearing ordinary clothes. Armor is hot and stuffy, particularly with the visor down; heat stroke was a real danger for the medieval knight. It is particularly fatiguing to march in full armor. This is not simply a matter of weight. Many modern infantrymen march with heavier weights on their backs, but leg harness is not like a weight you simply carry on your back, since it also slows your leg each time you take a step. Marching footsoldiers in the Middle Ages almost never wore leg armor. The armored man-at-arms depended on his horse to get him to the battlefield in fighting condition.

Armor demanded a good deal of maintenance. The metal component was principally carbon steel—essentially iron treated with carbon to make it harder than pure iron. Unlike modern stainless steel, carbon steel is very susceptible to rust; since armor was often exposed to sweat, rain, and mud, it had to be cleaned and polished frequently. This was especially difficult with mail—mail components were typically placed in a special rotating barrel with sand and vinegar to scour them free of rust.

The typical fourteenth-century shield was made of wood; this was covered with canvas, leather, or both, and then covered with **Shields** a gypsum-based sealant called gesso and painted. A gentleman's shield usually bore his personal emblem or "arms." The man-at-arms used a fairly small shield, about 2' long, often curved and shaped like the bottom of an iron (whence its modern name, a "heater"). It was equipped with a complicated arrangement of straps so he could keep it in position and still use his hands to control the reins of his horse. When he dismounted, his armor gave him enough protection that he could put the shield aside to use a weapon with both hands.

Ordinary infantry shields were larger. They were either circular, oval, or rectangular, and equipped with a simple pair of straps, or strap and handle, for the arm. Small round shields called "bucklers" had a single handle in the center behind a protruding iron boss or spike. Because the buckler could be carried conveniently when not in use, it was particularly popular with archers and travelers. It was also used in the medieval precursor to fencing. One surviving example has a hook in the front and could be hung from a belt, ready for a "quick draw."

WEAPONS

During the fourteenth century, weapons evolved to meet the advances in armor. As plate armor improved, the thrust became more important. It could find the weak points in a harness; moreover, a thrust driven by the force of both arms, when concentrated on the tiny area struck by an acute weapon point, could pierce the heaviest plate. For this reason the spear was highly popular and effective throughout the period, wielded either from horseback or on foot. The basic spear was an ash shaft 9' to 12' long topped by a steel head.

Foot combat, c. 1400. Pole weapons include spears, axes, and war-hammers [McLean].

Sword design also changed to emphasize the thrust. The older, parallel-sided, blunt-pointed blades, substantially unchanged since Viking times, began to be replaced by stiffer, more pointed blades. The new type of sword generally had a diamond cross-section, sometimes with a pronounced ridge near the hilt for stiffness. The edges were straight and converged at the tip, making a point narrow enough to punch through mail. The typical sword of this period had a blade about 30" to 35" long and 2" broad at the hilt, weighing 2 to 3 lbs. Some swords, called "estocs," were designed purely for thrusting; these had square, diamond, or triangular cross-sections, an almost straight taper from hilt to point, and no edge to speak of. The blunt edge let the user grasp the blade with one hand for greater control and power, using the weapon like a short spear.

Sword pommels, designed both to make the grip more secure and to help balance the weight of the blade, were also an opportunity for decoration. Some were of round or oval shape; but the "fig" shape, sometimes faceted, became increasingly common, being easier to grip with a second hand. The quillons, which protected the hand, were of square or octagonal section. They were typically either straight or turned slightly away from the hand towards the tips, the better to catch an opponent's weapon. The grip was of wood wrapped with cord or fine wire; sometimes the cord was covered with a layer of thin leather or parchment. The grip of a single-handed sword was short enough that the pommel rested snugly against the hand, affording better control.

Scabbards were made of wood covered with leather, as thin and light as possible, following the contours of the sword. Eelskin was a popular leather for covering scabbards, being available in convenient dimensions. Scabbards had metal mounts, often cast: these were generally a "chape," which protected the tip of the scabbard, a "throat" at the opening of the scabbard, and sometimes an intermediate mount in between. The throat might have rings on either side for attaching belt straps, and the intermediate mount might have a single ring for a strap to hold the scabbard angled back. Other scabbards attached only at the throat, perhaps with a lace, short strap and buckle, or ring and hook to fasten them to the belt or directly to the body armor.

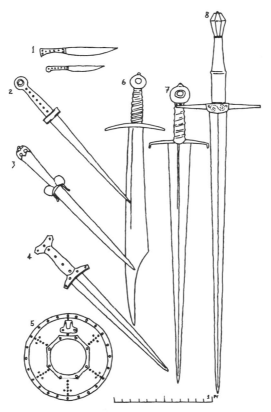

1. Common knives. 2. Rondel dagger. 3. Ballock knife. 4. Baselard. 5. Buckler. 6. Falchion. 7. Single-handed thrusting sword. 8. "Bastard" or "hand-and-a-half" sword [Vernier].

Other weapons relied on sheer force to smash through plate armor. The deadliest of these was the poll-axe (sometimes called a "pole-axe" today). With a heavy head on the end of a shaft 5' or longer, it possessed tremendous leverage. The head was often backed by a spike, fluke, or hammer head and topped by a spike as well. The bottom of the shaft was also used for thrusting; it was strengthened with a ring or spike. This type of axe was closely related to the pole-hammer, which bore a hammer head backed by a spike or fluke. Great heavy-headed mallets at the end of long shafts could also deal terrible blows. Single-handed weapons in this class included the mace, a single-handed club with a flanged steel head, and shorter versions of the poll-axe and hammer.

Some swords were similarly developed to deal the heavier blows needed to defeat plate armor. Hand-and-a-half grips became common; these allowed the owner to wield the sword with both hands if necessary. Some had blades over 40" long. This type of grip eventually led to the full two-handed sword of the fifteenth century. Another type was the falchion, which had a grip like a normal single-handed sword and a short, heavy, single-edged blade like a machete. Earlier examples, dating up to the first quarter of the fourteenth century, have a broad, single-curved tip, but later examples have a point like an exaggerated Bowie knife, designed for thrusting.

As a rule, swords and other large weapons were not a part of civilian wear; they were generally worn only by soldiers and by travelers on robber-infested roads. Hand-and-a-half swords were often mounted directly to a saddle, being cumbersome to carry on foot (there is no evidence that they were ever worn over the shoulder).

Daggers were ubiquitous during this period. They were worn by men of all classes, either with civilian clothes as the only weapon, or with armor, opposite the sword. The most common form was the "baselard"; this had a wooden handle, quillon, and pommel forming an H-shape. The blade was usually double-edged, of diamond section, and varied in length from a few inches to 2'.

Ballock daggers also were popular in the later fourteenth century. These were distinguished by their kidney-shaped lobes in the place of the quillon. The lobes gave the dagger a phallic appearance, a characteristic deliberately emphasized by the fashion for wearing this style of dagger at the front of the belt. Some ballock daggers had conical-shaped handles that widened towards the pommel. The blades were usually of heavy triangular section, intended to be inflexible for thrusting. Rondel daggers, with a round hand-guard in the place of the quillon, were also popular; these too had heavy thrusting blades. The rondel guard in the fourteenth century was usually small; often the pommel was a second rondel. Sometimes there was a ring at the end for attaching a chain (both swords and daggers sometimes had chains to attach them to the armor, lest they be lost in the heat of battle).

Daggers were weapons, not tools. Smaller, thinner knives were used for everyday cutting and for eating; their forms and dimensions were similar to modern steak knives. Several knives might be mounted in a single scabbard made with several pockets: there was usually a large knife with a smaller knife or two and a skewer for making holes—the equivalent of the modern Swiss Army Knife.

Men-at-arms disembarking. Detail after the tapestry of Jourdain de Blaye, Museo Civico, Padua, c. 1385. [Vernier].

One of the most significant weapons on the fourteenth-century battlefield was the English longbow, which consisted of a 6' bowstaff made of elm, ash, or (ideally) yew, with a bowstring of wax-coated linen. The arrows were a yard long. For war they were equipped with a small pointed tip that could penetrate mail or even—at close range with a solid, well-placed hit—plate armor. An experienced archer might wield a bow of

80 lbs. draw or more, even as much as 150 lbs.; the maximum range of the weapon was around 400 yards. Such bows were used almost exclusively by the English: they required enormous strength in certain muscles, so they were only effective in the hands of an archer who had practiced intensely for a long time.

Other armies relied on the crossbow instead. Early in the century it typically had a bowstaff made of wood reinforced with horn and sinew, but by mid-century it was largely replaced by a more powerful steel staff. The crossbow had a far lower rate of fire than the longbow, since it was much harder to load. Lighter ones had a foot stirrup in front: the bowman attached the string to a hook on his belt, crouched down to place his foot in the stirrup, and used the strength of his legs to string the bow. Other crossbows had to be strung with a lever or a small winch. The crossbow had much more power than a longbow, but its principal advantage was that it required little training to use.

During the course of the fourteenth century a new form of missile weapon made its appearance in battle—the cannon, or "gun." Large versions were used on board ships and to assail fortifications, but there were also smaller hand-cannons resembling a small cannon barrel mounted on a staff. Such weapons were as yet not a major factor on the battlefield, but they would eventually give rise to the firearms that rendered obsolete the armored knight of the Middle Ages.

8

Food and Drink

As with other aspects of medieval life, people's social and economic status determined the food they ate. Ironically, the diet of working commoners may actually have been healthier than that of the aristocracy, at least in terms of nutritional balance. The wealthy were able to indulge a taste for fine and rich foods with higher proportions of red meat, sugar, and fat, while the common people consumed more fiber and vegetables.

Bread was a staple food for all people, but aristocratic taste favored the whitest wheat bread possible (although it was less white than modern white bread—Wonder Bread might well have been considered the ultimate treat on the table of Edward III). The aristocratic diet also included a great deal of meat, principally beef, followed by pork and mutton, with game and poultry as the smallest component. Dairy and egg products were found in the aristocratic diet, but not particularly favored. Neither were vegetables, which mostly appeared as flavorings in the form of leeks, onions, garlic, or herbs. Sweets, including conserves and sugar candy, were also a feature of the aristocratic diet. The daily ration for a person living in an aristocratic household typically included 2 to 3 lbs. of wheat bread, 2 to 3 lbs. of meat or fish, and a gallon of ale.

A prosperous peasant might consume 2 to 3 lbs. of bread, 8 oz. of meat or fish, and 2 to 3 pints of ale per day. The bread was not likely to be fine white bread. Wheat was relatively expensive, so poorer people made use of rye, oats, barley, and even beans and peas. Meat was also expensive and was not necessarily a regular part of a commoner's diet. Those who could afford it ate the same sorts of meats as the aristocracy, although perhaps somewhat less beef and somewhat more pork and mutton. In place of meat, protein was more likely to be supplied by eggs, butter, and cheese; herrings were another inexpensive source of protein. Vegetables figured more prominently than in the diet of the aristocrat. Beans and bacon were the proverbial food of the peasant.

Further down the economic scale, people were more likely to drink water than ale and to consume their grains boiled whole in pottages, puddings, or gruel rather than in the form of bread. Nonetheless, the diet of the lower classes seems to have improved during this period, as a part of the general rise in the standard of living of the poor following the Black Death. Wage earners during this period were able to negotiate improved rations for their work: one contract from 1397 stipulates a daily ration of 2 lbs. of beef or mutton, 4 pints of ale, and 2 lbs. of wheat bread.[1]

An aristocratic feast. French, 1378-80 (*Grands Chroniques de France,* Bibliothèque Nationale MS Français 2813, f. 394) [McLean].

Fourteenth-Century Cuisine There is a popular misconception that medieval food had less variety than modern food, possibly due to the number of new ingredients introduced to the cuisine after the discovery of the New World. Yet the fourteenth-century aristocracy ate a much greater range of meats than is common today. Not only did they consume domestic livestock such as cows, sheep, pigs, chicken, geese, and ducks, but they also hunted game such as deer, boars, rabbits, and wildfowl. Commoners were generally not supposed to hunt, but they often poached rabbits and wildfowl in defiance of the laws. Moreover, fourteenth-century cooks used the animals more completely than we do today (with the possible exception of the production of hot dogs).

People also ate a variety of seafood, especially herring and cod; eels, mussels, and oysters were common as well. Dairy products were consumed in various forms. Plain milk could be curdled, and the curds either eaten as is or used to make cheese. Cheese was an extremely important staple, as it preserved better than unprocessed milk. The whey, a watery liquid remaining after the curds are removed, was also used as a drink.

The range of vegetables was probably less diverse than it is today, especially because of the difficulties of preservation. Onions, leeks, cabbage, garlic, turnips, parsnips, peas, and beans were all staples. Among fruits, plums, cherries, pears, grapes, strawberries, figs, and apples all grew in England. Nuts, particularly walnuts and hazelnuts, were also to be found domestically. Other vegetable foods were imported, such as almonds and dates.

An al fresco meal with white wine, pears, and cherries. The table is mounted on three-legged trestles. Italian, c. 1395 (TS Vienna, 86) [McLean]

The actual content of any given meal was much more dependent on the season than is the case today. Fruits and vegetables came into season at specific times of year, and not all could be preserved for consumption at other times. Meats could generally be preserved, but for many people fresh meat was available for only part of the year.

Most spices used in fourteenth-century cooking are still familiar today. It is often suggested that huge amounts of spice were used either to mask spoiled meat or to ostentatiously display wealth, but recent research suggests that this was not really the case. In fact, household accounts of the period suggest that no more spices were used per person than today, and in some cases even less. Spices were much more expensive in the fourteenth century than they are today, and smaller amounts would have been required to display wealth. Moreover, evidence suggests that imported spices were saved for special occasions. For daily use, people relied on ordinary seasonings such as salt, vinegar, mustard, onions, and garlic. Other domestic herbs included parsley, scallions, cress, and chervil. Another important flavoring agent was verjuice, the juice of sour apples or grapes.

Among imported spices, the most common were pepper, ginger, cinnamon, cloves, and nutmeg; of these, pepper and ginger were the cheapest. Sugar, a fairly expensive commodity, was also used as a spice rather than as a basic ingredient as we use it today. Candies and sweet dishes did exist, but desserts as we know them were not a feature of the fourteenth-century table. Honey was available domestically but was a relative luxury. For most people, the principal source of sugars was fruit; baked apples would be as close as one would get to what we might call a dessert.

Spices were often used in ways quite different from modern western cooking: medieval flavorings had more in common with modern Near Eastern and Indian cuisine. Some spices were used primarily or entirely for their coloring effects: saunders (ground red sandalwood) and the root of the plant alkanet gave a red coloring, and turnsole (a Mediterranean plant) yielded blue, for example. Part of the appeal of saffron, which features in many recipes, is the rich golden color it imparts.[2] Nonetheless, fourteenth-century recipes suggest that the high cuisine of the period was less elaborate than it was to become in the fifteenth century.

One item invariably present at meals was bread. Loaves of bread
Bread were always placed on the table to be eaten, in addition to sliced
bread used as plates, called trenchers (described below in the section on "The Table"). The type of bread served and its freshness depended on the status of the host and guest. The finest breads were known as pain-demain, wastel, cocket, and simnel; these were made with highly refined wheat flour (although even the finest was not as white as modern white flour). Such flour was finely sifted to extract bran and husk. Less expensive wheat breads were made with flour that had been sifted less finely and consequently had a higher proportion of bran and husk. This made the flour darker and more coarse but added bulk and significant nutritional value. The bread was not baked in pans, so it was typically round in shape.

Less expensive breads were made from rye, barley, oats, or a mixture of grains. Poor people also ate oat-cakes. Biscuits, which had a low water content and therefore preserved well, were useful for long journeys and sea-voyages. In times of scarcity, people sometimes had to eat bread made with peas or beans.

The simplest meal was breakfast, which was not normally reckoned as a meal at all: it appears to have been an informal, **Meals** catch-as-catch-can affair, consisting perhaps of leftovers from the previous day or of a sop, a popular snack consisting of bread dipped in wine, ale, milk, or water. As in England today, fish were sometimes eaten at breakfast. The principal meals of the day were dinner, served around midday, and supper, which took place in the evening. Practice varied as to which was the larger meal of the two. Some people also had a mid-afternoon snack of bread and ale called a "noon-shenche", or nuncheon, ultimately the source of the modern word "luncheon" or "lunch." The truly decadent ate an extra meal late at night called a "rear-supper."

Ordinary people ate their food all at once, but those of social pretensions had it served in a number of courses. Many menus survive for a variety of the more formal sorts of meals, ranging from the dinner and supper of a townsman to the coronation feasts of a monarch. Such menus generally consisted of three to six courses, each being made up of a number of dishes. More elaborate meals might include special dishes between courses (called an "entremess" or "subtlety"), sometimes artfully designed to delight the eye as well as the palate. One moderately fancy menu suggests the following:

> At the First Course: Boar's Heads Larded, Broth of Almain as Pottage, Baked Capons and Chevettes [small pies], and therewith Pheasants and Bitterns.
> The Second Course: Swans, Curlews, Pigs, Roast Veal, and Tarts, therewith Blandesire [white pottage] and Murrey [a dish colored with mulberries].
> Third Course: Coney, Partridge, and Woodcock, Roast Plovers and Larks, and therewith Fritters, Pot-wise, Sack-wise [forcemeat molded in pots and sacks], and Urchins [sausages made to look like hedgehogs], and therewith Egredoun [a sweet-and-sour dish].[3]

The Goodman of Paris (*Le Ménagier de Paris*), a French text of the same period, offers this slightly less elaborate menu for a Parisian supper:

> Another Meat Supper
> First Platter: Capons with herbs, a cominy, "daguenet" peas, loach in yellow sauce, venison in soup.
> Second Service: The best roast you can get, meat-jelly, blancmangier "parti" [see Recipes, "Blanc Manger"], little cream tarts well sugared.
> Third Service: Capon pies, cold sage soup, stuffed shoulders of mutton, pike in broth, venison with boar's tail, crayfish.[4]

The sequence of a medieval menu contrasts markedly from a modern one. Today we proceed from salad or soup to main course and dessert. Fancy medieval meals were more likely to proceed from the heavier dishes to the more delicate ones. There was no dessert as such, and sweet dishes were mingled among the rest. The diners' status might determine how many of the courses they received. Everyone present was served the first course, but sometimes only the most privileged tables received the last one.

Fish Days   An important feature of the medieval menu related to "fish days." The church designated certain days as occasions for religious penance. On these days people were forbidden to eat meat, which in strictest usage included eggs and dairy products but did not include fish or shellfish. Sea-mammals such as porpoises were considered fish for these purposes, as were barnacle geese (the name derives from the medieval belief that these birds hatched from barnacles), but such foods were not often found on the tables of ordinary people.

Fish days occurred every Friday and Saturday; they might also be observed on Wednesdays and on the evenings before major feast days. Not everyone observed the Wednesday and Saturday fasts, but they were especially called upon to do so on the "Ember Days": these were the Wednesday, Friday, and Saturday after the first Sunday in Lent (six weeks before Easter), after Whitsunday (six weeks after Easter), after Holy Cross Day (September 14), and after St. Lucy's Day (December 13). Fish days were also in force throughout all weekdays of Lent, and, for the pious, during Advent. Exception were made for pregnant or nursing women, the very young, the very old, the sick and the poor, and in some cases laborers. It was even possible to purchase an exemption. Nevertheless, the vast majority of the populace apparently followed the strictures to at least some degree. As a result, people consumed a great deal more fish than is common today.

One fourteenth-century menu for a fish day suggests the following:

The First Course: Oysters in Gravy, Pike and Smoked Herring, Fried Stockfish and Whiting.

The Second Course: Porpoise in Galantine, and therewith Conger and Fresh Salmon Gilded and Roasted and Gurnard, therewith Tarts and Flampoints [an egg and cheese pastry].

The Third Course: Rosee [a rose-colored dish] as Potage and Cream of Almonds, therewith Sturgeon and Whelks, Great Eels and Lampreys, Dariol [custard tart], Lechefres of Fruit [fruit tarts], and therewith Nirsebeke [a kind of fritter].[5]

Drinks   Ale, unhopped beer, was the staple drink of medieval England. It provided a significant portion of people's nutritional intake, women and children included. It was most often brewed from barley malt, but wheat and oats were also used. Ale was flavored with herbs. Because it had no hops, it lacked the bitter edge of modern beer but also lacked the preservative properties of the hops, so it did not keep very well. Daily intake appears to have been substantial, with allowances of a gallon per person being common in the households of the aristocracy, and

2 to 4 pints among peasants and laborers. However, medieval ale was not necessarily very strong. After the mash made by boiling the malted grain was poured off, water was poured through the malt several more times. Ale brewed from each successive pouring was progressively weaker. The different strengths of ale were consequently known as ale of the first, second, or third water; ale made from the last washing of the malt was called small ale. Toward the end of Chaucer's lifetime, ale was beginning to give way to beer in the city, although it remained the predominant drink in the country for centuries to come.

The figure on the left is drinking from a goblet of pale green glass. From a manuscript of before 1349 (Psalter of Bonne de Luxembourg) [McLean].

For those who could afford it, wine was also much favored. Wine had to be imported, and even a knight might find it expensive and rely on ale for daily use. France was probably the principal source, but wines were also imported from the Rhine valley, from Spain and Portugal, and even from as far away as Greece. Wines in this period were most often drunk young—vintage wines were just becoming fashionable at the end of the century. Wine was often watered or sweetened; sometimes it was spiced to make the drink known as hippocras.

Other drinks included cider (made from apples), perry (made from pears), and mead (made from honey). Distilled liquors were relatively rare and were generally consumed only for medicinal purposes. People at the lowest end of the economic scale had to rely on water, a drink less flavorful and less healthy than the alcoholic alternatives—particularly in towns, where overcrowding made water pollution a problem. Milk was not much favored by adults, although whey (the thin liquid remaining after the curds are removed from curdled milk) was sometimes consumed in poor households.[6]

The Table   It was uncommon to have a room permanently set aside as a dining room; a single room generally served for all public activities. For this reason, the medieval dining table was characteristically a temporary structure—a long board set up on trestles, which could be taken down after the meal to avoid cluttering the hall. The table was laid first with a boardcloth (a tablecloth) and with towels and napkins. In some households these might be coarse cloths of hempen canvas. Those who could afford it used white linen, while the wealthy used silk. Diners sat on wooden stools or benches, which could be made more comfortable with cushions. Salt was set out in salt-cellars, which might be quite ornate in aristocratic households. Drinks were served in pitchers made of pottery or of a metal such as pewter.[7]

The place settings for the guests were much less elaborate than modern formal settings. A typical medieval table setting included just a napkin, a "trencher," a bowl, a cup, and a spoon.

The trencher was a piece of old bread that served as a plate. The bread used for trenchers was less fresh than bread served as part of the meal—perhaps four days old, to ensure a good crust. The original round loaf was sliced in two to make two disks, and the edges were then squared off: a typical trencher would probably have been a rectangle 6" across and 4" deep. The trencher soaked up the juices from the meal and might afterwards be given to the dogs or the

A monk samples the drink from a bowl [Wright].

poor. During a fancy meal used trenchers might be replaced with fresh ones—often a new one was presented at the start of each course.[8]

Tableware varied with the means of the owner. Rich households made extensive use of silver; glass was also a relative luxury. Pewter was a cheaper alternative, so those of lesser means used it instead. The poorest relied heavily on wood and ceramics. Drinking vessels included glasses, cups, beakers, and even bowls.

An interesting feature of medieval table settings is the absence of knives. People generally carried their own knives and used these at the table. Note that knives were *not* the same as daggers: they were smaller, single-edged, and lacked the protective hand-guard of a dagger—besides, medieval people would probably not have been enthusiastic about eating with a tool used for killing people. The knives used at table were invariably pointed, since they had to serve for spearing as well as cutting. The fork was a cooking rather than an eating implement in fourteenth-century England, and it remained so until the seventeenth century.

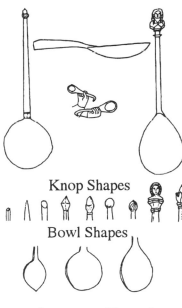

Knop Shapes

Bowl Shapes

Spoon types [Reames].

Spoons were made of wood (such as boxwood, juniper, poplar, or fruit woods), bone, horn, pewter, latten (a copper alloy containing zinc), silver, or gold.[9] Their bowls were generally round, fig-shaped, or—rarely—leaf-shaped. The stem was a slender stick with a cross-section either round, square, hexagonal, or diamond-shaped. Sometimes the stem ended in a sharp point, or was cut at right angles, or cut at a diagonal (called a "slip knop"). Otherwise there might be a fancy "knop," a decorative knob on the end of the stem. The knop might be in the shape of a simple diamond point, a simple round ball, a ball with spirals (called a "wrythen" knop), an acorn, a castle tower, or a figurehead or bust (called a "maidenhead"). Sometimes the spoon was quite fanciful: the entire stem and knop might be in the shape of a horse's leg, ending in a hoof for a knop. The typical length of the spoon was 6 to 7" overall.

There were several other popular styles of spoons. One was the fist-spoon, which had a shallow, round bowl and a very short, thick stem. There were also folding spoons, which had a hinged stem and were easy to carry—such spoons were particularly useful for travelers.

In a wealthy household, a large staff might be involved in bringing the food and drink from the **Serving the Meal** kitchen to the tables. One of the most skilled among these was the carver, who had the task of carving the various roasts according to an elaborate etiquette. The panter was responsible for the bread, both the trenchers and the table bread. It was he who trimmed the loaves and made sure that the appropriate types of bread went to the correct recipients. The role of the butler was very different from that associated with the butlers of today. His title was originally "bottler": he was responsible for the wine and ale, which included watering and spicing the wine as appropriate. The ewerer was responsible for the laving-water and towels with which the diners washed their hands.

Other servitors included the sewer, charged with arranging dishes before and after they reached the table; the almoner, guardian of the alms dish in which extra food was placed for distribution to the poor, and the surveyor, who controlled the surveying board to which the cook sent the individual serving platters; and the various servants who carried the food to the diners.

The servants might be ordinary hired help, but in the most important households the major serving positions were actually held by aristocrats. These could be sons, fosterlings, or squires living in the household. At important royal feasts the king might be waited on by leading noblemen.

Aristocratic feasters sharing a napkin. French, c. 1350 (Bibliothèque Nationale MS Français 1586, f. 55) [McLean].

Grace was customarily said both before and after a meal. It was also customary to wash one's hands before and after the **Manners** meal. In the better households, a servant would come around with a jug of "laving-water," sometimes scented with herbs such as sage or rosemary, a basin, and a towel. He would pour the water over the diner's hands into the basin, and the diner would dry them with the towel.

Medieval table manners were largely shaped by the sharing of food. Diners were supposed to use their knives rather than their fingers to obtain salt from the communal salt cellars. Plates were commonly shared between two to four people, and two people often shared a cup. In the absence of forks, it was common to dip fingers into common dishes; in fact, many rules of courtesy at the table centered around this. It was considered unmannerly to reach in with dirty fingers, and it was similarly rude to take all the best pieces for oneself. Likewise, when sharing a cup, it was polite to wipe one's mouth before drinking.[10] When children were learning their manners they were taught not to slurp, fidget at the table, speak with food in their mouths, or pick their teeth with their knives. When finished with their food, they were to remove their spoons from their dishes.

Not all meals were eaten indoors. Outdoor workers often brought food for a midday meal, or had it brought by **The Medieval** their wives: handy foods like bread, cheese, and meats **Picnic** could be carried in cloths or baskets for this purpose. Among the aristocracy, outdoor meals were especially common during a hunt. A glimpse of this sort of meal comes to us from the *Book of the Hunt* by Gaston Phebus, a French contemporary of Chaucer whose work was translated into English early in the fifteenth century by the Duke of York:

> The assembly that men call gathering should be made in this manner: . . . The place where the gathering should be made should be in a fair meadow, quite green, where fair trees grow all about, the one far from the other, and a clear well or some running brook besides. . . . The officers . . . should lay the towels and boardcloths all about on the green grass, and set diverse foods upon a great platter according to the lord's status, and some should eat sitting and some standing, some leaning upon their elbows, some drink and some laugh, some jangle, some joke, some play, and in short do all manner of disports of gladness.

A modern cook working in a medieval kitchen might very well give up in despair. Even in the most wealthy **The Kitchen** households, the circumstances of cooking were quite primitive by our standards. All cooking involved an actual fire. Meats were roasted on a spit by a fire—requiring the attention of someone to turn the spit, to ensure that the meat would be evenly cooked. It was customary to roast *beside* the fire rather than over it; this not only prevented flaring but allowed the fat to be caught in a dripping pan for later use. Frying and boiling took place above a fire or hot coals. Baking was the most involved process of all. Burning coals were placed in a clay oven until it was sufficiently heated, then the coals were raked out and the item to be baked was placed inside. Those who didn't own a proper oven could bake in a metal or ceramic vessel placed in the fire and covered with hot coals.

One early fifteenth-century chef offered the following suggestions for a lavishly appointed kitchen:

> There should be a provision of good big cauldrons to boil large cuts of meat, and a great number of moderate sized ones for making pottages . . . and for other cooking operations, and great suspended pans for cooking fish and other things, and a great number of large and ordinary-sized boilers for pottages and other things, and a dozen good big mortars. Decide on the place where sauces will be prepared. And you will need some twenty large frying pans, a dozen great kettles, fifty pots, sixty two-handled pots, a hundred hampers, a dozen grills, six large graters, a hundred wooden spoons, twenty-five holed spoons, both large and small, six pot hooks, twenty oven-shovels, twenty roasters, both those with turntable spits and those with spits mounted on andirons. You should not put your trust in wooden skewers or spits, because you could spoil all your meat, or even lose it; rather you should have six score iron spits which are strong and thirteen feet long; and you need three dozen other spits which are just as long but not as thick, in order to roast poultry, piglets and water birds. . . . And besides this . . . four dozen slender skewers for doing glazing and for fastening things.[11]

Stoking the fire [Wright].

Kettles (the pots used to heat water) were often three-legged and made of brass. Brass is not prone to rust and it heats more rapidly than iron; however, it is hard to clean and is thus less suited to cooking food. Although cast iron did exist, it is uncertain whether it was actually used for cooking vessels; iron cookware was generally wrought iron. Kitchen utensils might be made of iron or copper. Cooking pots were commonly made of clay. Spices were often stored in pouches, and kitchens generally had various ceramic vessels for storage. There would also be basins and cloths for washing dirty dishes.

Another major difference between medieval and modern kitchens is the technology of food preservation. There was no refrigeration, so other means had to be found to preserve foods, especially since the absence of high-speed transportation meant that it was impossible to import fresh foods. The means of preservation depended on the food. Fruits and vegetables were preserved by drying: raisins were one example. Peas and beans were important staples precisely because they dried well. Meats and fish could be preserved by drying, salting, or pickling. Salted meats were essential during the winter months in commoners' households; they had to be soaked several times before cooking to remove the excess salt, and even then they were tasted very salty. Of course, the best way to preserve meat was to keep it alive. Those who could afford the cost of winter fodder probably ate fresh meat all year round, and in general livestock were not slaughtered until the last possible moment. After all, not only did this preserve the meat longer, but beef was easier to transport when it could still walk on its own four legs!

Roasting. Flemish, 1338-1344 (RA) [McLean].

RECIPES

Quite a number of recipes survive from Chaucer's day. The following all derive from late fourteenth-century sources: the *Diversa Servicia*, the *Forme of Cury*, and British Library Manuscript Royal 17 A iii, a collection of medical recipes. In each case, the original recipe is given in italics (the language is somewhat modernized to aid the modern reader), followed by an interpretation for the modern cook.

Ground Beans

Take beans and dry them in an oast or in an oven. And hull them well, and winnow out the hulls, and wash them clean; and make them to seethe in good broth, and eat them with bacon.[12]

Place **1 lb. kidney beans** in a saucepan. Add **1/3 cup chopped onion** and **2 cups beef or chicken stock**. Add enough water to cover the beans, and simmer until tender (about 1 $^1/2$ hours). Chop up **1/4 lb. thick-sliced bacon**, mix in with the cooked beans, salt to taste, and serve.

This is one of the simplest recipes surviving from the period. It probably gives a good idea of the ordinary fare of most Englishmen of the period.

Cabbages in Pottage

Take cabbages and quarter them, and seethe them in good broth with minced onions and the white of leeks slit and chopped small. And add thereto saffron and salt, and season it with powder douce.[13]

Take **1 head of cabbage**, quarter it, and boil it for at least 30 minutes in **beef or chicken broth** with **1 diced onion** and **1 diced leek**. Season with **3 threads pounded saffron, salt** to taste, and **1/8 teaspoon cardamom** and **1/8 teaspoon coriander** and **1 teaspoon sugar**.

This is slightly finer recipe; the cabbages, onions, and leeks would have been found in an ordinary peasant's garden, but the saffron, cardamom, coriander, and sugar all indicate that this simple fare has been made more appealing to a richer diner's palate. A poor family might have eaten the same thing, seasoned only with salt.

Turnips in Broth

Take turnips and make them clean and wash them clean; quarter them; parboil them; take them up, cast them in a good broth and seethe them. Mince onions and cast thereto saffron and salt and serve it forth with powder douce. In the same wise make of carrots and parsnips.[14]

Peel and quarter **4 small to medium turnips**, and parboil them in salted water for about 5 minutes. Drain, and add to **2 cups meat broth**. Add **2 minced onions**, pinch of **saffron** and **salt**, and **1/8 teaspoon cardamom** and **1/8 teaspoon coriander** and **1 teaspoon sugar**. Simmer until tender. Carrots and parsnips may be cooked in the same way.

As with the cabbages above, this is a simple dish made somewhat more fancy for a wealthy table.

Fried Spinaches

Take spinaches; parboil them in seething water. Take them up and press out the water and hew them in two. Fry them in oil and add thereto powder douce, and serve forth.[15]

Parboil and drain **1 bunch spinach**. Fry in **2 tablespoons oil or grease,** season with **1 teaspoon sugar, 1/8 teaspoon cardamom** and **1/8 teaspoon coriander.**
Again, this is simple fare spiced for a rich family's table.

Salad

Take parsley, sage, green garlic, scallions, onions [one manuscript replaces this with "lettuce"], *leek* [three manuscripts add "spinach" here], *borage, mints, leeks, fennel, garden cress, rue, rosemary, purslane; rinse and wash them clean. Pick them clean. Pluck them small with thine hand, and mix them well with raw oil; lay on vinegar and salt, and serve it forth.*[16]

Wash and tear up **salad greens** (lettuce, *not iceberg lettuce,* spinach, borage). Drain well. Wash and finely slice **2 leeks, 1 bunch scallions** and **1 bunch green onions**. Add to greens. Next add at least 1 tablespoon each (fresh) or 1 teaspoon each (dried): **parsley, sage, mint, rosemary** (rue and purslane, if available). Add **2 cloves minced garlic** and **1/2 cup olive oil**. Mix well. Add **3 tablespoons vinegar** and **1 ¹/₂ teaspoon salt** just before serving (as the vinegar causes the greens to wilt).

Egurdouce of Fish

Take loaches or roches or tenches or soles; break them in pieces. Fry them in oil. Take half wine, half vinegar, and sugar, and make a syrup; add thereto chopped onions, dried currants, and great raisins. Add thereto whole spices, good powders, and salt; serve up the fish, and lay the sauce above and serve forth.[17]

Break up **2 filets of sole**. Fry in **2 tablespoons oil**. Mix **1/2 cup wine** with **1/2 cup vinegar** and **1 tablespoon sugar**. Add **1/4 cup chopped onions, 1/2 cup dried currants,** and **1/4 cup raisins**. Season with **1/2 teaspoon cinnamon, 1/2 teaspoon cloves, 1/2 teaspoon nutmeg, 1 teaspoon pepper,** and **salt** to taste. Pour the sauce over the fish and serve.
Fish would have been a regular part of most people's diet, although the fresh fish in this recipe would have been for a wealthy table; ordinary people were more likely to eat dried or pickled cod or herring.

Blanc Manger

Put rice in water all night, and in the morning wash them clean. Afterward put them to the fire until they burst, and not too much. Then take meat of capons, or of hens, boiled, and draw it small. After take milk of almonds and put into the rice and boil it. And when it is boiled, put in the meat and mix it therewith until it be thick, and mix it finely well so that it stick not to the pot. And when it is enough and thick add thereto a good part of sugar, and put therein almonds fried in white grease, and serve it forth.[18]

Soak **1 cup rice** overnight in water. Drain. Chop finely **1 lb. chicken breast**. To make almond milk, pound in a mortar **1/2 lb. blanched almonds**. Slowly add **3 cups water**, allow to soak, then strain through a cloth to get the almond milk. Add the almond milk to the rice and boil for 20 minutes. Add the chicken and stir. Add **1 1/2 tablespoons sugar**. Fry **1/2 cup blanched almonds** in **2 tablespoons butter**, and mix into the rice and serve.

This is the ancestor of the modern blancmange, which is now a dessert dish.

Mustard (for a Roast)

If you wish to provide for keeping mustard a long time do it at wine-harvest in sweet must. And some say that the must should be boiled. Item, if you want to make mustard hastily in a village, grind some mustard-seed in a mortar and soak in vinegar, and strain; and if you want to make it ready the sooner, put it in a pot in front of the fire. Item, and if you wish to make it properly and at leisure, put the mustard-seed to soak overnight in good vinegar, then have it ground fine in a mill, and then little by little moisten it with good vinegar: and if you have some spices left over from making jelly, broth, hippocras, or sauces, they may be ground up with it, and then leave it until it is ready.[19]

Add **4 teaspoons mustard seed** to **5 tablespoons vinegar**. Soak overnight. Mix in **1/4 cup vinegar**, a pinch of **ginger, cardamom, nutmeg, galingale** (if possible—it can sometimes be had from a specialty shop under the name "galangal" or "laos"), and a pinch and a half of **cinnamon**. Grind (a coffee mill can be used for this purpose).

This mustard would have been used to flavor a roast meat; it was also commonly used on herring. No roasting recipes survive from this period, but you may wish to follow a recipe from *The Joy of Cooking* or another modern cookbook.

Tarts of Flesh (Pork Dumplings)

Take boiled pork and grind it small with saffron; mix it with eggs, and dried currants, and powder fort and salt, and make a foil of dough and close the stuffing therein. Cast the tartlets in a pan with fair water boiling and salt; take of the clean flesh without eggs and boil it in good broth. Cast there powder douce and salt, and serve the tarts in dishes, and pour the juices thereon.[20]

Parboil **1/2 lb. ground pork** (about 1 cup). Drain and add **6 threads pounded saffron, 2 beaten eggs, 1 cup dried currants, 1 teaspoon pepper, 2 teaspoons ginger, 1 teaspoon mace, 1/2 teaspoon cloves**, and **salt** to taste.

For the shells, mix **2 cups flour, 2/3 cup water, 1/2 teaspoon salt**. Knead and roll to a thin sheet, about 1/16". Cut circles or squares of at least 3" diameter, and moisten the edges with water. Place filling into centers, fold in half, and seal the edges by pressing them firmly.

Boil about 3" of water in a pot. Set the dumplings carefully into the water, and simmer them for 10 minutes. Add to the water **1/8 teaspoon ground cardamom, 1/8 teaspoon coriander, 1 teaspoon sugar**, and **salt** to taste. Serve the dumplings forth, and pour the liquid over them.

Tart in Ember Day

Take and parboil onions and herbs and press out the water and hew them small. Take green cheese and bray it in a mortar, and temper it up with eggs. Add thereto butter, saffron, and salt, and dried currants, and a little sugar with powder douce, and bake it in a trap, and serve it forth.[21]

Pastry:

Mix **1 1/2 cups whole wheat pastry flour, 1/2 cup butter, 1 tablespoon sugar, 1/8 teaspoon salt, 1 thread saffron, 3 tablespoons water**. Knead to a stiff dough, refrigerate, roll out to 1/8" thickness, cut circles to make tarts fitting mini-muffin shells. Makes 12 tarts.

Filling:

Parboil, drain, and chop **1 medium onion**. Add **1/4 cup chopped parsley** and **1/4 cup chopped dill**. Add **6 oz. grated farmer's cheese, 2 beaten eggs, 2 tablespoons butter, 4 threads saffron**, and mix well. Mix in **1/2 cup dried currants**. Fill the pastry shells, and bake for 20 minutes at 375° F, or until golden brown.

The Ember Days were the Wednesday, Friday, and Saturday after the first Sunday in Lent, Whitsunday, Holy Cross Day, and St. Lucia's Day, which were supposed to be days for fasting and prayer. Accordingly, these tarts are made without meat.

Tart de Bry

Take a crust an inch deep in a trap. Take yolks of eggs raw and "rewen" [semi-soft] cheese and mix it and the yolks together. Add thereto ground ginger, sugar, saffron, and salt. Put it in a trap; bake it and serve it forth.[22]

For pastry recipe, see Tart in Ember Day, above.

For the filling, grate **8 oz. semisoft cheese** (e.g., Pont l'Eveque). Add **6 egg yolks, 1 teaspoon ground ginger, 1 teaspoon sugar, 4 threads pounded saffron, salt** to taste. Fill pastry shells and bake for 20 minutes at 375° F, or until golden brown. Makes twelve 1 1/2" tarts

This tart was another likely candidate for meals during periods of fasting.

Apple Tarts

Take good apples and good spices and figs and raisins and pears, and when they are well pounded in a mortar, color with saffron well and put it in a covered shell and set it forth to bake well.[23]

For the pastry recipe, see Tart in Ember Day, above.

Pare and core **3 apples, 2 pears**, and **3 figs**. Chop, and add **1 cup raisins, 1 teaspoon cloves, 1/8 teaspoon pepper, 1 teaspoon mace, 1 teaspoon cinnamon, 1/4 teaspoon salt, 4 threads saffron**, and crush. Fill pastry shells and bake for 20 minutes at 375° F, or until golden brown. You can add **1/4 teaspoon saunders (ground red sandalwood)** to the spices, if it is available to you.

Hippocras

Take a half lb. of choice cinnamon, of choice ginger a half lb., of grains of paradise [cardamom] 3 ounces, of long pepper 3 ounces, of cloves 2 ounces, of nutmegs 2 ounces and a half, of caraway 2 ounces, of spikenard [valerian] a half ounce, of galingale 2 ounces, of sugar 2 lb. If sugar is lacking, take a pottle [half-gallon] of honey.[24]

Add the following to **1 bottle red wine: 1 1/2 tablespoons sugar** or **3 tablespoons honey, 1 teaspoon cinnamon, 1 1/2 teaspoon ginger, 1/2 teaspoon cardamom, 1/2 teaspoon pepper, 1/4 teaspoon cloves, 1/4 teaspoon nutmeg, 1/4 teaspoon caraway**. Allow to sit at least overnight before drinking. You may want to filter it through a coffee filter to remove the dregs.

Hippocras was a spiced wine, reputed to be very good for the health—the name derives from Hippocrates, the Greek physician known today as the originator of the Hippocratic Oath. Galingale is similar to ginger.

Mead

Take honeycombs and put them into a great vessel and lay therein great sticks, and lay the weight thereon till it be run out as much as it will; and this is called live honey. And then take that forsaid combs and seethe them in clean water, & boil them well. After press out thereof as much as thou may and cast it into another vessel into hot water, & seethe it well and scum it well, and add thereto a quart of live honey. And then let it stand a few days well stopped, and this is good drink.[25]

Boil **1 cup honey** in **9 cups water** for 30 minutes, scumming the froth as it rises. Allow the liquid to cool, and pour it into a sealed container; a plastic milk jug or the like is a good choice, as it will expand to accommodate the carbon dioxide emitted by fermentation. Try to leave as little air as possible at the top. Allow to stand 4 days in the dark at room temperature. Keep an eye on the fermenting liquid, letting off excess pressure if necessary (it is wise to store it in a place that will be easy to clean if it bursts). If you like you can flavor it by adding **1 sliced and boiled apple, 1/2 teaspoon ground pepper**, and **1 teaspoon ground cloves** to the liquid before bottling it (all these additives are suggested in another mead recipe from the same manuscript).

This is a very quick and lightly fermented mead—it may sparkle slightly but has very little alcohol content. Finer meads are made to be kept for years before drinking.

Bread

Bread was a crucial part of any medieval meal, but, regrettably, no bread recipes survive from the period. The following recipe for a fairly ordinary sort of bread is based on early seventeenth-century sources:

Sift **3 cups unbleached whole wheat flour**. Dissolve **1 teaspoon active dry yeast** in **1 cup lukewarm water or beer** and stir in **1 teaspoon salt**. Make a well in the flour and pour the yeast mixture into it. Mix and knead for 5 minutes. Since the wheat can vary in initial moisture you might have to add water or flour to ensure that it is moist to the touch but not sticky.

Let the dough rise in a warm place for about an hour. Form into a flat round loaf, and prick it on top with a knife. Let the loaf rise again until it has doubled in volume, which should be about 45 minutes to an hour.

Preheat the oven to about 500° F. When the dough has risen, place it in the oven, and reduce the heat to 350° F. After about 20 minutes the bread should be golden and ready to remove from the oven.

9

Entertainments

LEISURE AND RECREATION

Leisure time for most people in the Middle Ages was more limited than now, yet entertainment remained an important part of their lives—perhaps even more so because of the limited opportunities to enjoy it. For the aristocracy, play was almost a characteristic way of life. In addition to their designated role as rulers and warriors, the culture of the aristocracy was in many respects defined by their recreations: hunting, hawking, tourneying, and courtly literature were among the pastimes which identified the aristocrat. Even the working commoner had at least some eight weeks of Sundays and holy days in the course of a year, so there was plenty of time to indulge a taste for entertainment.

Recreational activities were especially important because they served to give order and meaning to the rest of people's lives. The cycle of Sundays and holy days shaped the ritual year: it is sometimes said that the medieval peasant lived in memory of the last festival and in anticipation of the next. Through their games, amusements, and festivities, they expressed their values, their aspirations, and their sense of identity. As we shall see, the games people played have much to tell us about the way they saw their world.

Entertainment was somewhat more ritualized than it is today. This was partly because for most people the heavy schedule of work forced entertainment into certain restricted settings. For the medieval commoner, entertainment activities were concentrated on festival occasions, especially Sundays and

The Settings of Play

holy days after church. As can be seen from the calendar in Chapter 2, the various festivals of the year often had special entertainments associated with them.

Then as now, people would repair to a tavern to socialize indoors. Outdoors it was common to play in churchyards, which were one of the principal public spaces in a village—although some people felt this was a violation of the sacred space of the church. The common lands of a village were also places for play, as were the streets of a village or town.

For the aristocracy, opportunities for entertainment were less restricted: they did not have to conform to strict work schedules, and they had plenty of spaces for entertainment in their halls and on their lands.

Although people's opportunity for entertainment depended on their social status, the entertainments themselves were less stratified than were other aspects of medieval life. A few entertainments belonged especially to one class or another—hunting, for example, was an aristocratic pastime, whereas wrestling was more popular among common folk. Yet for the most part, entertainments seem to have crossed class boundaries more readily than other activities. The courtly poetry of the aristocracy may have been more refined than the folk verse of the commons, but both lord and peasant enjoyed many of the same stories; the dice used by the peasantry may have been made of simple bone or wood, but commoners played many of the same sorts of games as the nobility played with their dice of ivory.

Although games were surprisingly consistent across the social classes, there were important distinctions between the sexes. Both boys and girls played the same games freely, but adult women were more restricted in the games they could play. As a rule, women do not appear to have engaged much in physically demanding sports, although they were often present as spectators. However, they very commonly played table games and were especially likely to take part in dancing.[1]

Professional Entertainment   On the whole, entertainment in the Middle Ages was much more personalized than it is today. There were no mass media and no means of mass production. Even reading was more personal, in a sense—since there were no printing presses, every text had to be written out by hand. This is not to say that there was no professional entertainment. Rather, it means that professional entertainers generally had to do their entertaining in person. Medieval England was actually quite rich in such people: musicians, acrobats, animals trainers, and even puppeteers. Still, in the absence of mass dissemination of professional entertainment, people often had to provide their own fun.

Theatrical performances were also popular. Some of these were simple folk-plays or minor entertainments performed by strolling players, but the custom of major productions sponsored with church funds or public money was developing. It peaked in the fifteenth century, when a number of English towns staged major play-cycles telling the story of the Bible from the Creation to the Last Judgment. In Chaucer's day, plays were somewhat less ambitious and were more likely to tell a story of miracles performed by God, a saint, or the Virgin Mary.[2]

A puppet show, strongly suggestive of Punch and Judy.
Flemish, 1338-1344 (RA, f. 54v) [McLean].

One major form of entertainment was literature, in the very broadest sense. Poetry in particular was a common part **Literature** of people's lives and was composed on very diverse topics. There were courtly lyric verses about love. There were devotional poems about God, the saints, or the Virgin Mary. There were political prophesies and satires. There were epics and romances about the heroes of legend— King Arthur and his knights, the Siege of Troy, King Richard the Lion-Hearted, Robin Hood, and many others were the subjects of lengthy narrative poems. People delighted in lengthy versifications of the Bible or of English history. Chaucer's own major poetical work, *The Canterbury Tales*, is an excellent example. The poem is constructed as the account of a pilgrimage by diverse characters to the shrine of St. Thomas à Becket at Canterbury, and Chaucer has the characters tell an enormous variety of stories: chivalric epics, animal fables, bawdy farces, saints' lives, and more. *The Canterbury Tales* were an enormous hit in their own day and had many imitators in following centuries, testament to the popularity of narrative verse.

In addition to verse tales, there was prose storytelling, although fewer texts have survived—apparently people didn't find it as important to record the exact words of a prose narrative. It would seem that many of the same sorts of stories were told as were popular in poetic form. Of course, the single most important source of prose narratives was the Bible. People heard Bible stories every Sunday in church; they saw them illustrated in paintings, carvings, and stained glass windows. Biblical tales were taken seriously, but they were a form of entertainment too.

With more rapid cursive hands and less expensive paper supplanting expensive parchment, books were coming down in price but were still not cheap. An inexpensive romance might cost 2s., a primer 16d., and a calendar 8d. Thomas Walynton, a clothier, left two volumes in his will in 1402. By 1420 even a tailor like John Brinchley could leave two copies of Boethius' *The Consolation of Philosophy*, one in English and one in Latin, and a copy of *The Canterbury Tales*. Large libraries were rare, but this somewhat understates the number of books read. Books could be borrowed or purchased, read and then resold.

Because every book was written individually by hand, many volumes were personal anthologies containing a collection of texts of interest to the compiler. One example, probably collected by a Berkshire lawyer in the 1260s, contained formularies (model legal agreements), a treatise on accounting and on the laws of England, the *Romance of Horn*, Robert Grosseteste's *Le Chasteau de Amor* (a religious text), the *Fables* of Marie de France, and a bestiary (a moralized description of animals). More legal material was added by a later owner in the fourteenth century. *The Canterbury Tales* was in a sense a ready-made anthology. Another popular genre was the collection of moral tales, stories with edifying lessons derived from the Bible, the lives of saints, fables, and classical sources. Medieval readers of such works might be familiar with the characters of Æneas and Helen of Troy even if they never read Virgil or Homer, and a prosperous citizen like the Ménagier de Paris might be familiar with the Bible, the lives of the saints, and the works of St. Augustine, St. Gregory, St. Jerome, the classical historians Josephus and Livy, and Cicero, as well as such medieval works as *Romance of the Rose* and Petrarch's tale of Patient Griselda.

Music   Music was another pervasive form of entertainment. Some of it was provided by professional musicians, who were often hired by the aristocracy and rich townsfolk. Ordinary people could scarcely afford such a luxury; although they might occasionally have the opportunity to hear traveling musicians, they had to create most of their music themselves. It was common for people to sing for their own entertainment, sometimes as part of holiday revelry, sometimes during work to make the labor go more easily. The subjects of songs were diverse: there were love songs, drinking songs, and religious songs, songs about historical events and current politics, satirical songs about money or sex, and even nonsense songs.

People also enjoyed instrumental music. The instruments current in Chaucer's day were generally different from those used today. Bagpipes were one of the most popular instruments, especially among commoners: they were easy to hear at an outdoor festival, and their driving sound made them excellent for dancing. Also popular was the "pipe and tabor": the pipe was a three-hole recorder played with the left hand while beating a drum (the "tabor") with the right. This provided both melody and rhythm at once, and was especially favored among common folk. Simple flutes and recorders were also in use, as was the shawm, an extremely loud double-reeded ancestor of the oboe.

There were several sorts of bowed instruments. The most familiar is the fiddle, which was about the size of a modern viola, more plain in construction, and held against the chest rather than under the chin. The rebec was a smaller cousin, about the size of the musician's forearm, with a rounded back. The psaltery was a triangular box with strings running across it, comparable in appearance to a modern hammer dulcimer; it might be played with a bow or plucked with a plectrum. Other stringed instruments included the harp and the gittern, a plucked instrument vaguely comparable to a mandolin. Percussion was provided by drums, especially for dance music. Somewhere between percussion and wind instruments was the instrument known today as a Jew's harp, an inexpensive and common instrument in medieval England.

The sounds of all these instruments were generally coarser and harsher than is favored today, and many medieval instruments were quite loud. All this helped to ensure that the instrument would be audible. There were no amplifying systems, and one couldn't always count on good acoustics. The rhythms of fourteenth-century music were less rigid than in later centuries. In many respects, music of the period has affinities with the music of the Middle East.[3]

One common way of enjoying music was through dancing, which was widely popular throughout society and seems to have been fairly consistent at all social levels. People of Chaucer's day generally danced in a circle or chain, as is still common in some folk traditions of modern Europe. Courtly dancers liked to alternate men and women in the chain, but among ordinary people there seems to have been less concern about gender. It was especially common for women to dance together at all levels of society, while male-only dances seem to have been most popular among common folk. The music for the dance might be provided by musicians, but often the only music was the singing of the dancers themselves, a custom still found in a few parts of Europe.

Some entertainments were particularly the preserve of the aristocracy. One of these was hunting. In fact, it was generally illegal for commoners to hunt, as the rights to use land for hunting were generally reserved for the aristocratic **Hunting and Hawking** holders. The favorite targets of the aristocratic hunt were deer and boar—most of the other large game had become extinct in England. Smaller game included rabbits and foxes, although these were considered less interesting prey. The medieval hunt was highly ritualized: a skilled huntsman needed to know all about the habits of the quarry, to know the special vocabulary of the hunt, to recognize the various horn calls used during the hunt, to be able to interact with the hunting dogs, and to have mastered the art of carving up the quarry when it was killed. Hunting was a consuming art form for many aristocrats, in which the process of the hunt was as important as the actual killing of the prey.

Women did not generally hunt, but they did take part in the related sport of falconry. This sport was physically less demanding, but it had its own challenges. There were complex protocols as to what sorts of falcons should be sent after what quarry, and of course the handling of the falcon was much more demanding than the handling of a hunting dog. Hunting falcons were trained to bring down birds on the wing, especially waterfowl—falconry was generally practised near rivers, and the favored game were cranes, storks, and herons.

Combat at the barriers during a siege [McLean].

Another characteristically aristocratic pastime was the **Tournaments** tournament and related martial sports. The oldest form was **and Jousts** the tournament proper, which involved a mass of armored horsemen fighting as two teams. By Chaucer's day, this riotous sport had dwindled in popularity and had been ritualized to minimize casualties. Combat would take place within a limited area, typically about the size of a modern football field, surrounded by heavy barriers. The two sides might initially charge each other with lances and then fight out the combat with blunt swords, maces, or clubs. The awarding of prizes was in the hands of judges, often a panel of ladies.

Somewhat less chaotic was the joust, which gained favor as the tournament lost it. The joust pitted armored horsemen against each other one by one, charging with sharp or blunt lances. At any given occasion a number of horsemen would challenge each other, often divided into two teams of "holders" and "comers." In other forms of single combat, the participants might fight on foot with swords, axes, or daggers. Such contests were extremely dangerous and were generally only fought up to a certain number of blows, in order to reduce the risk.

The tournament was an occasion for rich display, costumes, and even play-acting. Large crowds of all classes might look on. Tournaments were sometimes officially organized by the king as a means of displaying the magnificence of his kingdom.

All these sports were extremely dangerous, especially those fought with unblunted weapons. In part this reflected the medieval willingness to risk serious injury in the course of play, but it also reflected the fine line between play combat and real fighting. Often these combats were fought by opposing knights involved in real wars, as English knights met their Scottish or French opponents. The risks were very real, and the antagonism was often real too.[4]

Young gentlemen fencing with sword and buckler. Italian, c. 1395
(TS Vienna, f. 96v) [McLean].

Commoners practiced martial sports too, although they were less elaborate. Their favorite weapons were cudgels, quarterstaves, and sword-and-buckler (the buckler being a small round shield). As with aristocratic

Common Physical Entertainments

combat, such pastimes could be very dangerous—or even more so, since commoners did not wear armor.

Perhaps somewhat less risky was wrestling, another favorite among commoners. Play could be full-contact or could allow grasping an opponent's clothes or a cloth sash worn over one shoulder. The aim could be either to give the opponent a simple fall, to pin him, or to throw him outside a circle. People also engaged in what is now called chickenfighting, with two wrestlers mounted on the shoulders of two supporters, each trying to throw his opponent off.

Some entertainments were pure demonstrations of athleticism. Men exhibited their strength by casting axles and heavy stones, or showed their speed in foot races. In the winter, people skated on frozen rivers and lakes on skates made of bone.

Ball games existed in a number of variations. An edict of 1363, attempting to stem the decay of English archery, forbade other sports including "handball", "football," "stickball," and "cambok." Medieval football was similar to its modern European namesake, known in North America as soccer. The game was invariably rowdy and sometimes extremely dangerous. In 1373 a group of tailors and skinners in London were arrested for playing football in Cheapside, a broad London street most noted for its market stalls—the players had been wearing daggers at the time.

A bat-and-ball game [Strutt].

Similar in structure was the game of Cambok, a sort of field hockey, named for the cambok or cammock, the curved stick often carried by shepherds. Variants (or other names) included Goff and Bandy. A rather more dangerous ball game was Camp-Ball, comparable to rugby and American football. There were two goals, which might be miles apart; each team would score by bringing the ball to the other team's goal. The ball could be conveyed by any means chosen: some versions of this game even included horsemen, and serious injury was common.

One family of ball-games was related to tennis. Commoners played a simple game called Handball, and aristocrats played an early version of tennis in which the ball was struck with the hand. Closely related was the game of Shuttlecock, the medieval equivalent of badminton, played with wooden paddles. Other ball games involved sticks or bats, and were related to baseball and cricket. A fifteenth-century text mentions Stoolball, which in later centuries involved one player pitching a ball at a stool and another attempting to ward it off, either with his hand or with a bat.

Shuttlecock [Strutt].

Another type of ball game was Bowls, in which the players would try to cast their balls as close as possible to a target. In the game of Quoits the players cast flat round stones at a target. Somewhere between medieval Bowls and modern ten-pin bowling was the game of Kailes or Loggats, in which a number of wooden or bone pins would be set up and the players would attempt to knock them over by casting a stick at them.

Playing with a whip-top [Wright].

Many of the games played by commoners were the object of official disapproval, since they encouraged idleness, rowdyism, and gambling. The one major exception was archery, which was strongly encouraged as a means of bolstering England's military might. In fact, archery was genuinely popular at all levels of society. The target might be a stick, a straw wreath mounted on an earthen butt, or even a hapless rooster.

Several popular games involved some sort of violence between or against animals. Bulls and bears were "baited," which involved setting dogs against them and betting on the outcome of the fight. Cockfighting was also popular: two cocks were set to fight each other, and the onlookers bet on which would win. Cocks were often the objects of violent sports. Not only were they used in cockfighting and as archery targets, but there was a sport called "cockthrashing," in which a blindfolded person would attempt to hit one with a stick.

Some games seem to have been particularly the pastimes of children. Such was Prisoner's Base, known as Base, or Post and Pillar, a game that had to be forbidden in Westminster because the noise it generated disturbed the deliberations of the government. Another was the whip-top, a form of top beaten with a scourge to make it turn.

Hot Cockles. Flemish, 1338-1344 (RA) [Wright].

Quite a few children's games were based on the giving and receiving of blows. In the game later known as Hot Cockles one player sat and took the head of the player who was "it" in his lap, to keep him from peeking; the other players took turns slapping the victim's rear, and if he correctly guessed who had struck the blow, that person became "it." Closely related was Hoodman's Blind, or Bobet, the ancestor of Blind-Man's Buff (also called Bear-Baiting after its more bloodthirsty cousin). In this game, one player had a hood pulled over his eyes and tried to catch one of the other players in order to change places with him or her. This was complicated by the fact that at the same time the other players were hitting him with their own hoods tied in a knot, or even with sticks—it is from these "buffets" that the game received its modern name. As in Hot Cockles, the object may sometimes have been to identify who had given the last blow. A similar game was Frog in the Middle, in which the player who was "it" crouched on the floor: the rest would try to touch, pinch, or slap him— anyone he caught would be "it." All these games were popular among both boys and girls.

Hoodman's blind. Flemish, 1338-1344 (RA, f. 54v) [McLean].

In addition to the physical games mentioned above, there were a number of popular table games. Chess **Table Games** occupied a prestigious position and was particularly favored as an aristocratic pastime. The form of chess played in fourteenth-century England was similar to the modern game, but there were a few substantial differences—notably in the moves of the Queen and the Bishop, which were much more restricted.[5]

After chess, perhaps the most popular class of board game was Tables, a family of games of which Backgammon is the only surviving descendant. The board and pieces were essentially the same as in modern Backgammon. Backgammon itself was not invented until the seventeenth century—in the fourteenth century there existed a variety of games at Tables, each with different initial set-ups and conditions for victory.

Another familiar game was that of Draughts or Jeu-de-Dame (called Checkers in North America today), which had originated by placing Tables pieces on the board for Chess. Even simpler was the game of Merels, usually known today as Nine-Man Morris or Six-Man Morris. Often a Tables set was built as a box, with two square halves folding together. The Tables board would be on the inside, on the back of one half would be a chessboard, on the back of the other a board for Merels.

One of the most simple, popular, and morally suspect forms of play was dicing, a practice that required almost no space and only the simplest equipment—two or three dice (bone was an inexpensive and popular material; ivory was used by the wealthy) and something to play for. The spots on the die had special names borrowed from French: ace, deuce, trey, cater, sink, and sise. Dice games were generally very simple, involving pure chance and almost no strategy, so their interest resided in the gambling.

Cross and Pile was another simple pastime, exactly the same as modern Heads or Tails—one side of the medieval coin had a cross on it, the other a face, or "pile."

Although games tend to be conservative, every now and then a
Cards   real change occurs. One major example was under way during
Chaucer's lifetime, with the introduction of playing cards to
Europe. These arrived from the Near East, perhaps through Venetian
trade with the Mameluk Turks. The first clear references to playing cards
in Europe occur in 1377, from which date onward there survive numerous
references from France, Italy, Spain, Switzerland, Germany, and the Low
Countries.[6] Many of these are laws banning card-playing on holidays, or
for tradesmen, or both, suggesting the broad popularity of the pastime
from its very first arrival.

The more isolated parts of Western Europe took to cards more slowly.
England appears to have been very backward in this respect. The earliest
references to playing cards in England date to the early fifteenth century.
Nonetheless, the close cultural contacts between England and the
Continent in this period suggest that at least some Englishmen must have
been exposed to the practice.[7]

Old playing cards have not generally survived, and no European
examples are known from before the fifteenth century. Most surviving
examples from before 1500 are cards that were never meant for ordinary
use—collectors' items displaying the wealth of the owner. They were hand
painted and illuminated by master painters, and were very expensive. Of
the millions of playing cards produced for common use, scarcely a single
card remains.

Playing cards are easily worn, torn, spoiled, or lost. This characteristic,
combined with the evidence of widespread popularity, indicates that a
large number of decks were being produced. For the tradesmen of Paris to
afford the cards that they were forbidden in 1377, cards must have been
cheap and plentiful enough for them to acquire the habit. The cards could
conceivably have been block-printed. An alternative would be the
stenciling technique that was commonly used to color block-printed
playing cards in the fifteenth century. Perhaps the cheapest cards were
rough sketches with quickly applied colors.

The modern deck of cards is almost always divided into suits of
Hearts, Spades, Clubs, and Diamonds. This suit system is only one of
many and did not appear until about 1480, in France, for which reason it is
called the French suit system. Several other standard suit systems
survived for hundreds of years in Europe.

Visual evidence suggests that the first playing cards in Europe were of
the Italian suit system of Coins, Cups, Swords, and Batons, similar to the
suits found on modern Tarot decks. This conclusion is supported by the
close resemblance between this system and the Mameluk suits of Coins,
Cups, Swords, and Polo-Sticks. In the Italian deck, the Swords are
invariably stylized and curved scimitars on the number cards, and they
are interlaced so as to cross each other at the hilts and near the points of

the sword. The suit of Batons is made of long straight staves that are also stylized and interlaced at the center of the card. Coins are large round disks, often with designs on their faces, and Cups are stylized basins with ornate tops. The Spanish suit system, probably slightly later in date, had more naturalistic swords and batons, not interlaced but arranged like modern suit signs.

A game at cards, after a French manuscript of the late fourteenth century. It appears to show the Italian suits of Coins and Batons (British Library MS Add. 12228, f. 313v) [McLean].

One of the first references in Europe is the *Tractatus de moribus et disciplina humanae conversationis*, written by a Dominican friar from Basel in 1377. The text describes the deck as having four suits, three court cards in each suit, and ten number cards in each suit. The number cards, as now, bear a number of pips of the suit sign equal to their value (i.e., twos have two pips, fives have five, and so on).[8] This description exactly parallels modern decks. The earliest surviving decks have the same pip cards as in a modern deck (i.e., 1 to 10), but the face cards might include a Knight as well as the Knave (the modern Jack), Queen, and King. This is reminiscent of the modern Tarot deck. German decks sometimes replaced the Queen and Knave with an Over and an Under, two figures holding the suit sign high and low respectively. The Joker was not a feature of medieval decks.

One important difference between medieval and modern
Gambling and   games is the role of betting. Physically demanding sports
the Element of   might be played for the pleasure of exercise, and chess for
Risk   the intellectual challenge, but most other games were
likely to involve some form of wager. Moralists railed against the vice of
gambling, and social reformers saw it as a destructive vice (particularly
among commoners, who were supposed to be working for their living),
but the excitement provided by a stake was treated as an integral part of
play. Even relatively poor people gambled, and for the aristocracy it was
practically a way of life. Most table games involved some degree of
gambling. In fact, the practice of gambling pervaded all sorts of games.
Some, like animal-fights, were gambling sports by definition, and many
other classes of games might be enlivened by the addition of a wager.

The penchant for gambling may well be related to the interest in
sports that were inherently dangerous, such as jousting or fencing with
sword and buckler. In general, medieval people seem to have been quite
willing to risk serious personal injury in the pursuit of entertainment,
which may reflect a generally lower value placed on life, However, it may
also be attributed to the greater importance of games. After all, games
gave meaning and interest to people's lives. Perhaps because medieval
society was quite static, people vented a natural desire for excitement and
challenge by deliberately choosing risky forms of play. In fact, games were
very much a part of people's everyday lives. In the modern world, people
tend to abandon game-playing as they mature; for medieval people,
games were likely to remain an important activity even in adulthood,
although only the aristocracy had the leisure to pursue them on a daily
basis.

RULES FOR GAMES

In reconstructing fourteenth-century games, we are obliged to
supplement contemporary and nearly contemporary sources with
additional information from later centuries. A few compilations of rules
for board games and dice games survive from the thirteenth to fifteenth
centuries, but for card games and physical games the rules must be
inferred from later sources. Fortunately, the conservatism of games has
meant that many of the games whose rules were first written down in the
seventeenth century had changed little, if at all, since the Middle Ages. In
fact, medieval games—especially physical games—were much less
formalized and rules-oriented than their modern counterparts and were
probably subject to regional and local variation; in this respect they
resembled modern playground games more than the games now played

as professional sports. It is therefore less important that the reconstructed rules be exactly correct, as long as they preserve the basic dynamic of the game.

Dice Games

Most of the excitement in these games comes from the betting. They are particularly amusing if you can provide yourself with a supply of medieval coins (see Appendix C). Details of medieval betting practices are sparse, but the modern conventions of similar games such as Craps are both workable and consistent with what we know of the medieval games. In all dice games, order of play can be determined by the roll of one die. The highest roll goes first, and ties roll again.

HAZARD

This was by far the most popular and enduring game at dice. Any number can play, forming a ring around the table or patch of ground where the dice are rolled and the bets are placed. The first player to cast the dice puts up the amount he is willing to bet, and any of the other players can wager against all or any part of the caster's bet, or against any remaining portion of it, at even odds. If two speak at once, the most recent loser takes precedence. The caster may at any time remove any part of his bet that has not been wagered against. As in modern Craps, you may also wish to allow side bets between any two players at any time on any outcome at mutually agreed odds. In an honest game, judging the correct odds to offer or accept on these side bets is the only element of skill in this kind of contest. Once a bet has been made and accepted, it can only be canceled by mutual consent. If the caster wins, he may retain the dice and declare a new center bet; if he loses, the dice pass to the next player on his left. New players should enter the game to the caster's right if possible and convenient.

There appear to have been two forms of this game, one played with three dice, the other with two. The three-dice version is found in a thirteenth-century Spanish treatise on games:

—The first player casts the dice. If the first cast is 15 or above or 5 or less, he wins and starts again.
—If the player casts a number from 6 to 14, that number becomes the opponent's "Chance." The player then rolls again.
—If the second cast is 15 or above or 5 or less, the player loses and passes the dice.
—If the second cast is between 6 and 14, that number becomes the player's Chance.

—The player then continues to cast until he either rolls the opponent's Chance and loses, or rolls his own Chance and wins.

The two-die version is described in a seventeenth-century treatise:

—The first player rolls two dice until he gets a "Main," which can be any number from 5 through 9. He then rolls again:
—On a 2 or 3, he loses (the former roll was known "ames-ace").
—If the Main is 5 or 9 and the player again rolls the Main, he wins. If he rolls an 11 or 12, he loses.
—If the Main is 6 or 8 and the player rolls the Main or a 12, he wins. If he rolls an 11, he loses.
—If the Main is 7 and the player rolls the Main or an 11, he wins. If he rolls a 12, he loses.
—Any other roll is called the "Mark," and the player continues to roll until he gets the Mark and wins, or gets the Main and loses.[9]

RAFFLE

This game is mentioned by Chaucer and described in a thirteenth-century Spanish treatise. Seventeenth-century sources imply a multiplayer game with all players putting in an equal stake. The caster throws until he gets doublets (two dice the same). He then throws the third die again and reckons the total of the three. The other players roll in turn in the same manner, and the highest score wins. If the score is tied, the game begins again with the pot carried over.[10]

PASSAGE

This game is attested from the early fifteenth century and described in the seventeenth. The caster throws three dice until he gets doublets (two dice the same). If the total of the three dice is under 10, he is "out" and loses; if over 10, he "passes" and wins. If the roll is 10, the dice pass to the other player but the pot is not collected.[11]

Board Games

CHESS

Medieval chess was somewhat different from the modern form. The form Chaucer probably played was Anglo-French Long Assize.[12] The moves of several pieces are different from those in the modern form:

King: Starts to right of Queen. On the King's first move (if not in check) he can move to any square he could reach in two moves, or

QKn1 or QKn2, provided he does not move through a space occupied by an opposing piece. This move cannot be used to capture a piece.

Queen: May only move one square diagonally. On her first move she too can go to any square she could reach in two moves, even if the intervening square is occupied; this move cannot be used to capture a piece.

Bishop: May move no more or less than two squares diagonally, but may jump over intervening pieces.

Pawn: As in the modern game, the pawn can capture *en passant*. It may only convert to a Queen upon reaching the final rank. On the pawn's first move as a Queen, the Queen's first move rules apply.

If one King has lost all his pieces, the game is over unless the opposing King also loses his last man on the next turn. A stalemate is considered a draw. This is a slower game than the modern version—more recent innovations were introduced specifically with the aim of speeding up play.

Fourteenth-century chess pieces were also somewhat different from their modern counterparts. Chess sets came in two forms, figurative and conventional. In figurative sets the Kings looked like kings, the Queens like queens, and so on. Surviving fourteenth-century French chessmen of this type are rather elegant in proportion but still well designed to stand up to rough handling, with a minimum of fragile projections. In conventional sets the pieces are stylized, as in most modern sets, although some of the conventions are different. For example, Bishops have a pair of upright horns, and Rooks a pair that curve downward. Other pieces are more like their modern form, although there are differences of detail and proportion.

TABLES

Backgammon as such had not yet been developed, but several forms of Tables are actually described in a fourteenth-century English manuscript.[13] The basic outlines of these games are similar to Backgammon. They typically involve two players, one sitting on side **a-l** of the board and moving towards point **x**; **a-f** is called his "entering table," **s-x** his "bearing table." The other player sits on side **m-x** and moves towards point **a**; **s-x** is his entering table, **a-f** his bearing table. At the beginning of the game, the pieces are set on certain points of the board. The players take turns rolling two or three dice, depending on the game. The roll of each die is assigned to a piece: on a roll of 6 and 5, one piece may be moved forward 6 points and another 5, or a single piece may be moved 6 and then 5. If a piece is left alone on a point and the opponent is able to move a man onto that point, the first piece is removed and must be played

in again onto the player's entering table. A point with more than one piece
on it cannot be landed on by the opponent and is said to be "doubled." A
player may not move any of his men until he has entered any that are
waiting off the board. No man may be borne from the board until all are in
the bearing table.

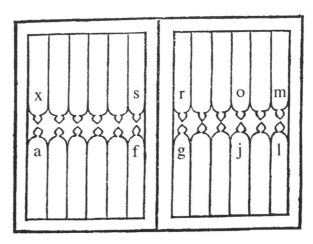

A fourteenth-century backgammon board (the letters have been added to help
explain the games) [Fiske].

Many of the games differ only in initial set-up, as suggested by these
three examples:

Imperial: Player 1 starts with 5 men on **f**, 5 on **g**, and 5 on **j**; his
opponent has 5 on **s**, 5 on **r**, and 5 on **o**. This game uses 3 dice.
Provincial: As Imperial, but Player 1 starts with 8 men on **f** and 7 on **g**,
Player 2 with 8 on **s** and 7 on **r**.
The English Game (*Ludus Anglicorum*): This was said to be the most
common form of Tables in England. Player 1 starts with all 15 pieces
on point **x**, and Player 2 has all his 15 on point **a**. This game uses 3
dice. A player's pieces cannot be doubled as long as they are on his
own side, so that a man cannot re-enter the board onto a point already
occupied by one of his men. In addition to the usual means of
winning, victory can be achieved by doubling the first 5 points on the
far side of the board while the opponent has one man in each of the 6
points in his table of entry, 8 on the last point of his bearing table, and
1 in his hand (this win is called "limpolding"). Another victory is
called "lurching," and occurs under the same circumstances, save that
the opponent has fewer than 8 men on the last point of his bearing
table.

MERELS

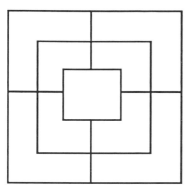

This was a very popular game; Merels boards were often placed on the reverse side of chessboards or on the outside of Tables boards. The game existed in several versions, including two that correspond to modern Nine Men's Morris and Six Men's Morris. In Nine-Man Merels, each player has nine pieces, each called a merel. Players draw lots to start and then take turns placing their merels on the board, one merel on each corner or intersection. After all merels are placed, the players take turns moving them. A merel can be moved to any adjacent corner or intersection, provided it is connected with the merel's current location by a line. A player who manages to place or move such that three of his merels come to be in a row removes one of his opponent's merels; and a player whose merels are so hedged in that they cannot move also has a merel removed by his opponent. To be in a row, the three merel must be connected by a single line. The last player on the board wins.

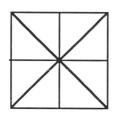

A simpler version of the game is Six-Man Merels. In this version, each player begins with three merels. Pieces are positioned and moved as in Nine Men's Merels, and the first player to get his three merels into a row wins.[14]

Cards

Although we know that playing cards appeared on the Continent in the last quarter of the fourteenth century, we have almost no idea of what games were played or what the rules were. The names of games do not appear until the fifteenth century, and rules were rarely written down prior to the late seventeenth century. The games included here are those mentioned in fifteenth-century sources.

All these games can be played with an ordinary modern deck. If you want something a bit more like a medieval deck, a Tarot deck is a good choice (leaving out the cards of the Major Arcana). In fact, it is even possible to buy Tarot decks that reproduce the appearance of surviving fifteenth-century decks.

ONE AND THIRTY

<u>Players</u>: 2 to 8

This is perhaps the simplest of traditional card games, and widely popular: games called Thirty-One appear frequently in literature from 1440 onwards in all of Western Europe. It is also the ancestor of modern Blackjack.

Players ante into the pot. The cards are cut for the deal, and the lowest card deals; the deal rotates clockwise among the players thereafter. Each player is dealt three cards. Next, each player in turn may ask the dealer to deal him cards, attempting to come as close as possible to 31 without going over—face cards count 10, and all others according to the number of their pips. Once all players are finished, the cards are turned up and reckoned. A player who has exactly 31 wins double the pot. If no player hits 31 exactly, the highest hand under 31 wins the pot. The eldest hand (i.e. the hand closest to the dealer's left) wins all ties.[15]

KARNOEFFEL

<u>Players</u>: 4 (partners)

The German game of Karnoeffel is the oldest documented card game, attested as early as 1426.[16] In the description below, the court cards in each suit are the King (K), Over (O), and Under (U). Depending on the deck, the Knight or Queen can serve as Over (the other being discarded), the Knave (Jack) as Under. Aces are discarded.

Players ante into the pot, and five cards are dealt to each. Opposite players are partners, and each side tries to win the most tricks. Each player's first card is dealt face up, and the lowest ranking of them (using the normal order: K O U 10 9 8 7 6 5 4 3 2) establishes a quasi-trump suit. If there are ties, use the suit dealt first for trump.

The eldest player (i.e., on the dealer's left) leads by playing a card, and each player does likewise in turn, proceeding clockwise. Players need not follow suit (i.e., play a card of the suit led by the first player), and partners may discuss between them what card to play. When each has played, the trick is taken by the highest card of the suit led, or by the highest trump if any are played. In plain suits the ranking of cards is normal, from King down to deuce. In the quasi-trump suit, the following cards are able to trump:

Card	Name	Rank
trump Under	Karnoeffel	beats any other cards
7 of trumps	the Devil	beats any cards except the Karnoeffel, but only if led
6 of trumps	the Pope	beats all plain suit cards
2 of trumps	the Emperor	beats all plain suit cards
3 of trumps	the Over-taker	beats all plain suit cards except Kings
4 of trumps	the Under-taker	beats all plain suit cards except Kings and Overs
5 of trumps	the Suit-taker	beats all plain suit cards except face cards

The other cards in the quasi-trump suit (i.e., the K, O, 10, 9, 8) do not trump—they act as a normal suit. The seven of trumps (the Devil) beats all other cards (except the Karnoeffel) only if it is the first card led to a trick, and it may not be led to the first trick. It will not beat any card in any other circumstance—it is thus second highest if led, and lowest otherwise. This gives the following order in the trump suit: U, (7), 6, 2, K, 3, O, 4, 5, 10, 9, 8, (7).

Play continues until either side has taken three tricks, at which point they collect the pot, and a new deal begins.

GLIC, POCHSPIEL

Players: 3 or more

Pochspiel, or Bockspiel, appears in the records as early as 1441 in Strasburg, Alsace, and regularly thereafter in other German-speaking areas. Glic appears first in 1454 in France and seems to be virtually the same game. Other names used for the same game are Boeckels, Poque, Bocken, and Bogel; the name is the ultimate source of modern Poker. Even without surviving rules, the names can be recognized as belonging to the same game by their playing boards—a number of brightly painted boards survive from the sixteenth century.[17]

Pochspiel is played with a board, usually with eight compartments or spaces, labeled Ace, King, Queen, Knave, Ten, Marriage, Sequence, and Poch (a board can be improvised by writing with chalk on a piece of wood). Some of the earliest boards omitted the Marriage and Sequence spaces, or substituted Over and Under for Queen and Knave. First the players place stakes in each compartment except Poch. This can be done starting at the dealer, with each player in sequence putting a single coin into a compartment until one coin has been put in each. Five cards are then dealt to each player, and the top remaining card is turned up for trump.

There are three separate phases to a round of Pochspiel. The first phase is a "sweepstakes." Anyone who holds the Ace of trump wins the stakes in the Ace compartment, and likewise for the King, Queen, Knave, and Ten compartments. Marriage is won by the player holding the King and Queen of trump (who also wins the stakes in the King and Queen compartments). The Sequence compartment is won by the player who holds the 7-8-9 of trump. If any compartment is not claimed, the stakes in it remain for subsequent hands.

The second phase is a betting phase, like Poker, and focuses on the Poch compartment (so called from the German word *pochen*, to brag). The winning hand is that with the best combination. Four of a kind beats three of a kind, three of a kind beats a pair, and a pair beats a hand without a pair. Higher valued cards beat lower ones in the same class (i.e., a pair of Kings would beat a pair of sixes but would be beaten by three Knaves). Each player in turn may put a stake into the Poch compartment. Other players may see it, raise it, pass, or fold. When the betting returns to the first player, he may bet again. You may want to set a limit on the total bet—say, 12 pence on a 1 penny stake. Betting stops only when every player has passed or folded. When betting stops, if only one player remains he wins the stakes in the Poch compartment. If two or more players remain (having all bet the same amount), the winner is the one with the best hand.

The third phase involves playing cards in a sequence, building up to 31. This is similar to modern Cribbage: each player in turn lays down a card so that the total of the cards laid does not exceed 31. When no one can play a card and remain under 31, each player must pay one penny to the person who laid the last card. Then the person who laid the last card plays the first card of the next sequence. As soon as one player runs out of cards, all the players who have cards remaining must pay him one penny for each card they still have remaining in their hands, and the game begins again.

Physical Games

BASE

The rules for this game are first recorded in the seventeenth century. A number of players are divided into two sides. Each side has a designated Base and a designated Prison. One player on each side touches the Base, a second player touches him, a third touches the second, and so on. One of the outermost players "leads out" by leaving contact with his chain. The outermost player on the other side may chase him; if he does, the new outermost player on the first side may chase him, and so on. A player caught by his pursuer is taken to his pursuer's Prison, where he begins a chain as before. A player who can reach any of his imprisoned teammates without being caught releases them, and they may walk untroubled back to their Base. A player who reaches his own Base cannot be caught.[18]

FOOTBALL

Equipment:

 —1 Football (this would have been round, probably a bit smaller than a soccer ball, and made of an inflated bladder encased in a leather covering)
 —2 Goals (e.g., two pairs of stakes set up at opposite sides of the field)

The rules for this game are first recorded in the seventeenth century. Two sides are chosen, and separate to their respective sides of the field. A third party throws the ball out into the center, and each side tries to kick it through the opponent's goal. After each goal, the ball can be thrown out again, or given to the side scored against.

A ball game, probably football [Ashdown].

The game Cambok was similar in outline, except that the ball was smaller and harder and had to be driven with sticks comparable to modern field hockey sticks. The ball might be made of leather or sturdy canvas stuffed with cloth (the cloth might be wrapped in twine for extra hardness).[19]

BOWLS/QUOITS

<u>Equipment:</u>

—2 Wooden Balls for each player, about the size of an apple (each pair
   of balls should be color-coded to distinguish them from other
   pairs)
—1 Mistress (a wooden cone, a stake, or some other object that can be
   set upright in the ground) or 1 'Jack' (a ball smaller than the
   others, preferably of a bright and contrasting color)

The rules for this game are first recorded in the seventeenth century. A
point is designated as the casting spot, and the Mistress is set up on the
pitch some distance away (two Mistresses can be set up, each serving as
the other's casting spot, which will save walking back and forth); if using a
Jack, the first player casts it out onto the pitch. Each player in turn casts
one ball onto the pitch, trying to get it as close to the Jack or Mistress as
possible; then each in turn casts the second ball. The player whose ball is
closest at the end scores 1 point, 2 points if he has the two closest balls. A
ball touching the target counts double. Balls can be knocked about by
other balls, and the Jack can also be repositioned in this way. Play is
normally until one player reaches 5 or 7.

Quoits is played in the same manner, save that the bowls are replaced
by quoits, large flat stones or pieces of metal, and the Mistress by an iron
stake, or Hob, driven into the ground (or the Jack by a small quoit).[20]

Bowling at a stake [Strutt].

KAILES

Equipment:

—6-8 Pins (wooden cones or other objects that can be made to stand
   upright without fixing them into the ground). One of these should
   be taller than the others; it is called the King Pin.
—1 Casting Stick

No rules for this game survive, but some help is afforded by
seventeenth-century rules for the game of Nine-Pins, a close relative
played with a ball rather than a casting stick. A casting spot is marked,
and the players set up the pins some distance away in a row, a square, or a
circle, with the King Pin in the middle. One player then throws the casting
stick at the pins and scores as many points as he can knock over pins. The
King Pin is worth 10 if it can be knocked over by itself, but only 1 if any
other pins are knocked over. The pins are then set up again for the second
player. The first player to reach 31 wins; a player who goes over 31 goes
back to 15 but gets another cast.

Kailes [Wright].

SONGS

Very little popular music has survived from Chaucer's lifetime; the songs
that follow include some from fifteenth-century manuscripts, in some
cases with modern melodies.

ANGELUS AD VIRGINEM

Text and music: Fourteenth-century [Furnivall (1902), 687-88].

An- ge- lus ad vir- gi- nem sub- in- trans in----- con-
Vir- gi- nis for- mi- di- nem de- mul-cens in------ quit
Ga- bri- el from hea-ven's king sent to the mai---- den
Brought her bliss- ful ti--------- dings and fair he did----- her

cla- ve A- ve re- gi- na vir------ gi- num
"A- ve!
sweet---- "Hail be thou, full of grace---- a- right,
greet-----

Cœ- li ter- ræ que do----- mi- num con------
For God's own son, this hea- ven-ly light, for-------

ci- pi- es et pa- ri- es------- in- tac----------- ta sa-
love of man will man be- come--- and take-------------- flesh

lu- tem ho------- mi- num tu-------- por- ta cœ------- li
of the mai----- den bright, man---- kind free for------- to

fac----------- ta me- de- la cri------- mi- num."
make-------------- of sin and de------- vil's might."

"Quomodo conciperem quae virum non cognovi?
Qualiter infringerem quod firma mente vovi?"
"Spiritus sancti gratia perficiet haec omnia,
Ne timeas sed gaudeas, secura quod castimonia
Manebit in te pura Dei potentia."

Ad haec virgo nobilis respondens inquit ei,
"Ancilla sum humilis omnipotentis Dei;
Tibi cœlesti nuntio tanti secreti conscio,
Consentiens et cupiens videre factum quod audio
Parata sum parere Dei consilio."

Eia mater Domini quæ pacem reddidisti
Angelis et homini cum Christum genuisti;
Tuum exora filium ut se nobis propitium
Exhibeat et deleat peccata, præstans auxilium
Vita frui beata post hoc exilium.

Mildly to him answered then the maiden ever mild,
"How should I, untouched by men, be now to bear a child?"
The angel said, "Now dread thee nought,
Through Holy Ghost shall it be wrought,
This very thing, whereof tidings I bring,
Mankind shall be rebought
Through thy most sweet childing
And out of pain be brought."

When the maiden understood and had the angel heard,
Mildly then and mild of mood the angel she answered,
"Our Lord's handmaiden I am in this,
His that in heaven eternal is,
By way of me, fulfilled be what you say,
That I, since it His will is,
A maid contrary to way
Of motherhood have such bliss."

Maiden, mother without peer, with mercy sweet and kind,
Pray to Him that chose thee here, with Whom thou grace did find,
That He forgive us sin and mistake
and clean of every guilt us make
And heaven's bliss, when our time is to perish
Us give, for thy sweet sake,
That we Him here may cherish
and He us to Him take.

This religious song was extremely popular in the fourteenth century—
the merry scholar Nicholas in Chaucer's *The Miller's Tale* sings it. It is a
rare example of surviving popular music of the period. It commemorates
the Annunciation, the occasion on which the Archangel Gabriel
announced to the Virgin Mary that she was to bear Jesus. The English
version is modernized from a translation found in a manuscript of around
1300.

The Latin would have been pronounced with more or less the same
sounds as in Spanish. The letters *c* and *g* are hard (as in *cat, get*) before
consonants and before *a*, *o*, and *u*, soft (as in *cedar, general*) before *i*, *e*, *æ*,
and *œ*. *Æ* and *œ* would be pronounced as *e*. Otherwise each vowel in a
combination is pronounced; *tuum* is pronounced *tu-um*; *eia* is pronounced
ey-a. The combinations *-tium, -tia* and *-tio* would be pronounced as *-ci-um,
-ci-a, -ci-o*.

KYRIE ELEYSON

Text: Fifteenth-century [Greene #457]; Music: T. Postle.

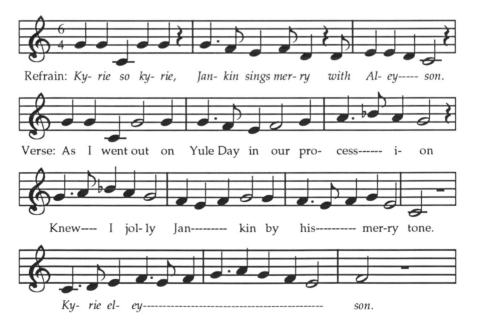

Refrain: *Kyrie, so Kyrie, Jankin sings merry with Aleyson.*

As I went out on Yule Day in our procession
Knew I jolly Jankin by his merry tone
    Kyrie eleyson

Jankin began the office on the Yule Day
And yet me think it does me good, so merry did he say
   "Kyrie eleyson"

Jankin read the pistle full fair and full well
And yet me think it does me good, as ever have I soul
   Kyrie eleyson

Jankin at the Sanctus cracked a merry note
And yet me think it does me good; I paid for his coat
   Kyrie eleyson

Jankin cracked notes a hundred to a knot
And yet he hacked them smaller than herbs in a pot
   Kyrie eleyson

Jankin at the Agnus carried the Paxbred,
He winked but said nothing, and on my foot he tread
   Kyrie eleyson

Benedicamus Domino, Christ from shame me shield!
Deo Gracias, also; alas, I go with child.
   Kyrie eleyson

This song is the charming lament of a woman who has fallen in love with a minor clergyman   Jankin was the proverbial name for a cleric. The Jankin of this song is probably only in minor orders, and not sworn to a life of celibacy, but he knows that he should not be eyeing female parishioners during Mass: his treading on the woman's foot, like the wink, is a sly form of flirtation.

"Kyrie eleison" is one of the chants in the ceremony of the Mass—it is Greek for "Lord have mercy"; but "Alison" was also one of the most common names for women in medieval England. A play on words is obviously intended.

The music is modern but in a medieval style; the refrain can be repeated for full effect. The meter of the text is fairly loose.

procession: a religious procession
office: the ceremony of the Mass
pistle: an "epistle," one of the letters of the apostles included in the New
       Testament, read aloud as part of the Mass
Sanctus: one of the chants in the Mass
Agnus: one of the chants in the Mass
Paxbred: a sacred tablet used in the Mass

Benedicamus Domino: "Let us bless the Lord"
Deo Gracias: "Thanks be to God"

DOLL THY ALE

Text: Fifteenth-century [Greene # 423]; Music: Traditional.

Ale makes many a man to stick upon a briar,
Ale makes many a man to slumber by the fire,
Ale makes many a man to wallow in the mire.
[Chorus] *So doll, doll, doll thy ale, doll, doll thy ale.*

Ale makes many a man to stumble on a stone,
Ale makes many a man to stagger drunken home,
Ale makes many a man to break his bone.

Ale makes many a man to brandish forth his knife,
Ale makes many a man to make great strife,
Ale makes many a man to beat his wife.

Ale makes many a man shed tears upon his cheeks,
Ale makes many a man to lie in the streets,
Ale makes many a man to wet his sheets.

Ale makes many a man to stumble at the blocks,
Ale makes many a man to break his head with knocks,
Ale makes many a man to languish in the stocks.

Ale makes many a man to run across the fallows,
Ale makes many a man swear by God and All Hallows,
Ale makes many a man to swing upon the gallows.

All Hallows: All Saints

THE FALSE FOX

Text: Fourteenth-century [Robbins (1952) #49]; Music: T. Postle.

The false----- fox came un- to our croft, and
so-------- our geese full fast he------- sought, With how-----
------------------- fox------------ how! and hey------ fox
hey! Come no more un- to---------- our croft to
bear-------- our geese----------- a--------- way!
[2nd part:] a---------------- way!

The false fox came unto our sty,
And took our geese there by and by.

The false fox came unto our yard,
And there he made the geese afeared.

The false fox came unto our gate,
And took our geese there where they sat.

The false fox came to our hall door,
And shrove our geese there on the floor.

The false fox came into our hall,
Absolved our geese both great and small.

The false fox came unto our coop,
And there he made our geese to stoop.

He took a goose fast by the neck,
And then the goose began to queck.

The goodwife came out in her smock,
And at the fox she threw her rock.

The goodman came out with his flail,
And smote the fox upon the tail.

He threw a goose upon his back,
And forth he went then with his pack.

The goodman swore if that he might,
He would him slay ere it were night.

The false fox went into his den,
And there he was full merry then.

He came again the very next week,
And took away both hen and chick.

The goodman said unto his wife,
"This false fox liveth a merry life."

The false fox came upon a day,
And with our geese he made affray.

He took a goose fast by the neck,
And made that goose say "Wheckumqueck!"

"I pray thee fox," she did entreat,
"Take of my feathers but not of my feet!"

The fox was a constant threat to the rural household's livestock and was the subject of numerous stories and songs. In this example, the fox is implicitly compared to a priest—he "shrives" and "absolves" the geese, an allusion to the sacrament of Confession and Absolution that priests adminstered to their parishioners. This was a popular image, embodied in a medieval proverb: "When the fox preaches, look to your geese."

The goodwife's "rock" in this song is not a stone, but an archaic word for the distaff used in spinning linen. "Queck" was the Middle English word for the sound made by geese and ducks.

BRING US IN GOOD ALE

Text: Fifteenth-century [Greene #422];
Music: Fifteenth-century [Chappell 42].

Bring us in no beef, for that is full of bones, but bring in ale e-nough, for that---- goes down at once! *And bring us in good ale, good ale, and bring us in good ale! and for our dear La-dy's love, bring---- us in good ale!*

Bring us in no bacon, for that is passing fat,
But bring us in good ale, and bring us enough of that.

Bring us in no mutton, for that is tough and lean,
Nor bring us in no tripes, for they be seldom clean.

Bring us in no eggs, for there are many shells,
But bring us in good ale, and give us nothing else.

Bring us in no capons, for that is often dear,
Nor bring us in no ducks, for they wallow in the mere.

This song offers a good survey of some of the staples of the medieval diet, including ale itself, the unhopped form of beer that was the standard form of liquid refreshment.

DANCE

There survive no detailed descriptions of dance before the fifteenth century, so any reconstruction of fourteenth-century dance must rely on visual evidence in comparison with later treatises on dancing and with more recent folk-dancing traditions. The reconstructions offered here cannot be a precise re-creation of fourteenth-century dances, but they appear to preserve the general shape and feel these dances would have had.[21]

The Forms

The typical fourteenth-century dance was a circle or chain dance, which we can call a "carole." This term was used in the Middle Ages to describe dances of this sort, especially if the music was sung. The reconstructed carole may be done in two forms, here called the "single bransle" (pronounced "brawl") and the "farandole."

SINGLE BRANSLE

The single bransle is a style of dance described in a sixteenth-century treatise. It is one of the most archaic dance forms in Europe—versions are still danced in places from the Faeroe Islands to the Balkans. The dancers form a circle or a chain. They may be all men, all women, or a mixed group, not necessarily of even numbers. There are a number of possible grips: the dancers may link hands, link hands and elbows, or hold onto kerchiefs or garlands. The dance is very simple: it consists of two steps to the left and one to the right in time with the music, repeated throughout the dance. This type of carole has no figures and relies for its interest on the song or music, the elegance or spirit of the dancers, and the interaction among them.

FARANDOLE

In the farandole type of carole, the dancers form a chain, linking up as in the single bransle. The dance consists of a simple walking step, moving to the left. The dancers follow the leader, who decides at will to begin any of the following figures:

The Snail: The leader leads the chain around into a circle, then spirals inward towards the center. Once there, he may turn back and spiral out again, or he and the second dancer may lift their joined hands to make an arch under which the rest of the dancers pass (without anyone dropping hands) until they are all out of the spiral.

Threading the Needle: The leader turns to face the second dancer, who drops hands with the third, and the two make an arch perpendicular to the direction of the chain. The third dancer passes under the arch. He may choose to become the leader and lead the entire chain under the arch. In this case the previous leader takes the free hand of the last dancer with his left as he passes underneath the arch, and passes under himself, so that the second dancer becomes last. Otherwise, the third dancer may form an arch with the fourth, the rest following suit. In this case, the leader takes the last dancer's hand as before, and the other odd-numbered dancers follow suit.

The Arches: The leader doubles back to the space between the second and third dancers. They raise their joined hands, as do all the other dancers. The leader passes under the arch, then backwards under the arch between the third and fourth dancers, then forward under the arch between the fourth and fifth, and so on, pulling the rest of the dancers through behind him.

The Hey: The leader turns to face the second dancer, dropping hands, and the rest of the dancers drop hands too. The leader and the second dancer take right hands and pass each other, then the leader and the third dancer pass each other taking left hands. Then the leader passes the fourth dancer taking right hands, while the second dancer turns around and passes the third taking left hands, and so on. When any dancer comes to the end of the line, he turns around and gives hands with the dancer coming towards him, and the chain continues until the original order is restored.

Music

The carole may be danced to any music with a strong and lively beat, either in a duple or a quick treble time. The music for the carole may be either vocal or instrumental. If the music is vocal, it is important to remember the singer's need for air. Either the dance should be slow enough not to leave the singer breathless, or the singing should be done by several people, or the singer should not actually dance. The singer may accompany herself on a tambourine (it seems to have been more common for the music to be sung by women than by men). Among the songs in this book, "Angelus ad Virginem," "Bring Us In Good Ale," and "Doll Thy Ale" would be suitable for any carole; "Kyrie Eleison" would be suitable for a single bransle type of carole.

Ladies dancing—the music is provided by a singer who accompanies herself on the drum. Italian, c. 1365 (Andrea Buonatuti da Firenze, fresco from the Spanish Chapel [detail], Santa Maria Novella, Florence) [McLean].

Glossary

acolyte A cleric in minor orders who assisted a priest or deacon in his duties.

alderman A member of a city council.

ale A form of beer made without hops.

apprentice A young person learning a craft or trade.

archdeacon A church officer assigned to assist the bishop in administering his bishopric, having especial authority for church courts.

aristocracy The second estate of medieval political theory, the warrior class. The term is a modern one: medieval English had no clear-cut word for this class as a whole, although the adjective "gentle" was applied to people of this class.

astrolabe An astronomical instrument.

Ave Maria A formulaic prayer to the Virgin Mary, deriving from the words spoken by the Archangel Gabriel to Mary announcing the conception of Christ.

banneret See **knight banneret**.

bascinet A form of close-fitting helmet.

brazier A vessel for holding coals to provide heat.

breech A man's undergarment, vaguely comparable to modern boxer shorts.

canon law The body of law administered by the Church, pertaining to such topics as morality, religious observation, and marriage.

carding The process of brushing wool so that the fibers are free of tangles and run in a single direction.

champion settlement A system of agricultural organization in which each holding consists of strips of land scattered about a village, as contrasted with **woodland settlement**.

citizen An inhabitant of a town having the full rights and privileges of the town.

coat-armor A military cloth overgarment, typically padded and quilted and sometimes bearing heraldic symbols.

coathardie A close-fitting civilian coat.

cob-iron An iron supporter for a spit.

coif A small, close-fitting head covering made of fabric or leather, sometimes padded for military use; also, a "mail-coif," a comparable head covering made of mail, covering the head, neck, and upper shoulders.

commons The third estate of medieval political theory, those obliged to work for a living.

communion The religious ceremony in which the communicants receive wine and/or bread as the blood and body of Christ.

confession The religious observation in which a person confesses his or her sins to a priest or friar.

confirmation The religious ceremony by which a young person is fully admitted as a member of the church.

cottar The smallest sort of landholding commoner, holding insufficient land to support a family without doing additional labor.

couter A piece of armor protecting the elbow.

Credo The formulaic statement of Christian belief, also called the Creed.

cuirbouilli Leather made pliable by soaking or boiling, molded into shape, and hardened by exposure to low heat. It was commonly used as material for armor.

cuisse A piece of armor protecting the thighs.

dagging A notched or zig-zag edge on fabric or armor.

dean A church administrator subordinate to an archdeacon, or in charge of the chapter of clergymen at a cathedral.

demi-greave A small piece of armor protecting the upper shin.

doublet A fabric undergarment, sometimes padded and quilted, designed to provide extra warmth and support for the hose; also, a similar military undergarment providing extra protection as well as support for the arm and leg armor.

ember days The Wednesday, Friday, and Saturday after the first Sunday in Lent (six weeks before Easter), after Whitsunday (six weeks after Easter), after Holy Cross Day (September 14), and after St. Lucy's Day (December 13). These days were observed with fasting and penance.

estate One of the three divisions of society according to medieval theory (clergy, aristocracy, commons).

ewer A water-jug.

extreme unction The religious ceremony preparing a person for death.

fallow field A field left idle for a season to allow it to recover for future planting.

franklin The most prosperous form of landholding free commoner.

friar A member of a mendicant order of regular clergy. Like monks, friars were subject to the rule of their order; unlike monks, they were not allowed to own personal property.

Galen The ancient Greek physiologist who formulated the theory of the Four Humors.

gentle See **aristocracy**.

gesso A solution of gypsum and glue used to seal a surface for painting.

greave A piece of armor protecting the shin.

groom A male common servant ranking below a yeoman and above a page.

guild The modern term for medieval organizations which regulated the practice of a craft or trade in a particular town; in medieval England they were known as "misteries."

gusset A small piece of fabric inserted into a garment for additional room, or a piece of mail inserted to cover a vulnerable point in a harness of armor.

habergeon A mail shirt.

hainselin A kind of short jacket.

harness An assembly of armor.

holding See **landholding**

hose Cloth leggings, reaching to the groin on men and to the knee on women.

husbandman A small but self-sufficient landholding commoner; also, a general term for a farmer.

journeyman A craftsman or tradesman who has completed apprenticeship but does not possess a business of his own, working instead for others.

knight bachelor An ordinary knight.

knight banneret A class of knight ranking above an ordinary knight bachelor.

lame An articulated band of armor, comparable to the individual shell pieces on a lobster's tail.

landholding A parcel or quantity of land rented to a holder in accordance with the custom associated with that landholding.

latten A copper alloy, of variable composition, but sometimes containing zinc, tin, and lead.

laver A special water jug designed for washing.

lay peerage The secular aristocracy of the House of Lords in Parliament, as opposed to the Bishops and Abbots who also sat in the House of Lords.

lower house The House of Commons in Parliament.

lye An alkaline solution obtained by percolating water through wood ashes.

mail A form of armor consisting of small interlocked rings of iron.

man-at-arms A fully armored soldier, typically equipped with a horse.

Martinmas The feast of St. Martin, November 11.

master A fully qualified craftsman or tradesman having his own shop.

master of arts A graduate of a university.

minor orders A status of clergyman not fully a priest; clerks in minor orders did not take a vow of celibacy.

order An organization of regular clergy (such as monks, friars, or nuns) belonging to a single structure and following a common rule of religious life.

ordination The religious ceremony by which a person is admitted into the priesthood.

page The lowest rank of servant, usually a young boy.

parson The priest of a parish church.

Pater Noster The Lord's Prayer, especially in its Latin form.

pauldron The piece of armor covering the shoulder.

poleine The piece of armor covering the knee.

poll tax A "head tax" on every person in England, first levied in 1377.

pommel The knob on the end of a sword-grip.

pottage Stew.

prior A monastic official ranking just below an abbot, either assisting the abbot in running the monastery or administering a priory, a less substantial version of the monastery.

quillons The lateral projections on a sword, designed to protect the hand.

reader A cleric in minor orders who read the biblical lessons for church services.

rector The person or institution receiving the income associated with a parish church.

regular clergy Clergy subject to a specific rule of religious life, such as monks, friars and nuns, in contrast with **secular clergy**.

rerebrace The piece of armor covering the upper arm.

rule A particular system of life and organization for an order of regular clergy.

sabaton The piece of armor covering the foot.

secular clergy Clergymen such a priests, whose primary function is to serve the religious needs of the public.

slop A kind of loose outer garment, which might be "cutted," reaching only to the hips.

splint A style of armor consisting of long strips of metal riveted to cloth or leather.

squire A man of aristocratic estate ranking below a knight; also, an aristocratic assistant to a knight.

surcoat A civilian or military overgarment, which might be loose or tailored.

tabard A loose, poncho-shaped overgarment, typically with flaring sleeves and skirt.

tablet-weaving A style of weaving in which the "warp" or lengthwise threads are manipulated with small pierced cards.

tonlet A horizontal piece of armor skirting attached to a breastplate to protect the abdomen.

tonsure The distinctive hair style of the clergy, involving the shaving of the crown of the head and cropping the rest of the hair.

trivet A three-legged gridiron for cooking over a fire.

vambrace The piece of armor covering the forearm.

vicar A priest who administers a parish church for an absentee rector.

villein An unfree common landholder, subject to more feudal taxes, services, and restrictions than a free landholder.

weft In weaving, the thread that is passed back and forth horizontally through the longitudinal, or "warp," threads.

woodland settlement A system of agricultural organization in which each holding is a discrete parcel of land, as contrasted with **champion settlement**.

yeoman The highest rank of male common servants; in the fourteenth-century the name was coming to be applied to the upper rank of landholding free commoners as well, replacing the older term **franklin**.

Appendix A: The Medieval Event

As well as being a general introduction to daily life in the fourteenth century, this book is intended to facilitate medieval living history. We have included enough information to allow a group to organize a living history event, or to allow an individual to participate in such an event. The suggestions in this appendix are geared towards a living history event, but elements will apply equally to medieval fairs or feasts, school pageants, and other sorts of activities in which there is some attempt to recreate a historical milieu.

If you think you might be interested in trying medieval living history, the easiest route is to find an already existing organization. There are relatively few medieval living history organizations in North America; all of those known to the authors at the time of writing this book are listed in Appendix B. There are a few more overseas, particularly in England, although most of them focus on the fifteenth century.

Among the organizations in North America involved in medieval living history, the Society for Creative Anachronism (SCA) is by far the largest, with chapters all over the continent and a fair number abroad. The SCA covers a broad temporal scope (roughly AD 500-1600) and accommodates very diverse interests, some of them oriented towards history, others not. The educational quality of the SCA's activities is therefore quite variable. However, the SCA does provide a context for many people with a genuine interest in the Middle Ages to pursue their interests and meet others of like mind, and it has helped foster a good deal of valuable research, particularly in the field of medieval crafts.

TAKING PART

For the individual preparing to take part in a living history event, the first step will be to choose what sort of person you will be representing and to assemble an appropriate kit of personal equipment. For the beginner, we strongly suggest someone towards the lower end of the social scale, as this makes the equipment easier and cheaper. The higher your social status, the richer and more elaborate your personal property would be, the more servants you would have, and the more sophisticated your entertainments.

The chapter on clothing is designed to provide all necessary information to assemble a basic outfit. For a man, an outwardly plausible outfit would require at least **headgear** (probably a hood), a **kirtle, hose**, and **shoes**. For a woman, it would require **headgear**, a **kirtle**, and **shoes**. Both men and women might also want a **belt** and **purse**. Depending on the circumstances of the event, you may also need to provide basic eating equipment, all of which is described and/or illustrated in the text. This would mean a **bowl, knife, spoon**, and **drinking vessel**. To assist in assembling equipment, Appendix C lists suppliers of goods that are useful for medieval living history.

You will probably have more fun at the event if you look at the section on entertainments and, if possible, practice some of them beforehand. Many can be learned on the spot, but the more you know ahead of time the more comfortable you are likely to feel.

You will probably also get more out of the re-enactment if you devote some time to the person inside the clothes. What would you have known or believed? What was your place in society? This book should help in addressing some of these questions. For a more intimate view of how medieval people saw themselves, you might take a look at some of the books they wrote. The section on Further Reading in the Bibliography offers some useful suggestions.

ORGANIZING

If you are actually organizing a medieval living history event, you will need to attend to the following:

1. *Define and Disseminate the Goals*: The first step in organizing an actual event is to define its purposes. The following discussion addresses the issue from scratch; but if you are operating within an existing living history organization, your choices will naturally be shaped by the traditions of your group.

You may want to hold a fourteenth-century aristocratic tournament with twenty knights on a side, perfectly equipped in every detail, but unless you are incredibly wealthy or immensely fortunate in your choice of friends, something is going to have to give. You can be forgiving in the degree of authenticity you require in the knights' equipment, or perhaps a small deed of arms with three men-at-arms on a side will suffice. These are less ambitious goals, but you will still only be able to achieve them in a reasonable time if some of your participants are experienced re-enactors who already have some of the necessary equipment.

Even if you don't have a stable of armored knights at your disposal, there are plenty of viable alternatives. You might decide to hold a medieval picnic, with less expensive amusements, or a village festival, or a gathering of pilgrims at an inn. Your choice of setting should reflect your goals and resources.

So should the standards of authenticity you decide to set. The more accuracy you require, the more authentic your experience will be, but the smaller the number of people able or willing to take part. This is an important factor, since a larger number of participants will generally tend to add to the energy of the event.

You may choose to have somewhat easier standards for beginners or for your entire group while it is getting started. Some groups have several levels of acceptability in permitted items. Some things may be perfectly acceptable. Others are tolerated, but the owner is expected to replace them as soon as possible. Yet others would be allowed on a one-time basis, but permission would have to be renewed for each use.

You must make your own decisions about what level of authenticity to require, but here are some suggestions. Clothing of the wrong color, the wrong shape, or the wrong cut is more likely to spoil an effect than anything else. One basic test is to ask "Does it look right from ten feet away?". Some areas require a disproportionate amount of time or expense to bring up to the standard of the rest of the costume. Shoes are one example. You might want to be a little more flexible there. Not all inaccuracies are equally grievous; one that is unobtrusive, or dictated by overwhelming necessity, may be less a matter of concern.

If you expect people to meet a certain standard of authenticity, that standard needs to be clearly articulated. We recommend compiling a list of "authoritative sources," people or texts one can turn to as a guide for how to prepare for the event. A source need not be perfect to be considered authoritative: it need only represent a degree of authenticity that you consider adequate for the purposes of your re-enactment. This book is in part written to provide an authoritative source of this sort.

Another question you will want to bear in mind is that of "playing character" or "playing persona". Not everyone is good at this kind of theatrics, and few people can keep it up for extended periods of time. It will help if you enunciate clear and realistic ideas as to what you expect in this direction.

Above all, we strongly recommend honesty: be absolutely clear about what you are doing. There is nothing inherently wrong with inauthenticity except when it gives people a misleading impression. For this reason, you should hold yourself to a higher standard if you are doing some sort of re-enactment for the public. Making compromises when you are amusing yourself is one thing, but the general public is less likely to recognize the difference between historical accuracy and practical compromises.

Always remember that complete accuracy is never really possible. Historical authenticity is best understood as a process, not a state. We could never actually *be* medieval people; at best, we can only strive to approach that goal without ever attaining it. At any given living history event, we are representing the Middle Ages only to the best of our current knowledge. If this is done well, we may actually achieve an atmosphere that does reflect historical reality, but we should never delude ourselves into believing that an experience of a living history event is tantamount to an experience of the past.

Whatever you decide, make sure that everyone knows what is expected of them. Writing up some sort of description of the event and circulating it among prospective participants is always a good idea.

2. *Provide for Creature Comforts*: No event can hope to work without certain essentials, notably food, drink, utensils, seating, and shelter. Food in particular can absorb a lot of effort. If your organizing group is small, we recommend keeping it as simple as possible, choosing dishes that will provide the greatest satisfaction for the least preparation unless some member has a desire to explore medieval cooking. You may want to rely on foods that can be prepared several days ahead of time.

3. *Define the Space*: As medieval buildings are few and far between, some effort is required to make the setting feel right. In the absence of a medieval hall, an outdoor event is one possibility, especially if you can provide some sort of medieval pavilion. If your event is held outdoors, don't overlook the importance of shade—and have an alternate plan in case of rain.

If the event is held indoors in a less-than-medieval setting, it will help if you can furnish the site with medieval household accoutrements of some sort. Wall hangings, tablecloths, banners, and candlelight can help to disguise the intrusions of the modern world (decorated wall hangings can be made with relative ease by tracing medieval designs onto a transparency and projecting them onto fabric with an overhead projector).

In any case, but particularly if you will be meeting outside, give some thought to climate and weather. In most parts of North America, seasonal differences are much more extreme than anywhere in northern Europe. If you want to be comfortable dressed like a medieval Englishman, you might want to schedule an outdoor event as early in spring or as late in fall as weather will permit. Another possibility is to set the event in southern France, parts of which were in English hands throughout the fourteenth century.

You will have a hard time making everything authentic, so it pays to concentrate your efforts. It is better to have half the site all medieval than the whole site half medieval. Clear boundaries can help keep the modern world from spilling into the re-creation. It helps to define which particular portions of the event space are to be "authentic." It is also useful to demark the beginning and end of the re-creation by some pre-arranged signal. Someone might welcome the guests at the official beginning and thank them at the end, or a special banner might be raised during the "authentic" portion of the event. If the event will be a long one, it may help to have "authentic" periods set off from "informal" ones. An entire day is a long time to stay in character as a medieval person, or to manage without eyeglasses, but many people can manage it for an hour or two at a time.

4. *Arrange Entertainments*: If the event is not fun, it will not succeed. In this book we have attempted to assemble a good selection of easily re-created entertainments. They will not only provide enjoyment and diversion but will make it easier to experience the event as a medieval person. Talking or consciously acting like a person from the fourteenth century requires a positive effort of will,

but taking part in a medieval amusement makes it easier to forget your modern self. The most convivial entertainments are those that several people can take part in at once. You will need to ensure that any necessary equipment is available, and it will help if the participants have some practice beforehand.

Another kind of entertainment is "scripting." If one can have some sort of plot or plots happening at the event—comparable perhaps to the "host a murder mystery" idea that has become a popular party theme in recent years—this may contribute to the interest of the occasion.

5. *Prepare the Participants*: It is not always easy to re-create the past, and it will help if the group takes an active part in preparing people for the event. Try to ensure that beginners have guidance available to them in assembling their outfits—sewing get-togethers are a good way of doing this. You might even set up a buddy system, teaming beginners with experienced people responsible for making sure they have everything they need.

The event will work best if there is a core of participants who know what they are doing. For this reason, it is worth having a series of workshops prior to the event at which people can practice games, dances, songs, social interaction, and the like. In addition, the day of the event is a good time to hold workshops for the benefit of out-of-town visitors.

You should also be prepared to take an active hand in arranging the social relationships between the participants' characters. Left to their own devices, participants will probably all attend as people of the same rank (usually knight or lady), with few relationships among them. This tends to make the event both unrealistic and dull. Encourage participants to come with pre-arranged social relationships among them. One good possibility is for some to come as servants to others: a servant is a comparatively easy and cheap character to re-create, and it can be a great deal of fun. Other possibilities might be relatives, neighbors, and friends.

For groups as for individuals, a modest social rank is easier to portray than a high one. Chaucer's Canterbury pilgrims are a good slice of society to emulate: nobody higher than a simple knight, nobody lower than an honest plowman, and most falling well between the two extremes. They are not a full cross-section of English society, but a good sample of what you might find on the Canterbury road in the 1380s—and they're a fun bunch of people (after all, they've been entertaining audiences for 600 years). Again, you may find it worthwhile organizing sessions to help arrange social relationships, before and/or on the day of the event.

6. *Do It Again*: If the event was enjoyable, it will be even more so next time. You will already have assembled your basic equipment and core of participants, and you can build on it. Think of the things you can improve for your next event. Keep at it long enough, and you will be amazed what you can accomplish.

Appendix B: Contacts

There is at present very little medieval living history in North America, but a fair amount in Europe and some in other areas of the globe. The following are the contacts we have been able to identify as of the time of publication.

Journals

Smoke and Fire News. A newspaper-style publication covering all periods of re-enacting, with some information on medieval groups. A good way to find out about what other kinds of re-enactment groups are doing. PO Box 166, Grand Rapids OH 43522; (419) 832-0303.

The Living History Register. Publishes a newsletter on living history activities in the United Kingdom. 21 Oak Rd., Woolston, Southhampton, Hants. SO2 9BQ ENGLAND.

Call to Arms. An absolute must for any re-enactor for the medieval period, this journal carries an extensive listing of groups and suppliers around the world, many of them involved in fourteenth- and fifteenth-century living history. 7 Chapmans Crescent, Chesham, Bucks. HP5 2QU ENGLAND

Australasian Register of Living History Organisations. A living history directory covering Australia and New Zealand. Tony Cryan, PO Box 12325, Brisbane Elizabeth St., Brisbane, Queensland 4002 AUSTRALIA.

Organizations

Will McLean. McLean hosts an annual fourteenth-century tournament on his land in Pennsylvania. This event is by invitation. Will McLean, RD 1, Box 95, Yellow Springs Rd., Malvern PA 19355; (610) 827-1360. McLean also supplies boards for Glic.

La Belle Compagnie. This group sets up a fourteenth-century military encampment at the annual "Military through the Ages" display in Jamestown, VA. Robert Charrette, 7875 Wintercress Lane, Springfield VA 22152.

Southern California Historical Reenactment Society. A small fourteenth-century re-enactment organization re-creating various aspects of life during the period covered by the Hundred Years' War, emphasizing the lives of common people, soldiers, and camp followers. Daniel R. Jennings, 4342 Gentry Ave. #9, Studio City CA 91604; (818) 980-2207.

The Company of Saint George. Recreates the life of an artillery company of the late fifteenth century; they have an excellent newsletter and are in contact with other similar groups in Europe. Time Machine, Gerry Embleton, CH-1425 Onnens, SWITZERLAND.

Order of the Black Prince. A living history group for the period 1330-1376, based at Dover Castle. John Buttifint, 9, Saxon St., Dover, Kent, ENGLAND.

The Society for Creative Anachronism. Holds tournaments, feasts, and other activities inspired by the Middle Ages. Publishes *Tournaments Illuminated*, a useful quarterly magazine. PO Box 360743, Milpitas CA 95036-0743.

ELECTRONIC RESOURCES

By far the most efficient means of obtaining information on living history activities is the World Wide Web. The newsgroups **alt.history.living** and **soc.history.living** are a good forum in which to air any queries—the readers will be only too happy to answer. Most of the contacts listed above are in direct or indirect contact with both of these newsgroups. Other newsgroups exist for many of the specific subjects treated in this book, and are well known to the living history newsgroups.

Appendix C: Suppliers

General

Buzzard's Nest, William Ruppert, Jr., PO Box 146, Barhamsville VA 23011; (804) 566-2259. Leather and wrought iron goods.

Cumberland General Store, Dept. EAL, Route 3, Box 418, Clarksburg, WV 26301. Buckets, barrels, etc.

The Dragon's Hoarde, James M. Keith, 3100 Franor Ave., Alton IL 62002-2933; (618) 462-3336. Books and accessories.

G. Gedney Godwin, Box 100, Valley Forge PA 19481; (215) 783-0670. Accessories and camping equipment.

Marianne Hansen, 520 Adam Ave., Ithaca NY 14850. Lead-free pewter spoons, badges, buttons, buckles, fittings. Also cards and dice.

Past Times, 280 Summer St., Boston MA 02210-1182; (800) 621-6020. Games.

Claire A. Rutiser, 1952 Highland Dr., State College PA 16803; (814) 867-8678. Coins, coin-dies.

Douglas W. Strong, 240 E. Palmer, Northlake IL 60164. Belt fittings and other castings.

Track of the Wolf, Inc., Box Y, Osseo MN 55369; (612) 424-2500. Camping equipment.

Clothing and Accessories

Alister's Fine Footwear, Andrew Guy, Rte. 2 1768 S 600 W, Russiaville IN 46979; (317) 883-5870.

Kirstie Buckland, Chippenham Gate, Monmouth, Gwent NP5 3DH, UNITED KINGDOM; 600-71-2469. Knit caps.

J. & L. Cooke, #3 Ronald Cir., Spencerport NY 14559; (716) 352-4730. Historical fabrics.

Andrew Guy, 224 Little Switzerland Lane, Knoxville TN 37920; (615) 577-2785. Shoes.

K & K Historic Fabrics Ltd., Dennis Krowe, 2372 Rose St., Scotch Plains NJ 07076. Woolen fabrics.

Istvan Kostka (Ted Fleming), Shoemaker, 1623 Lincoln "A," Topeka KS 66604; (913) 233-8663. Shoes.

Lion's Paw Boots, c/o Gavin Danker, 5056 Tujunga Ave. #20, North Hollywood CA 91601; (213) 281-7759. Boots.

Metropolitan Museum of Art, 255 Gracie Station, New York NY 10028; (800) 468-7386. Books, jewelry.

Plantagenet Shoes, Morgan Hubbard, 92 Cozens Hardy Rd., Sprowston, Norwich, Norfolk NR7 8QG ENGLAND. Shoes.

Signals, WGBH Educational Foundation, PO Box 64428, St. Paul MN 55164-0428; (800) 699-9696. Jewelry.

Textile Reproductions, Box 48, West Chesterfield MA 01084; (413) 296-4437. Thread, fabrics, dyestuff. Also sells swatches of fabric dyed with many of the dyes used in the Middle Ages.

Timefarer Footwear, Gorthleck, Inverness, IV1 2YS SCOTLAND; 0456 486 696. Shoes.

Knives, Weapons, and Armor

John Buttifint, 9, Saxon St., Dover, Kent, ENGLAND. Knives, lanterns.

Gordon Osterstrom, P.O. Box 9216, Phoenix AZ. Welded and riveted mail.

Robert MacPherson, 520 Adam Ave., Ithaca NY 14850. Armor.

Museum Replicas, Box 1840, Conyers GA 30207; 1 (800) 241-3664; 404-922-3700. Arms and armor.

Daniel Rotblatt, 20888 Waveview Dr., Unit C, Topanga CA 90290; (310) 455-1475. Knives and scabbards.

J. S. Schroter Antique Arms, PO Box 10794, Costa Mesa CA 92627. Arms and armor.

Eldrid Tremayne, Armourer, c/o Tom Justus, 1120 West Webb Ave., Burlington NC 27217; (919) 227-6044. Armor.

Vorhut Fähnlein Arms, Jeffrey E. Hedgecock, 17228 Voorhes Ln., Ramona CA 92065; (619) 789-6644. Arms and armor.

Household Goods

Frederick the Kohler, PO Box 5264, Westport OR; (503) 458-6246. Spoons.

Fulk's Woody Works, Michael Martin, 61-20 Grand Central Pky. #B4, Forest Hills NY 11375; (212) 865-7571. Stools.

Good Erthe Pottis, Glenn Herbert, Box 83, Ouaquaga NY 13826; (607) 655-1376. Pottery.

Goose Bay Workshops, Peter Goebel, Rte. 1, Box 297-C, Crozet VA 22932; (703) 456-8717. Tinware and copperware.

Tents

Tentmasters, 4221 Livesay Rd., Sand Creek MI 49279; (517) 436-6245.

Tentsmiths, Box 496, North Conway NH 03860; (603) 447-2344.

Entertainments

The Early Music Shop, 38 Manningham Lane, Bradford, West Yorkshire BD1 1BR
  ENGLAND. Instruments (finished and kits), written music.
The Early Music Shop of New England, 59-65 Boylston St., Brookline MA 02146.
  New and used instruments, written music.
U.S. Games Systems, 179 Ludlow St., Stamford CT 06902. Card decks.

Notes

CHAPTER 2: CHAUCER'S WORLD

1. On the structure of society, see Scott L. Waugh, *England in the Reign of Edward III* (Cambridge: Cambridge University Press, 1991); Christopher Dyer, *Standards of Living in the Later Middle Ages* (Cambridge: Cambridge University Press, 1989).

2. Translation of the Pater Noster from a fourteenth-century version in William Maskell, *Monumenta Ritualia Ecclesiae Anglicanae* (Oxford: at the Clarendon Press, 1882), III.249; translations of the Ave Maria and Credo from the *Book to a Mother*, ed. Adrian James McCarthy, Elizabethan and Renaissance Studies 92 (Salzburg: Institut für Anglistik und Amerikanistik, 1981), 1.

3. On religious education, see *Dives and Pauper*, ed. Priscilla Heath Barnum, Early English Texts Society 275, 280 (London: Oxford University Press, 1976, 1980), I.329; John Mirk, *Instructions for Parish Priests*, ed. E. Peacock. Early English Texts Society 31 (London: Kegan Paul, Trench and Trübner, 1868), 151 ff.; *DMA* s.v. "Religious Instruction."

4. Emmanuel Le Roy Ladurie, *Montaillou* (New York: Braziller, 1978).

5. On religious services, see Robert Mannyng, *Handlyng Synne*, ed. F. J. Furnivall, Early English Texts Society 119, 123 (London: Kegan Paul, Trench and Trübner, 1901, 1903), ll. 4260, 1045; Mirk ll. 404 ff.; G. R. Owst, *Preaching in Medieval England* (Cambridge: Cambridge University Press, 1926), 144-45.

6. On confession, see Mirk ll. 236 ff., 771 ff., 805, 1590 ff.; Mannyng ll. 4783 ff., 10297 ff., 10300, 11607; *DMA* s.vv. "Confession," "Religious Instruction". See also W. A. Pantin, *The English Church in the Fourteenth Century* (Cambridge: Cambridge University Press, 1955).

7. On the medieval world and cosmos, see C. S. Lewis, *The Discarded Image* (Cambridge: Cambridge University Press, 1964).

8. *A Collection of Ordinances and Regulations for the Government of the Royal Household Made in Divers Reigns from King Edward III to King William and Queen Mary* (London: Society of Antiquaries, 1790), 9; James E. Thorold Rogers, *A History of Agriculture and Prices in England* (Oxford: at the Clarendon Press, 1882), I.282, 314, 322; II.582-83.

9. Dyer (1989), 147, 194. The landholder incomes are based on a per-acre yield of 4s. 6d.

10. Rogers I.348-50, 362-63, 451, 453-54, 593, 641, II.584; *MED* s.v. "brech"; Edith Rickert, *Chaucer's World* (New York: Columbia University Press, 1948), 29-30, 113, 237, 338; Earnest Savage, *Old English Libraries* (London: Methuen, 1912), 243, 248-49; C. Pendrill, *London Life in the Fourteenth Century* (London: Allen and Unwin, 1925), 37, 177, 181-82; Dyer (1989), 80, 167.

CHAPTER 3: THE COURSE OF LIFE

1. John Trevisa, *On the Properties of Things. John Trevisa's translation of Bartholomeus Anglicus'* De Proprietatibus Rerum, gen. ed. M. C. Seymour (Oxford: at the Clarendon Press, 1975), 305.

2. Robert S. Gottfried, *Doctors and Medicine in Medieval England 1340-1530* (Princeton: Princeton University Press, 1986), 87. Principal sources on growing up are Barbara Hanawalt, *Growing Up in Medieval London. The Experience of Childhood in History* (New York and Oxford: Oxford University Press, 1993); Barbara Hanawalt, *The Ties That Bound. Peasant Families in Medieval England* (New York and Oxford: Oxford University Press, 1986); Nicholas Orme, *From Childhood to Chivalry. The education of the English kings and aristocracy 1066-1530* (London and New York: Methuen, 1984).

3. Cf. Mirk 85 ff.; Mannyng ll. 9585 ff.

4. On names, see P. H. Reaney, *A Dictionary of British Surnames* (London: Routledge and Kegan Paul, 1977).

5. Trevisa 299, 304.

6. Josiah Cox Russell, *British Medieval Population* (Albuquerque: University of New Mexico Press, 1948), 183.

7. See John Lydgate, "Stans Puer ad Mensam", in *The Minor Poems of John Lydgate*, ed. H. N. MacCracken, Early English Texts Society 192 (London: Trübner, 1934), 2.739-44.

8. Hanawalt (1986), 180-81; Hanawalt (1993), 65.

9. Trevisa 303, 310-11.

10. Trevisa 300-301, 302.

11. Mirk 7; *DMA* s.v. "Confirmation."

12. Mirk 216.

13. Hanawalt (1993), ch. 8.

14. Hanawalt (1993), ch. 11.

15. Hanawalt (1993), 205-6.

16. Mirk 190 ff.; *Dives and Pauper* 2.61; Mannyng ll. 203 ff.; *DMA* s.v. "Family and Marriage, Western."

17. Josiah Cox Russell 183.

18. Gottfried 86-89. See also Charles Talbot, *Medicine in Medieval England* (London: Oldbourne, 1967).

CHAPTER 4: CYCLES OF TIME

1. On mornings, see G. G. Coulton, *Medieval Panorama* (New York: Macmillan, 1938), 302; G. T. Salusbury-Jones, *Street Life in Medieval England* (Oxford: Pen in Hand, 1938), 171.

2. On daily labor, see Hanawalt (1993), 177; Christopher Dyer, *Standards of Living in the Later Middle Ages* (Cambridge: Cambridge University Press, 1989), 224.

3. On evenings, see Mannyng 1. 4712; Pendrill 40; Hanawalt (1993), 30; *MED* s.v. "curfew."

4. On the weekly schedule, see Pendrill 171; Mannyng ll. 845 ff.; *Dives and Pauper* 1.287.

5. On Sundays, see Pendrill 171.

6. On Sunday afternoons, see Owst 179; *Dives and Pauper* I.293-94; Mannyng ll. 985 ff.

7. R. H. Robbins, *Secular Lyrics of the XIVth and XVth Centuries* (Oxford: at the Clarendon Press, 1952), 62.

8. C. R. Cheney, *Handbook of Dates for Students of English History* (London: Offices of the Royal Historical Society, 1970); John J. Bond, *Handy Book of Rules and Tables for Verifying Dates within the Christian Era* (New York: Russell and Russell, 1966).

9. These are based on the holidays listed in a Masons' Ordinance of 1474 [L. F. Salzman, *Building in England Down to 1540* (Oxford: at the Clarendon Press, 1952), 64-65] and on those mentioned in the journals of John Dernell and John Boys, two Norfolk carters of the early fifteenth century [*Norfolk Archaeology* 14 (1904), 125-57].

10. On the yearly cycle, see George Caspar Homans, *English Villagers of the Thirteenth Century* (Cambridge, MA: Harvard University Press, 1942); *Walter of Henley's Husbandry*, ed. E. Lamond (London: Longman's, Green and Co., 1890); Nicholas of Lynn, *Kalendarium*, ed. Sigmund Eisner (Athens: University of Georgia Press, 1980); William Maskell, *Monumenta Ritualia Ecclesiae Anglicanae* (Oxford: at the Clarendon Press, 1882).

CHAPTER 5: THE LIVING ENVIRONMENT

1. On villages, see Frances and Joseph Gies, *Life in a Medieval Village* (New York: Harper and Row, 1990); Maurice Beresford and John Hurst, *Wharram Percy. Deserted Medieval Village* (London: Batsford/English Heritage, 1990); Stuart Wrathmell, *Wharram. A Study of Settlement on the Yorkshire Wolds VI. Domestic Settlement 2: Medieval Peasant Farmsteads*, York University Archeological Publications 8 (York: York University, 1989).

2. On houses, see Silvia Thrupp, *The Merchant Class of Medieval London* (Chicago: University of Chicago Press, 1948), 130-31; Dyer (1989), 203; L. F.

Salzman, *Building in England Down to 1540* (Oxford: Clarendon Press, 1952); Margaret Wood, *The English Mediaeval House* (London: Phoenix House, 1965).

3. On towns, see Dyer (1989), 189; A. R. Myers, *London in the Age of Chaucer* (Norman: University of Oklahoma Press, 1974); D. W. Robertson, *Chaucer's London* (New York: John Wiley and Sons, 1968).

4. Coulton (1938), 312; *MED* s.v. "rishe"; Trevisa 137, 1149; William Woods, *England in the Age of Chaucer* (New York: Stein and Day, 1976), 56a.

5. Coulton (1938), 310. On furniture, see Penelope Eames, *Furniture in England, France and the Netherlands from the Twelfth to the Fifteenth Century* (London: Furniture History Society, 1977); Eric Mercer, *Furniture 700-1700* (New York: Meredith Press, 1969).

6. G. G. Astill, "An early inventory of a Leicestershire knight," *Midland History* 2 (1974), 279-81.

7. For a description of bathing, see John Russell, *The Boke of Nurture*, ll. 975 ff., in F. J. Furnivall, *The Babees Book*, Early English Texts Society (London: Trübner, 1868), 61-114.

8. John Russell ll. 931 ff.

9. Rickert 258-59.

Other important sources on the living environment include:

Alexander, Jonathan, and Paul Binski, eds., *Age of Chivalry. Art in Plantagenet England 1200-1400* (London: Royal Academy of Arts, 1987).

Blair, John, and Nigel Ramsay, eds., *English Medieval Industries* (London: Hambledon Press, 1991).

London Museum, *Medieval Catalogue* (London: Her Majesty's Stationery Office, 1967).

Metropolitan Museum of Art, *The Secular Spirit: Life and Art at the End of the Middle Ages* (New York: Dutton, 1975).

CHAPTER 6: CLOTHING AND ACCESSORIES

1. *CT* I.415 ff. Principal sources on clothing include:

Boucher, François, *2000 Years of Fashion* (New York: Abrams, 1957).

Crowfoot, E., F. Pritchard, and K. Staniland, eds., *Medieval Finds from Excavations in London. Vol. 4: Textiles and Clothing* (London: Her Majesty's Stationery Office, 1992).

Cunnington, Q. W. and P., *Handbook of English Medieval Costume* (London: Faber and Faber, 1952).

Cunnington, Q. W. and P., *The History of Underclothes* (London: Faber and Faber, 1981).

Davenport, Millia, *The Book of Costume* (New York: Crown Publishers, 1948).

Egan, G., and F. Pritchard, eds., *Medieval Finds from Excavations in London. Vol. 3: Dress Accessories* (London: Her Majesty's Stationery Office, 1991).

Hartley, Dorothy, *Medieval Costume and Life* (London: Batsford, 1931).

Houston, Mary G., *Medieval Costume in England and France* (London: Black, 1939).

Kelly, Francis M., *A Short History of Costume and Armour* (London: Batsford, 1931).

Köhler, Carl, *A History of Costume* (London: Harrap, 1928).

Lester, Katherine Morris, and Bess Viola Oerke, *Accessories of Dress* (Peoria, IL: Manual Arts Press, 1954).

Newton, Stella Mary, *Fashion in the Age of the Black Prince* (Woodbridge, Suffolk: Boydell Press, 1980).

Nockert, Margareta, et al., eds., *Bokstensmannen Och Hans Drakt* (Falkenberg: Falkenberg Tryckeri, 1985). Describes a bog-find from Sweden that yielded a set of woolen and leather clothes and accessories, probably from the fourteenth century. Includes an English summary and captions.

Norlund, Poul, "Buried Norsemen at Herjolfsnes," *Meddelelser om Groenland* 67 (1924), 87-192. Describes extensive finds of hoods, hose, tunics, and gowns from a site in Greenland, probably from the fourteenth or fifteenth century.

Scott, Margaret, *A Visual History of Costume. The Fourteenth and Fifteenth Centuries* (London: Batsford, 1986).

Semenzato, Camillo, *Le Pitture del Santo di Padova* (Vicenza: Pozza, 1984). Contains plates of very realistic frescoes by Altichiero, an Italian contemporary of Chaucer.

DMA s.v. "Textile Technology."

2. *DMA* s.v. "Textiles."

3. On knitting, see Richard Rutt, *A History of Hand Knitting* (Loveland, CO: Interweave Press, 1987).

4. *MF* 4.19-20, 199-200; *DMA* sv. "Dyes."

5. *MED* s.v. " brest."

6. Norman Davis, ed., *Paston Letters and Papers of the Fifteenth Century* (Oxford: at the Clarendon Press, 1971), 1.351. The shirt pattern is after Dorothy Burnham, *Cut My Cote* (Toronto: Royal Ontario Museum, 1973), 12.

7. On shoes, see F. Grew and M. de Neergard, eds., *Medieval Finds from Excavations in London. 2: Shoes and Pattens* (London: Her Majesty's Stationery Office, 1988).

8. For examples, see *MF* 3.35.

9. On knives, see J. Cowgill, M. de Neergard, and N. Griffiths, eds., *Medieval Finds from Excavations in London. 1: Knives and Scabbards* (London: Her Majesty's Stationery Office, 1987).

10. Coulton (1938), 311.

11. For jewelry, see *MF* 4 and *AC*.

12. The original Middle English text was edited by Eric Stanley as "Directions for making many sorts of laces" in B. Rowland, ed., *Chaucer and Middle English Studies in Honour of Russell Hope Robbins* (London: Allen and Unwin, 1974), 95-103.

CHAPTER 7: ARMS AND ARMOR

1. Useful sources on fourteenth-century arms and armor include:

Arthur, Harold, Viscount Dillon, "On a MS. Collection of Ordinances of Chivalry of the fifteenth century," *Archaeologia* 57 (1840), 29-71.

Blair, Claude, *European Armour circa 1066 to circa 1700* (New York: Macmillan, 1959).

Cripps-Day, F. H., "The Armour at Chartres," *Connoisseur* 110:486 (1942), 91-95, 158.

Edge, David, and John Miles Paddock, *Arms and Armour of the Medieval Knight* (New York: Defoe, 1988).

ffoulkes, C., *The Armourer and His Craft* (New York: B. Blom, 1967).

Macklin, H. W., *Monumental Brasses* (London: Sonnenschein, 1891).

Mann, J. G., *Wallace Collection. European Arms and Armour.* Vol. 1 (London: Printed for the Trustees of W. Clowes, 1962).

Mellini, G. L., *Altichiero e Jacopo Avanzi* (Milan: Edizioni di Comunita, 1965).

Metropolitan Museum of Art, *The Bashford Dean Collection of Arms and Armor in the Metropolitan Museum of Art* (Portland, ME: Southworth Press for the Armor and Arms Club of New York, 1933).

Norman, A. Vesey, *Arms and Armour* (New York: Putnam's, 1964).

Rothero, Christopher, *The Armies of Crécy and Poitiers*, Osprey Men-at-Arms Series 111 (London: Osprey, 1981).

Thordeman, B., *Armour from the Battle of Wisby 1361* (Stockholm: Kungl. vitterhets historie och antikvitets akademien, 1939).

Trapp, O., *The Armoury of the Castle of Churburg*, tr. J. G. Mann (London: Methuen, 1929).

CHAPTER 8: FOOD AND DRINK

1. Important sources on food include:

Cosman, Madeleine Pelner, *Fabulous Feasts* (New York: Braziller, 1976). Lavishly illustrated, containing much information about medieval food and cooking, with over a hundred adapted recipes, although their authenticity is not reliable.

Dyer, Christopher, "English Diet in the Later Middle Ages," in *Social Relations and Ideas*, ed. T. H. Aston, P. R. Coss, et al. (Cambridge: Cambridge University Press, 1983), 191-216.

Freeman, Margaret, *Herbs for the Mediaeval Household* (New York: Metropolitan Museum of Art, 1943).

Friedman, David, et al., *A Collection of Medieval and Renaissance Cookbooks*, 6th ed. Vol. I (private printing, 1991).

Friedman, David, ed., *A Collection of Medieval and Renaissance Cookbooks*, 4th ed. Vol. II (private printing, 1991).

Henisch, Bridget Ann, *Fast and Feast: Food in Medieval Society* (University Park: University of Pennsylvania Press, 1976).

Hieatt, Constance B., and Sharon Butler, *Curye on Inglisch*, Early English Texts Society special series 8 (London: Oxford University Press, 1985). The principal collection of fourteenth-century English recipes. These recipes do not come with modern adaptations; a good glossary is included at the end.

Hieatt, Constance B., and Sharon Butler, *Pleyn Delit* (Toronto: University of Toronto Press, 1979). Medieval recipes with modern adaptations that are quite close to the originals.

Hieatt, Constance B., and Robin F. Jones, "Two Anglo-Norman Culinary Collections," *Speculum* 61:4 (1986), 859-82. Recipes from the early fourteenth century.

Le Ménagier de Paris (Paris: Crapelet, 1846). A fourteenth-century French collection of recipes and household advice. Translations include Tania Bayard, *The Medieval Home Companion* (New York: HarperCollins, 1991); Eileen Power, *The Goodman of Paris* (London: Routledge, 1929), and one printed in Vol. II of Friedman's *Collection*.

Scully, Terence, ed. and trans., *Chiquart's "On Cookery"* (New York: P. Lang, 1986). A scholarly edition and translation of an early fifteenth-century cookery book. It does not include a huge quantity of recipes but is the only contemporary source that actually describes how a feast is put together, from kitchen set-up, equipment, staffing, to menu planning.

Taillevent, *The Viandier of Taillevent*, ed. and trans. Terence Scully (Ottawa: University of Ottawa Press, 1988). A fourteenth-century French cookbook.

Willan, Anne, *Great Cooks and Their Recipes from Taillevent to Escoffier* (Boston, Toronto, and London: Bulfinch, 1992).

Wilson, C. Anne, *Food and Drink in Britain from the Stone Age to Recent Times* (London: Constable, 1973).

On diet, see Dyer (1989) 60, 63-64, 156-57; Dyer (1983) 193, 196, 202, 206, 209-10, 214.

2. On seasonings, see Dyer (1989) 63; Wilson 285; Bruno Laurioux, "Spices in the Medieval Diet: A New Approach," *Food and Foodways* 1 (1985), 43-76.

3. Hieatt and Butler (1985), 41.

4. *Ménagier de Paris* 2.100.

5. Hieatt and Butler (1985), 40-41.

6. On drinks, see Dyer (1989), 62; Wilson 375; Coulton (1938), 314.

7. On the table, see John Russell ll. 62, 185 ff.; Michael R. McCarthy and Catherine M. Brooks, *Medieval Pottery in Britain A.D. 900-1600* (Leicester: Leicester University Press, 1988).

8. On trenchers, see John Russell l. 56.

9. On spoons, see Peter Hornsby, Rosemary Weinstein, and Ronald Homer, *Pewter: A Celebration of the Craft 1200-1700* (London: Museum of London, 1990); Arthur MacGregor, *Bone, Antler, Ivory and Horn* (London: Croom Helm, 1985).

10. On etiquette, see Lydgate, "Stans Puer ad Mensam."

11. Scully (1986), 12-13.

12. Hieatt and Butler (1985), 4.3.

13. Hieatt and Butler (1985), 4.6.

14. Hieatt and Butler (1985), 4.7; Hieatt and Butler (1979), recipe 16.

15. Hieatt and Butler (1985), 4.188.

16. Hieatt and Butler (1985), 4.78, adapted by David Tallan.

17. Hieatt and Butler (1985), 4.137.

18. Hieatt and Butler (1985), 4.200.

19. *Ménagier de Paris*, p. M-36, in David Friedman and Betty Cook, *A Miscelleny* [sic], 5th ed. (private printing, 1990), 75, adapted by David Tallan.

20. Hieatt and Butler (1985), 4.51.

21. Hieatt and Butler (1985), 4.173.

22. Hieatt and Butler (1985), 4.174.

23. Hieatt and Butler (1985), 2.82.

24. Hieatt and Butler (1985), 5.148-49.

25. Hieatt and Butler (1985), 5.151.

CHAPTER 9: ENTERTAINMENTS

1. General sources on entertainments include:

Alfonso X, *Das spanische Schachzabelbuch des Königs Alfons des Weisen vom Jahre 1283* (Leipzig: Hiersemann, 1913).

Brand, John, and Sir Henry Ellis, *Observations on Popular Antiquities* (London: Chatto and Wyndus, 1913).

Cotton, Charles, *The Compleat Gamester* [1674], in *Games and Gamesters of the Restoration* (London: Routledge, 1930).

DMA s.v. "Games and Pastimes."

McLean, Theresa, *The English at Play in the Middle Ages* (Windsor Forest, Berks.: Kensal Press, 1983).

Nelson, Walter, *Ye Merrie Gamester* (private printing, 1993). An excellent source on medieval games, including card, dice, board, and physical games. Available from the author, 7341 Etiwanda Ave., Reseda CA 91335.

Strutt, Joseph, *Sports and Pastimes of the English People* (London: Methuen, 1903).

Willughby, Francis, *Francis Willughby's Treatise on Games*, ed. David Cram, Dorothy Johnston, and Jeffrey L. Singman (Leicester: Scolar Press, forthcoming).

2. On theater, see E. K. Chambers, *The Medieval Stage* (Oxford: at the Clarendon Press, 1903).

3. Useful sources on music and song include:

Chappell, W., *Popular Music of the Olden Time* (London: Chappell, 1859).

Gleason, Harold, *Examples of Music Before 1400* (Rochester, NY: Eastman School of Music, 1942).

Greene, R. L., *The Early English Carols* (Oxford: at the Clarendon Press, 1935).

Robbins, R. H., *Historical Poems of the XIVth and XVth Centuries* (Oxford: at the Clarendon Press, 1959).

Robbins, R. H., *Secular Lyrics of the XIVth and XVth Centuries* (Oxford: at the Clarendon Press, 1952).

Stainer, J. F. R. and C., *Early Bodleian Music* (London: Novello, 1901).

Wilkins, Nigel, *Music in the Time of Chaucer*, Chaucer Studies 1 (Cambridge: D. S. Brewer, 1979).

4. On tournaments, see Richard Barber and Juliet Barker, *Tournaments* (New York: Weidenfeld and Nicholson, 1989); Juliet Barker, *The Tournament in England 1100-1400* (Woodbridge, Suffolk: Boydell Press, 1986); F. H. Cripps-Day, *The*

History of the Tournament (London: BernardQuaritch, 1918). A pamphlet on martial sports is forthcoming from Will McLean (see Appendix B).

5. On chess, see H. J. R. Murray, *A History of Chess* (Oxford: at the Clarendon Press, 1913).

6. Dummett, David, *The Game of Tarot* (London: Duckworth, 1980), 10. On cards, see

Beal, George, *Playing-Cards and Their Story* (Newton Abbot: David and Charles, 1975).

Dummett, Michael, "The Earliest Spanish Playing Cards," *Journal of the International Playing Card Society* 18:1 (Aug. 1989).

Hoffmann, Detlef, *The Playing Card: An Illustrated History* (Greenwich, CT: New York Graphic Society, 1973).

Parlett, David, *The Oxford Guide to Card Games* (Oxford: Oxford University Press, 1990).

Varekamp, T., "A Fifteenth-Century French Pack of Painted Playing Cards with a Hunting Theme (Part 1)," *Journal of the International Playing Card Society* 14:2 (Nov. 1985).

Varekamp, T., "A Fifteenth-Century French Pack of Painted Playing Cards with a Hunting Theme (Part 2)," *Journal of the International Playing Card Society* 14:3 (Feb. 1986).

Wintle, Simon, "A 'Moorish' Sheet of Playing Cards," *Journal of the International Playing Card Society* 15:4 (May 1987).

7. *MED* s.v. "carde" n. (2) and "carder" n. (2). See also Strutt 261.

8. Dummett (1980), 11.

9. The three-die version is from Alfonso, the two-die version from Cotton.

10. Rules from Alfonso.

11. Rules from Cotton 81; Nelson 29.

12. Murray (1913), 464 ff.

13. Described in H. J. R. Murray, "The Medieval Games of Tables," *Medium Ævum* 10 (1941), 57-69; edited in W. Fiske, *Chess in Iceland* (Florence: Florentine Typographical Society, 1905).

14. Rules from Willughby.

15. Parlett 80-81; rules from Willughby.

16. Parlett 165.

17. Thierry Depaulis, "Pochspiel: An 'International' Card Game of the Fifteenth Century," *Journal of the International Playing Card Society* 19:2-4 (Nov. 1990, Feb. 1991, May 1991), 2; cf. also Parlett; Dummett (1980).

18. Rules from Willughby.

19. Rules from Willughby.

20. Rules from Willughby.

21. The earliest European dance treatises are from early fifteenth-century Italy. The earliest treatise from north of the Alps is a mid-fifteenth-century French collection of basse dances, a translation of which printed in 1521 is the earliest dance text in English. No independent English source exists before the late sixteenth century, and there is no source for popular English dance before 1651. Some useful sources for the reconstruction of fourteenth-century dance are:

Arbeau, Thoinot, *Orchesography* (New York: Dover, 1967). Originally published in French in 1589; the earliest text on circle and chain dances.

Castelli, Patrizia, Maurizio Mingardi, and Maurizio Padovan, eds., *Mesvra et Arte del Danzare* (Pesaro: Gualtieri, 1987). A rich source of illustrations for fourteenth-century Italian dance.

McGee, Timothy, *Medieval Instrumental Dances* (Bloomington: Indiana University Press, 1989). Contains all known medieval instrumental dance melodies, with some current discussion of medieval dances and dance music.

Nonsuch Early Dance Series. Uses Melusine Wood as its basis for medieval dances, which are to be found in Volume 1 and in the First Supplement in this series. Ordering information is available from Mrs. J. McKay, 97 Queensborough Gardens, Glasgow G12 9RY Scotland.

Wood, Melusine, *Historical Dances* (London: Imperial Society of Teachers of Dancing, 1952). One of the classic older sources for historical dance. Not extremely reliable, yet useful for the wary reader.

Bibliography

The titles listed below are cited recurrently in the notes. For bibliographies on specific topics, see the notes to the relevant chapters.

ABBREVIATIONS

AC   Alexander, Jonathan, and Paul Binski, eds., *Age of Chivalry. Art in Plantagenet England 1200-1400*

CT   Geoffrey Chaucer, *The Canterbury Tales*

DMA   *The Dictionary of the Middle Ages*

MED   *Middle English Dictionary*

MF 3   Egan, G., and F. Pritchard, eds., *Medieval Finds from Excavations in London. Vol. 3: Dress Accessories*

MF 4   Crowfoot, E., F. Pritchard, and K. Staniland, eds., *Medieval Finds from Excavations in London. Vol. 4: Textiles and Clothing*

Alexander, Jonathan, and Paul Binski., eds. *Age of Chivalry. Art in Plantagenet England 1200-1400*. London: Royal Academy of Arts, 1987.

Alfonso X. *Das spanische Schachzabelbuch des Königs Alfons des Weisen vom Jahre 1283*. Leipzig: Hiersemann, 1913.

Brewer, Derek. *Chaucer and His World*. New York: Dodd, Mead and Co., 1978.

Chappell, W. *Popular Music of the Olden Time*. London: Chappell, 1859.

Chaucer, Geoffrey. *The Riverside Chaucer*. Boston: Houghton Mifflin, 1987.

Contamine, Philippe. *La vie quotidienne pendant la guerre de Cent ans: France et Angleterre*. Paris: Hachette, 1976.

Cotton, Charles. *The Compleat Gamester* [1674]. In *Games and Gamesters of the Restoration*. London: Routledge, 1930.

Coulton, G. G. *Chaucer and His England*. New York: Putnam's, 1900.

Coulton, G. G. *Medieval Panorama*. New York: Macmillan, 1938.

Crowfoot, E., F. Pritchard, and K. Staniland, eds. *Medieval Finds from Excavations in London. Vol. 4: Textiles and Clothing.* London: Her Majesty's Stationery Office, 1992.

The Dictionary of the Middle Ages. New York: Scribner, 1982.

Dives and Pauper. Priscilla Heath Barnum, ed. Early English Texts Society 275, 280. London: Oxford University Press, 1976, 1980.

Drogin, Marc. *Medieval Calligraphy: Its History and Technique.* Montclair: Allanheld and Schram, 1980.

Dummett, David. *The Game of Tarot.* London: Duckworth, 1980.

Dyer, Christopher. "English Diet in the Later Middle Ages." In *Social Relations and Ideas,* ed. T. H. Aston, P. R. Coss, et al. Cambridge: Cambridge University Press, 1983.

Dyer, Christopher. *Standards of Living in the Later Middle Ages.* Cambridge: Cambridge University Press, 1989.

Egan, G., and F. Pritchard, eds. *Medieval Finds from Excavations in London. Vol. 3: Dress Accessories.* London: Her Majesty's Stationery Office, 1991.

Furnivall, F. J. *The Cambridge MS. Dd.4.22. of Chaucer's Canterbury Tales.* London: Kegan, Paul, Trench, and Trübner, 1902.

Gottfried, Robert S. *Doctors and Medicine in Medieval England 1340-1530.* Princeton: Princeton University Press, 1986.

Greene, R. L. *The Early English Carols.* Oxford: Clarendon Press, 1935.

Halliday, F. E. *Chaucer and His World.* New York: Viking, 1968.

Hanawalt, Barbara. *Growing Up in Medieval London. The Experience of Childhood in History.* New York and Oxford: Oxford University Press, 1993.

Hanawalt, Barbara. *The Ties That Bound. Peasant Families in Medieval England.* New York and Oxford: Oxford University Press, 1986.

Hart, Roger. *English Life in Chaucer's Day.* London: Wayland Publishers; New York: G. P. Putnam's Sons, 1973.

Hartley, Dorothy. *Lost Country Life.* New York: Pantheon, 1979.

Hartley, Dorothy, and Margaret M. Elliot. *Life and Work of the People of England. A pictorial record from contemporary sources. The Fourteenth Century.* London: Putnam's, 1929.

Hieatt, Constance B., and Sharon Butler. *Curye on Inglisch,* Early English Texts Society special series 8. London: Oxford University Press, 1985.

Hieatt, Constance B., and Sharon Butler. *Pleyn Delit.* Toronto: University of Toronto Press, 1979.

Hussey, Maurice. *Chaucer's World. A Pictorial Companion.* Cambridge: Cambridge University Press, 1967.

Loomis, Roger. *A Mirror of Chaucer's World.* Princeton: Princeton University Press, 1965.

Lydgate, John. "Stans Puer ad Mensam." In *The Minor Poems of John Lydgate,* ed. H. N. MacCracken. Early English Texts Society 192. London: Trübner, 1934. 2.739-44.

Mannyng, Robert. *Handlyng Synne.* F. J. Furnivall, ed. Early English Texts Society 119, 123. London: Kegan Paul, Trench and Trübner, 1901, 1903.

Le Ménagier de Paris. Paris: Crapelet, 1846.

Middle English Dictionary. Ann Arbor: University of Michigan Press, 1952-.

Mirk, John. *Instructions for Parish Priests*. E. Peacock, ed. Early English Texts Society 31. London: Kegan Paul, Trench and Trübner, 1868.

Murray, H. J. R. *A History of Chess*. Oxford: Clarendon Press, 1913.

Nelson, Walter. *Ye Merrie Gamester*. Private printing, 1993.

Owst, G. R. *Preaching in Medieval England*. Cambridge: Cambridge University Press, 1926.

Parlett, David. *The Oxford Guide to Card Games*. Oxford: Oxford University Press, 1990.

Pendrill, C. *London Life in the Fourteenth Century*. London: Allen and Unwin, 1925.

Quennell, Marjorie. *A History of Everyday Things in England. Volume 1: 1066 to 1499*. London: Batsford, 1918.

Rickert, Edith. *Chaucer's World*. New York: Columbia University Press, 1948.

Robbins, R. H. *Historical Poems of the XIVth and XVth Centuries*. Oxford: Clarendon Press, 1959.

Robbins, R. H. *Secular Lyrics of the XIVth and XVth Centuries*. Oxford: Clarendon Press, 1952.

Rogers, James E. Thorold. *A History of Agriculture and Prices in England*. Oxford: Clarendon Press, 1882.

Russell, John. *The Boke of Nurture*. In *The Babees Book*, F. J. Furnivall, ed. London: Trübner, 1868. 61-114.

Russell, Josiah Cox. *British Medieval Population*. Albuquerque: University of New Mexico Press, 1948.

Salzman, L. F. *Building in England Down to 1540*. Oxford: Clarendon Press, 1952.

Scully, Terence, ed. and trans. *Chiquart's "On Cookery."* New York: P. Lang, 1986.

Serraillier, Ian. *Chaucer and His World*. London: Lutterworth, 1967.

Strutt, Joseph. *Sports and Pastimes of the English People*. London: Methuen, 1903.

Trevisa, John. *On the Properties of Things: John Trevisa's translation of Bartholomeus Anglicus' De Proprietatibus Rerum*. M. C. Seymour, gen. ed. Oxford: Clarendon Press, 1975.

Willughby, Francis. *Francis Willughby's Treatise on Games*. David Cram, Dorothy Johnston, and Jeffrey L. Singman, eds. Leicester: Scolar Press, forthcoming.

Wilson, C. Anne. *Food and Drink in Britain from the Stone Age to Recent Times*. London: Constable, 1973.

Woods, William. *England in the Age of Chaucer*. New York: Stein and Day, 1976.

NOVELS

Druon, Maurice. *The Iron King* (New York: Scribner, 1956), *The Strangled Queen* (New York: Scribner, 1957), *The Poisoned Crown* (New York: Scribner, 1957), *The Royal Succession* (New York: Scribner, 1958), *The She-Wolf of France* (New York: Scribner, 1961), *The Lily and the Lion* (London: R. Hart-Davis, 1961). A series of novels centering around the history of the French crown in the fourteenth century.

Eco, Umberto. *The Name of the Rose* (San Diego: Harcourt, Brace, Jovanovich, 1983).

Hanse, Hella S. *In a Dark Wood Wandering* (Chicago: Academy Chicago, 1989).

FURTHER READING

There are quite a few books available on life in medieval England, although they do not necessarily focus on the fourteenth century. Sheila Sancha's *The Luttrell Village* (New York: Crowell, 1982) and *Walter Dragun's Town* (New York: HarperCollins, 1987) are vivid introductions to medieval life in the country and town in a period slightly earlier than the scope of this book; they are aimed at the young reader, relying heavily on rich illustrations of reconstructed daily life, but both are well researched and an excellent starting point. More narrative accounts of similar topics are two books by Frances and Joseph Gies: *Life in a Medieval Village* (New York: Harper and Row, 1990) and *Life in a Medieval City* (London: Barker, 1969).

For an accessible, scholarly study of English society in this period, Scott L. Waugh, *England in the Reign of Edward III* (Cambridge: Cambridge University Press, 1991) is a useful source. A readable narrative account of the fourteenth century (although it may offer an excessively bleak picture of the period) is Barbara Tuchman, *A Distant Mirror: The Calamitous Fourteenth Century* (New York: Knopf, 1978). Good visual histories of the period are *Chronicles of the Age of Chivalry* (London: Weidenfeld and Nicholson, 1987) and *The Chronicles of the Wars of the Roses* (London: Viking, 1988). For general reference, *The Dictionary of the Middle Ages* (New York: Scribner, 1982) is a good starting point.

For literary images of the period, Chaucer's own *Canterbury Tales* (Boston: Houghton Mifflin, 1987) are a good source; they span a diverse range of stories and voices, from the knight's chivalric romance to the miller's bawdy farce to the parson's pious sermon. The alliterative romance of *Sir Gawain and the Green Knight* (Harmondsworth: Penguin, 1974), dating to the late fourteenth century, is one of the finest examples of Middle English romance; it offers both chivalric adventure and sophisticated humor. Giovanni Boccaccio's *Decameron* (Harmondsworth: Penguin, 1972) is also worth a look: written in Italy in the mid-fourteenth century, it shares the diversity of *The Canterbury Tales*; indeed, many of Boccaccio's tales are told by Chaucer as well. For a female perspective on society, Christine de Pisan, *The Treasure of the City of Ladies* (New York: Persea, 1982), written in 1405, is an invaluable source. Among contemporary historical works, Jean Froissart's *Chronicles* (London: Penguin, 1978) are vivid and detailed. All these works are available in modern English translations. Also noteworthy is John of Trevisa, *On the Properties of Things* (Oxford: Clarendon Press, 1975), a fourteenth-century translation of a thirteenth-century Latin encyclopedia, an excellent source of information on a variety of topics ranging from medieval science to geography to family life.

Additional readings on individual topics are suggested in the chapter notes.

VISUAL SOURCES

Arano, Luisa Cogliati, ed. *The Medieval Health Handbook. Tacuinum Sanitatis*. New York: Braziller, 1976.

Avril, François. *Manuscript Painting at the Court of France*. New York: Braziller, 1978.

Backhouse, Janet. *The Luttrell Psalter*. London: British Library, 1989.

Dupont, Jacques and Cesare Gnudi. *Gothic Painting*. New York: Rizzoli, 1979.

Erlande-Brandenburg, Alain. *Gothic Art*. New York: Abrams, 1989.

James, M. R. *The Romance of Alexander: A Collotype Facsimile of MS Bodley 264*. Oxford: Oxford University Press, 1933.

The Four Seasons of the House of Cerruti. New York: Facts on File, 1984.

Ring, G. *A Century of French Painting 1400-1500*. London: Phaidon Press, 1949.

Thomas, Marcel. *The Golden Age of English Manuscript Painting*. New York: Braziller, 1979.

Trivick, Henry, *The Picture Book of Brasses in Gilt*. London: John Baker, 1971.

Warner, George F. *Universal Classic Manuscripts*. Washington and London, M. W. Dunne, 1901.

AUDIO-VISUAL SOURCES

The Return of Martin Guerre. This film is set around the year 1500, but it is probably the best existing cinematic view of medieval village life.

Medieval Video Collection. A wide variety of videos on various aspects of medieval life and civilization, including a series of reconstructed medieval dramas; available for purchase or rental. Media Centre Distribution, University of Toronto, 563 Spadina Ave., Toronto, Ontario, Canada M5S 1A1; (416) 978-6049.

For those interested in learning to pronounce Middle English, there exist a number of recordings of Chaucer's works, notably a series of tapes issued by Argo.

ILLUSTRATION SOURCES

Ashdown, Emily Jessie. *British Costume*. London: T. C. and E. C. Jack, 1910.

Bateson, Mary. *Mediæval England. English feudal society from the Norman conquest to the middle of the fourteenth century*. New York: G. P. Putnam's sons; London: T. F. Unwin, 1904.

Clinch, George. *English Costume*. Chicago and London: Methuen and co., 1910.

Fiske, W. *Chess in Iceland*. Florence: Florentine Typographical Society, 1905.

Furnivall, F. J. *The Harleian Manuscript of Chaucer's Canterbury Tales*. London: Kegan Paul, Trench, Trübner, and co., 1885.

Gay, Victor. *Glossaire Archéologique*. Paris: Librairie de la Société Bibliographique, 1887.

Griffiths, Nick, in J. Cowgill, M. de Neergard, and N. Griffiths, eds. *Medieval Finds from Excavations in London. 1: Knives and Scabbards*. London: Her Majesty's Stationery Office, 1987.

Hewitt, J. *Ancient Armour and Weapons in Europe*. Oxford and London: John Henry and James Parker, 1860.

Lundwall, E., in Nockert, Margareta, et al., eds. *Bokstensmannen Och Hans Drak.t* Falkenberg: Falkenberg Tryckeri, 1985.

Mitford, Susan, in F. Grew and M. de Neergard, eds. *Medieval Finds from Excavations in London. 2: Shoes and Pattens*. London: Her Majesty's Stationery Office, 1988).

Norlund, Poul, "Buried Norsemen at Herjolfsnes." *Meddelelser om Groenland 67* (1924), 87-192.

Parker, John Henry. *Some account of domestic architecture in England from Edward I to Richard II*. Oxford and London: J. H. Parker and co., 1882.

Ruding, Rogers. *Annals of the Coinage of Great Britain*. London: J. Hearne, 1840.

Santarem, Manuel visconde de. *Atlas composé de mappemondes, de portulans et de cartes hydrographiques et historiques*. Paris: E. Thunot, 1849.

Strutt, Joseph. *Sports and Pastimes of the English People*. London: Methuen, 1903.

Unwin, Christina, in E. Crowfoot, F. Pritchard, and K. Staniland, eds., *Medieval Finds from Excavations in London. Vol. 4: Textiles and Clothing*. London: Her Majesty's Stationery Office, 1992.

Woods, William. *England in the Age of Chaucer*. New York: Stein and Day, 1976.

Wright, Thomas, *History of Domestic Manners and Sentiments in England during the Middle Ages*. London: Chapman and Hall, 1862.

Zylstra-Zweens, H. M. *Of his array telle I no lenger tale*. Amsterdam: Rodophi, 1988.

Additional illustrations by Will McLean, John Vernier, Karen Weatherbee, and Kitten Reames.

Where possible, manuscript sources have been given for the illustrations. The following manuscripts recur frequently with abbreviated designations:

LP: *Luttrell Psalter*. British Library MS Add. 42130.
RA: *Roman d'Alexandre*. Oxford Bodleian MS 264.
TBH: *Tres Belles Heures*. Bibliothèque Nationale nouv. acq. lat. 3093.
TS: *Tacuinum Sanitatis*. Cited by manuscript location (Casanatense, Paris, Vienna).

Index

Page numbers in *italics* indicate illustrations.

absolution, 29, 211. *See also* sacraments
Advent, 76, 164
agriculture, 14, 15, 16, 31-32, 65, 67-76 *passim*, 80. *See also* harvesting; land and landholdings
ale, 33, 37, 92, 159, 160, 163, 164-65, 167, 212. *See also* drinks
alehouses. *See* inns and taverns
animals. *See* horses; livestock and poultry
apprentices, 22, 23, 25, 52, 53, 55, 83. *See also* craftsmen and tradesmen; guilds
archers and archery, 2, 21, 36, 67, 137, 138, 157-58, 186, 187
aristocracy, 2, 9, 14-19, 22, 25, 36, 47, 50, 52, 53, 80-81, 94, 159, 168, 179, 180, 182
armor, 85, 105, 106, 137ff. *See also* clothing

Backgammon, 189, 195-96
baptism, 40-41. *See also* godparents
barbers, 56, 113
barley, 32, 67, 159, 162, 164

basins, 85
bathing. *See* washing
beans, 32, 68, 159, 171, 172
beds, 73, 85, 86-87. *See also* furniture
beer. *See* ale
belts, 98, 109, 117-18, 131
benches, 86, 166. *See also* furniture
Bible, 6, 28, 37, 45, 181, 182
bishops, 9, 11, 47, 64. *See also* clergy
Black Plague. *See* plague
Black Prince. *See* Edward of Woodstock
Boccaccio, Giovanni, 5
Boksten, 102, 107
bondmen. *See* villeins
books, 37, 45, 182. *See also* Bible; reading and writing
bowling, 187, 202
bowls, 85, 166. *See also* tableware
bread, 33, 37, 159, 160, 162, 163, 166, 167, 177-78. *See also* food
breakfast, 62, 163
breeches, 37, 97, 98, 101, 122-23, 140. *See also* clothing
bridges. *See* roads and bridges
brooches, 103, 107, 119. *See also* jewelry

butter, 37, 160. *See also* dairy work and produce

buttons, 103, 105, 106, 107, 108, 111, 116, 131

calendar, 65ff.

Cambok, 186, 201

candles and candlesticks, 37, 68, 84, 85. *See also* light and lighting

Canterbury Tales, 45, 93, 181, 182. *See also* Chaucer, Geoffrey

canvas and hemp, 37, 87, 95, 166. *See also* cloth

cards, 190-91, 197-200

Chaucer, Geoffrey, *xiii*, 4, 5, 6, 7, 45, 181, 206. *See also Canterbury Tales*; literature

cheese. *See* dairy work and produce

chess, 189, 194-95

children, 39-47, 51, 52, 53, 164, 169, 188

Christmas, 65, 76, 77. *See also* holidays and holy days

church and religion, 10, 11, 26-30, 40-41, 43, 47, 53, 59, 65, 66, 80, 180. *See also* clergy; pope; parishes; prayers; sacraments; saints

churching, 40, 68

cleaning, 52, 85, 153. *See also* laundry; washing

clergy, 9, 10-14, 47, 50, 207. *See also* church and religion; priests; monks; nuns; bishops

cloth, 32, 33, 37, 94-95. *See also* canvas; cotton; dyes; embroidery; linen; silk; thread; wool

clothing, 9, 10, 37, 93ff., 140. *See also* cloth; thread; belts; breeches; coathardies; doublets and pourpoints; gloves; gowns; headgear; hose; houppelandes; kirtles; mantles; shirts; shoes and footwear; surcoats

coat-armors, 146, 152

coathardies, 95, 105. *See also* clothing; doublets and pourpoints

coifs, 112, 129, 140. *See also* headgear

combs, 37, 113. *See also* hair

commoners, 9, 10, 14, 18, 19-24, 53, 159-60, 179, 180, 185

communion, 29, 59, 72. *See also* sacraments

confession, 29, 59, 211. *See also* sacraments

confirmation, 47. *See also* sacraments

cooking, 47, 52, 169ff.

Cornwall, 1

cosmetics, 113

cottars, 21, 23, 36. *See also* land and landholding

cotton, 87, 88, 95. *See also* cloth

craftsmen and tradesmen, 23, 32-33, 36, 51, 82. *See also* apprentices; guilds; shops

Credo, 26, 28, 29

cups, 85, 166, 169. *See also* tableware

daggers, 118, 156, 186. *See also* knives

daily schedule, 62-63

dairy work and produce, 33, 52, 70, 159, 160-61, 164, 166. *See also* butter; milk

dancing, 77, 183, 212ff.

death. *See* mortality and death

dentistry, 55, 56. *See also* medicine

desserts, 162, 163. *See also* food

dice, 189, 193-94

disease. *See* health.

dinner, 62, 163. *See also* food

doublets and pourpoints, 101, 105, 106, *106*, 140, 141, 142, 146. *See also* clothing

drinks, 119, 164-66, 167, 176-77. *See also* ale, wine

dyes, 96, 121. *See also* cloth

Easter, 29, 65, 69. *See also* holidays and holy days

education, 4, 13, 27, 43, 47, 51-52. *See also* reading and writing; universities

Edward III, 2, 3, 5, 6, 17

Edward of Woodstock, Prince of Wales (The Black Prince), 2, 3, 5, 6

eggs, 37, 159, 164. *See also* food
elements, 30, 55, 57
Ember Days, 69, 71, 75, 77, 164, 175.
    See also holidays and holy days
embroidery, 47, 52, 99. *See also* cloth
English language, 2, 27, 28, 40, 45-46
entertainments, 64, 77, 179ff. *See also*
    dancing; games and sports;
    literature; music; plays
etiquette, 9, 43, 169
eyeglasses, 37, 118-19

fairs, 66-67, 92. *See also* markets;
    shops
families. *See* households
fasting, 63-64, 164
feudalism 14-17, 19-20. *See also* land
    and landholding
fire and fires, 62, 63, 84, 88, 169. 170.
    See also cooking; light and lighting
fish and seafood, 37, 63, 159, 160,
    163, 164, 171, 173. *See also* food
fish days. *See* fasting.
flax, 94-95. *See also* linen.
food, 30, 36, 37, 159ff., 212. *See also*
    barley; breakfast; cooking; dairy
    work and produce; desserts;
    dinner; drinks; eggs; fasting; fish;
    kitchens and kitchen utensils;
    meat; nuts; oats; peas; rye; supper;
    vegetables; wheat
football, 186, 201
France, 2, 3, 4, 5, 6, 95, 137, 190
franklins, 21, 23, 36. *See also* land and
    landholding
French language, 45, 50, 51
friars, 10, 12-13, 23, 29. *See also* clergy
fruits, 161, 162, 171, 176
fur, 95-96, 109
furniture, 37, 85-87. *See also* beds;
    benches; stools; tables

gambling, 187, 192
games and sports, 64, 77, 184ff. *See*
    also cards; chess; dice; football
gardens, 33, 52, 80, 82, 83

garters, 101, 116-17, 131. *See also*
    clothing
geography, 30-31
girls. *See* women and girls
glass, 113, 166
gloves, 95, 118, 148. *See also* clothing
godparents, 40, 43. *See also* baptism
gowns, 37, 46, 85, 95, 108. *See also*
    clothing
guilds, 22, 52. *See also* apprentices;
    craftsmen

hair, 10, 113
halls, 80-82, 85, 166
handkerchiefs, 119
harvesting 14, 63, 73. *See also*
    agriculture
hats. *See* headgear
hay, 68, 71, 72
headgear, 37, 73, 109, 110, 112. *See*
    also clothing; coifs; hoods; veils
    and wimples
health, 22, 56-58. *See also* medicine;
    plague
Henry IV (Henry Bolingbroke), 4,
    5, 7
herbs. *See* spices and seasonings
Herjolfsnes, 103ff., 109
hockey. *See* Cambok
holidays and holy days, 179-80. *See*
    also Advent; Christmas; Easter;
    Ember Days; Holy Cross Day;
    Lammas; Lent; Michaelmas; St.
    Lucy's Day; Twelfth Day; Whitsun
Holy Cross Day (Holy Rood Day),
    71, 75, 176. *See also* holidays and
    holy days
honey, 162, 165, 177
hoods, 37, 95, 97, 109-11, 128-29, 151,
    188. *See also* headgear
horn, 84, 113, 116, 167
horses, 37 68, 89, 137, 138. *See also*
    livestock and poultry
hose, 37, 93, 97-98, 100-1, 105, 113,
    116, 119, 123-25, 140. *See also*
    clothing
hospitals, 39

houppelandes, 97, 108-9. *See also* clothing

houses and buildings, 37, 79, 80-83. *See also* halls; kitchens and kitchen utensils

households, 16, 25, 53, 81-82, 83

humors, 55, 57

Hundred Years' War, 2, 5

hunting, 169, 183-84, 160

husbandmen 21, 23, 36, 51. *See also* agriculture; land and landholdings

incomes. *See* wages and incomes

inns and taverns, 63, 90, 92, 180

Ireland, 1, 4, 6

jewelry, 119-20. *See also* brooches; rings

Jews, 30

John of Gaunt, 3, 4, 5, 6, 7

jousting. *See* tournaments

Kailes, 187, 203

kings, 14, 16, 17-18, 22, 168

kirtles, 37, 97, 99, 101, 105, 119, 127-28

kitchens and kitchen utensils, 81, 85, 169ff.

knights, 9, 18, 23, 25, 36

knives, 37, 117, 118, 139, 157, 166-67, 169. *See also* daggers

laborers, 21, 23, 36, 51, 53, 160, 164

laces, 96, 101, 102, 103, 105, 114, 116, 132-5, 141, 142. *See also* points

Lammas, 65, 73

land and landholdings, 14, 15, 19-20, 21. *See also* cottars; feudalism; franklins; husbandmen; villeins

Latin language, 26, 27, 28, 40, 45, 50, 51, 206

laundry, 47, 97. *See also* cleaning; washing

law, 4, 51, 52

leather, 101, 106, 112, 113, 116, 117, 139, 143

Lent, 65, 69, 176. *See also* fasting; holidays and holy days

life expectancy. *See also* mortality and death

lights and lighting, 62, 63, 84, *84, 85. See also* candles and candlesticks

linen, 37, 87, 88, 94-96, 97, 98, 101, 102, 106, 111, 112, 118, 120, 122, 141, 166, 211. *See also* flax

literacy. *See* reading and writing

literature, 181-82. *See also Canterbury Tales; Piers Plowman*

livestock and poultry, 37, 80, 83, 86, 160, 174, 211

Lollards, 6, 28, 45. *See also* Wycliffe, John

London, 4, 22, 83. *See also* towns

Low Countries, 2, 94, 95, 190

mail, 139, 142, 145, 149, 151

manners. *See* etiquette

mantles, 85, 95, 97, 107, 119. *See also* clothing

markets, 33, 37, 62, 64, 89. *See also* fairs; shops

marriage, 19, 24, 53-55, 119

Mass, 29, 64, 207. *See also* sacraments

meat, 37, 63, 66, 69, 74-75, 76, 159, 160, 161, 164, 167, 169, 171. *See also* food

medicine, 51, 55-56. *See also* health; hospitals; physicians; surgeons

Ménagier de Paris, 51, 163, 182

merchants, 4, 36

Merels, 189, 197

Michaelmas, 65, 73, 75

milk, 161, 163. *See also* dairy work and produce

mirrors, 113

money, 14, 15, 34-37, *34,* 118. *See also* prices; wages and incomes

monks and monasteries, 10, 11, 12, *13,* 23, *166. See also* clergy

mortality and death, 26, 40, 43, 44, 55, 58-59

music, 47, 51, *160, 168,* 182-83. *See also* dancing; songs

names, 41-42
napkins, 85, 166
Nine-Man Morris. *See* Merels
Normans and Normandy, 1, 2, 41, 45
nuns, 13
nurses, 42
nuts, 37, 161

oats, 32, 67, 159, 162, 164
old age, 58-59
Oxford, 6, 28, 51. *See also* universities

pages, 23, 36
parents, 44-45
parishes, 11, 66, 71, 80. *See also*
    church and religion
Parliament, 6, 11, 13, 18
Pater Noster, 26, 27, 29, 62. *See also*
    prayers
peas, 32, 67, 159, 171
Peasants' Revolt, 4, 6, 19, 20, 51
pewter, 116, 119, 120, 166, 167
physicians, 12, 13, 39, 55. *See also*
    medicine; surgeons
Piers Plowman, 5, 45. *See also*
    literature
pilgrimage, 30, 89, 120. *See also* travel
pins, 112, 117
plague, 3, 5, 6, 9, 15, 34, 43, 58, 73,
    160. *See also* health; medicine;
    mortality and death
plays, 43, 180-81
points, 101, 106, 119. *See also* laces
Pope, 6, 26. *See also* church and
    religion; clergy
population, 3, 9, 21, 22, 58, 59, 83
pouches. *See* purses and pouches
poultry. *See* livestock and poultry
pourpoints. *See* doublets and
    pourpoints
poverty, 23-24, 39, 160
prayers, 26, 27, 29, 62, 63, 169. *See*
    also church and religion; Pater
    Noster
prices, 3, 34-37, 137, 182. *See also*
    money

priests, 10, 11, *12*, 23, 29, 40, 59, 211.
    See also church and religion; clergy
purses and pouches, 98, 103, 117,
    118, 131-32

Quoits, 187, 202

reading and writing, 14, 15, 43, 47-
    50, 118, 180. *See also* books;
    education; literature
religion. *See* church and religion
Richard II, 3, 4, 6, 7, 17
rings, 53, 119. *See also* jewelry
roads and bridges, 14, 90. *See also*
    streets; travel
Rome, 6, 26, 89
rye, 32, 75, 159, 162

sacraments, 27. *See also* absolution;
    communion; confession;
    confirmation; marriage; Mass;
    mortality and death; church and
    religion
saints, 41, 42, 65ff., 181, 182
St. Lucy's (Lucia's) Day, 76, 176
salt, 162, 166, 169, 171. *See also* spices
    and seasonings
sanitation, 56, 83, 88
Saturdays, 64, 164. *See also* weekly
    schedules
schools. *See* education
Scotland, 1, 2, 3, 4, 5, 6, 137
serfs. *See* villeins
servants, *10*, 19, 22-23, 25, 33, 53, 82, 83,
    112, 167-68. *See also* pages; squires
sexuality, 10, 12, 13, 47, 54, 55. *See*
    also marriage
shaving, 113
shields, 153
ships, 90
shirts, 63, 97, 98, 99, 101, 125-26, 140.
    See also clothes
shoes and footwear, 37, 101, 113-16,
    130-31, 140, 141
shops, 37, 64, 82-83. *See also* fairs;
    markets

silk, 95, 96, 97, 106, 109, 111, 118, 120, 166. *See also* cloth
soldiers and the military, 10, 14, 15, 16, 17, 18, 19, 36, 70, 74, 137-39
songs, 182, 203ff.
Spain, 3, 5, 190
spices and seasonings, 37, 80, 159, 161-62. *See also* salt; sugar
spoons, 85, 166, 167, 170. *See also* tableware
sports. *See* games and sports
squires, 18-19, 22, 23, 36, 168
stools, 37, 166. *See also* furniture
straw, 37, 73, 79, 85, 88, 112
streets, 64, 83, 180, 186. *See also* roads and bridges
sugar, 37, 159, 162. *See also* honey; spices and seasonings
Sundays, 29, 64, 179-80. *See also* weekly schedules
supper, 62, 163. *See also* food
surcoats, 37, 95, 107, 146, 152
surgeons, 55-56. *See also* medicine; physicians

tabards, 146, 152
tables, 10, 85, 86, 161, 166. *See also* furniture
tableware, 166-67, 169. *See also* bowls; knives; spoons
taxes, 3-4, 6, 18, 52
tents, 91, 92
thread, 32, 33, 121
time, 61-62
toilets. *See* sanitation
tournaments and jousting, 184-85
towels, 85, 166, 167, 169
towns, 11, 22, 51, 52, 62, 63, 72, 82-83, 180. *See also* London
travel, 89-92, 162. *See also* pilgrimage; roads
Trevisa, John of, 39, 42, 44, 45, 46
Twelfth Day, 65, 67. *See also* holidays and holy days

universities, 12, 51, 55. *See also* Oxford
vegetables, 80, 159, 161, 171, 172-73. *See also* food
veils and wimples, 111-12, 129-30. *See also* headgear
villages, 11, 80, 180
villeins, 4, 15, 19-20, 21, 51. *See also* land and landholdings

wages and incomes, 3, 5, 11, 18, 19, 34-36, 138. *See also* feudalism; land and landholdings; money; prices
Wales, 1, 2
Wars of the Roses, 5, 17
washing, 62, 87, 88, 97, 87-88, 167, 169. *See also* cleaning; laundry; towels
water, 62, 80, 83, 87, 90, 160, 163, 170
weapons, 137, 138, 153ff., 184-85. *See also* archery; daggers
Wednesdays, 63, 164
weekly schedules, 63-64. *See also* Wednesdays; Saturdays; Sundays
wheat, 32, 75, 164
Whitsunday, 71, 176. *See also* holidays and holy days
widows, 23-25, 59. *See also* women
wimples. *See* veils and wimples
wine, 37, 163, 165, 167, 176. *See also* drinks
women and girls, 24-26, 32, 33, 39, 42, 43, 47, 51, 52, 53, 56, 59, 92, 97, 98, 101, 104, 107, 111, 113, 164, 180, 183, 184, 188. *See also* nuns; widows
wool, 15, 32, 33, 37, 52, 87, 88, 94, 95, 96, 97, 101, 109, 112, 118, 120. *See also* cloth; thread
writing. *See* literacy and writing
Wycliffe, John, 6, 28. *See also* Lollards

year, 64ff.
yeomen. *See* franklins

About the Authors

JEFFREY L. SINGMAN is an editor at the *Middle English Dictionary* project at the University of Michigan. He is a practitioner of Elizabethan living history as a founding member of the University Medieval and Renaissance Association (Tabard Inn Society) of Toronto and the Trayn'd Bandes of London, an international living history organization. Singman has published and lectured on games literature and game theory, medieval languages and literatures, and the Robin Hood legend.

WILL McLEAN is an author and illustrator who has been active in medieval living history for 20 years. He runs reenactments of medieval tournaments and has written several articles on the subject.